Who Will Rule in 2019?

Who Will Rule in 2019?

Jan-Jan Joubert

Jonathan Ball Publishers
Johannesburg & Cape Town

All rights reserved.
No part of this publication may be reproduced or transmitted,
in any form or by any means, without prior permission
from the publisher or copyright holder.

© Text Jan-Jan Joubert 2018
© Published edition 2018 Jonathan Ball Publishers

Originally published in South Africa in 2018 by
JONATHAN BALL PUBLISHERS
A division of Media24 (Pty) Ltd
PO Box 33977
Jeppestown
2043

ISBN 978 1 868428 70 0
EBOOK ISBN 978 1 868428 71 7

Every effort has been made to trace the copyright holders and to obtain their permission for the use of copyright material. The publishers apologise for any errors or omissions and would be grateful to be notified of any corrections that should be incorporated in future editions of this book.

Twitter: www.twitter.com/JonathanBallPub
Facebook: www.facebook.com/JonathanBallPublishers
Blog: http://jonathanball.bookslive.co.za/

Cover by publicide
Editing by Mark Ronan
Proofreading by Kathleen Sutton
Index by George Claassen
Design and typesetting by Triple M Design, Johannesburg
Set in 11.25/18pt Sabon MT Std

Printed by paarlmedia, a division of Novus Holdings

To my parents,
who have always believed in me, especially when it was hard to,
and to Henry, Lisa and Jan for providing a safe haven
in which to write this book.

Contents

Acronyms and abbreviations ix
Preface xi

1 The day Jesus walked in Nelson Mandela Bay 1
2 Reading the tea leaves or, rather, the stats 14
3 How the 2016 opposition deal was done – the back story 28
4 Cyril Ramaphosa's impact on coalition politics 56
5 The two biggest opposition parties and their options for 2019 82
6 The smaller opposition parties and their options for 2019 111
7 Burning issues I: It's the economy, stupid! 140
8 Burning issues II: Land and the power of perception 154
9 Burning issues III: Labour and black economic empowerment 175
10 Burning issues IV: Nationalisation and tackling corruption 192
11 Coalitions – lessons learnt from the past and the present 217
12 Who will rule in 2019? 234
    How to put a coalition together: A user's guide 247

Notes 253
Index 255

Acronyms and abbreviations

ACDP	African Christian Democratic Party
ANC	African National Congress
ANCWL	ANC Women's League
COPE	Congress of the People
Cosatu	Congress of South African Trade Unions
DA	Democratic Alliance
EFF	Economic Freedom Fighters
IDP	integrated development plan
IEC	Independent Electoral Commission
IFP	Inkatha Freedom Party
MEC	Member of the Executive Council
MP	Member of Parliament
NDP	National Development Plan
NEC	National Executive Committee
NPA	National Prosecuting Authority
PAC	Pan Africanist Congress
RDP	Reconstruction and Development Programme
SAA	South African Airways
SABC	South African Broadcasting Corporation

SACP	South African Communist Party
SOE	state-owned enterprise
UDF	United Democratic Front
UDM	United Democratic Movement

Preface

Political journalism is at the same time the most wonderful and the most difficult of professions. It shows you the best and worst sides of people in times of great personal triumph and huge personal distress.

If you choose to answer its calling, political journalism offers a magnificent but dangerous opportunity to witness humanity in all its fallibility and to write, to the best of your limited ability, what the erstwhile *Washington Post* proprietor Philip Graham called 'a first rough draft of history'.

Political journalism has been my profession since 2001. I love it because it has offered me the opportunity to witness and record firsthand South African history as it was made from that point onwards. Some of the key events were the break-up of the Democratic Alliance (DA) in 2001 when the New National Party broke away, which set back the opposition project for almost a decade; the resultant demise of the once all-powerful National Party; the battle between Thabo Mbeki and Jacob Zuma that unfolded between 2002 and 2008; the hope offered by the Motlanthe era; the rise and fall of the Zuma presidency; the tragedy of state capture, and power of ordinary South Africans' opposition to it, and the dawn of the Ramaphosa era – as well as the elections and debates and many other events in between.

For me, what sets political journalism apart from other forms of journalism is that it is about a continuous process rather than separate events. A crime reporter, for instance, would report on one crime on one day and a different one the next – mostly, these events are unrelated. But, with political reporting, one reports on a related set of developments – as well as the human condition in all of its manifestations. Much of what one covers in political journalism follows on from or is related to other events, and depends on the changing relationships between people. To a large degree, everything in politics builds on everything that has gone before, and everything has the potential to influence future events. A good political reporter must therefore be able to connect the dots and understand the relational and policy undercurrents – the things that are not apparent on the surface or that are often left unsaid by politicians.

My profession has afforded me the opportunity to interact with and interview the great and the good – Nobel laureates like Nelson Mandela, FW de Klerk and Desmond Tutu. Other great South Africans I have crossed paths with include former public protector Thuli Madonsela, late politician Frederik van Zyl Slabbert, Olympic medallist Ryk Neethling, academic Russel Botman, education expert Jonathan Jansen, the late academic Jakes Gerwel and businessman Johann Rupert.

As anyone who loves South Africa and is interested in its past, present and future will know, South African politics is a messy contact sport where hope and despair can arise in quick succession. Covering it is like being in the front row at a boxing match. Writers who have been

PREFACE

in such a position will be able to testify that while you have a ringside seat and an unimpeded view of the fight, it also means that the sweat, and even the blood, of the fighters sometimes lands on you, despite your best efforts to avoid it.

When you cover political punch-ups, those who are on the ropes will often even climb through the ropes and punch you in the face for their own ends, even if this is against the rules. Political journalism has therefore also exposed me to the pettiness, viciousness and pointless score-settling of some people whom many South Africans hold in high esteem, but who shall remain nameless because I took a decision long ago not to become or imitate what I dislike.

To use a different metaphor, as a political journalist you must try to fly close enough to the sun for you to have maximum light to guide your reporting, but not so close that you get burnt. If you can manage that, it will be an intellectually rewarding, even if constantly challenging, exercise.

I will try to take you behind the scenes to the back rooms where the deals are made that have an impact on us all. I will try to do justice to the joy my profession has afforded me and to the hope it has always engendered in me for the future of our beloved country. I will respect confidentiality and protect sources, and, as ever, I will take full responsibility for the accuracy of my facts and interpretation.

Political journalism, if practised at a level above the mediocre, becomes a matter of study, reading, thinking, assessment, developing trust and building relationships, and even, especially, having some fun. Even though all the reading can at times be tedious, it's crucial that your knowledge of the subject is comparable to or even better than that of the politician you are interacting with.

One must study and attempt to understand the content and, more importantly, the impact of legislation, regulation and party political documentation. This is valuable foundational knowledge and serves as a breakwater against the unscrupulous, who may attempt to mislead you. However, once you venture beyond the safety of that theoretical breakwater, you enter the great, exciting and dangerous sea of true, gritty and gutsy political reporting. Then, you start dealing with politicians.

By far the majority of South African politicians are wonderful people who aim to serve and work hard in a profession that the general population is quick to judge negatively. Countless politicians have shown me incredible kindness over the years, have provided excellent argument and discussion, and a few have even become friends. Politicians are people, after all – even though many of their critics tend to forget this.

However, whenever I lecture university students about political reporting, I tell them the story of the old lady and the snake.

There was an old lady who lived outside a town and was very lonely. Every day, she would walk into town to buy groceries. One day, on her way back, she passed a snake. The snake was not in a good way. It was, in fact, about to die. The old lady picked it up, took it home and nursed it back to health. Over time, they became friends. The old lady's lonely days seemed over. Then, one day, the snake bit her.

As she lay dying, she called out: 'Why did you do this? I saved you, I cared for you and I fed you. I thought we were friends. How could you?'

The snake answered: 'Because I'm a snake.'

PREFACE

There is much truth in this old story. Some politicians are snakes. The trick is to keep your distance and try to behave as courteously as your mother would expect you to, even at times of extreme provocation. Sometimes, when you write what politicians do not want to read about themselves or their parties, you become a target. They will easily attack you if they get it into their heads that you are driving an agenda or waging a vendetta.

As a political journalist, you must therefore constantly investigate your own motives to ensure that you are being as balanced and objective as humanly possible. Still, it is important to understand that those attacks will come, regardless of what the true facts are – it comes with the territory. Political journalism is not about winning popularity contests. It quickly teaches you to toughen up.

In all the years I have covered politics, I have met only three truly toxic and malicious politicians, who had the ability and desire to poison my career, and in all three instances tried to do so. Needless to say, this is extremely unpleasant, but, once again, you must find ways to deal with the situation. A saving grace is if the media house you work for supports you when such things happen. Unfortunately, that is not always a given for political journalists.

When, as a journalist, you deal with politicians, discretion is the better part of valour. At the same time, if your aim is insightful political reporting and you practise informed punditry, you need to build a position of trust with at least some politicians. Trust is a weird thing – it must come from both sides.

A professional relationship with a politician comes down to give and take; it is face-threatening and it is risky, yet necessary. It cannot be coldly transactional. The journalist should trust the politician to give him the correct information and an honest interpretation, and the politician should trust the journalist to write accurately and in a balanced way.

It is much like investing in the stock exchange – even when you make an informed and careful choice, the dividend for both parties is unpredictable. Sometimes your judgement lets you down and you notch up a loss; other times the risky mutual decision to open up bears good fruit.

For me, political journalism remains an intellectual challenge worth tackling every day. It is a privilege to record the journey of the country I love for all those who find it important and worthwhile reading about.

I will conclude with an Afrikaans poem that has become my daily motto and which I have translated into English. It is framed and hangs on the wall of my home. It is called '*Soet is die Stryd*' ('Sweet is the Battle') and was written by ID du Plessis:

You say the battle is lost,
Our nation too poor and too small,
Our language born of an urge
Which will disappear someday soon?
My friend, you may well be correct,
Who knows what the future will bring?
Tomorrow we may be required
To let go of this wonderful dream.
But, if we can only strive
For those victories easily guaranteed,
What use then the battle of life
Where one must not be overconfident?
If your intentions are noble,

PREFACE

Distress over failure is void,
Just persevere and be brave –
It's the effort of trying which counts!
Ah, sweet is the battle to the warrior,
Even if, in the end, he must lose;
But those who refuse to take part
Shoot the nation through its weary heart!

– '*Soet is die Stryd*' by ID du Plessis, from the volume *Land van ons Vadere*, Unie-Volkspers, Cape Town, 1945

CHAPTER 1

The day Jesus walked in Nelson Mandela Bay

In the early hours of Friday morning, 5 August 2016, battle-axe trade unionist Zwelinzima Vavi claimed his eyes had seen the glory of the coming of the Lord. 'Jesus was seen walking in the streets of Nelson Mandela Metro last night – he is back!' tweeted Vavi, giving President Jacob Zuma a taste of his own medicine.

It was two days after the local-government elections and the unimaginable had just happened. The ANC had been unseated from the largest metro government in its Eastern Cape heartland. Several times since 2004, Zuma had said publicly that the ANC would rule 'until Jesus comes back', raising the ire of opposition supporters and many Christians of all political persuasions. But he was wrong.

Not only did the ANC lose Nelson Mandela Bay Metro, by the next evening, the Independent Electoral Commission (IEC) had confirmed that ANC municipal governments had fallen in two more metros: Johannesburg and Tshwane, and in more than 30 municipal and district councils across the country. In the following weeks and months, South Africans watched in disbelief as coalition politics became a new part of our lives.

To this day, many South Africans believe the ANC is destined to govern. But those who still blindly believe this is a given need to study the cold, hard figures. Nationally, the ANC's support fell from 62% in the 2014 national election to 53% in the 2016 local-government elections.

Since then, the ruling party has been further wracked by evidence of state capture, leadership disputes and further upheavals, and its position among voters has hardly improved.

Zuma's resignation and Cyril Ramaphosa's appointment as president lifted the national mood in early 2018, but many of the issues the ANC has to grapple with remain.

The ANC's slide since 2016 is also borne out by the numbers. Exactly 118 by-elections took place between the local-government elections on 3 August 2016 and 31 December 2017. The ANC put up candidates in each of these, and registered an average swing against it in these by-elections, countrywide, of 7.4%. An average swing of 7.4% against it in more than 100 by-elections should make any governing party extremely nervous.

While one swallow does not make a summer, it was interesting that the ANC made no dent in DA support in the first two by-elections since Ramaphosa's ascension to the presdency.

Quite frankly, the ANC may be in trouble in the 2019 elections. Until 2016, South Africa was a perfect example of a one-party dominant state, so how could losing power even have become a possibility for the ANC, let alone the probability it currently is? The answer to the question how the ANC gambled away arguably the largest moral, political and liberation dividend in the history of the world will be examined in this book – as will the fascinating dynamics of how a non-ideological opposition cooperative agreement came into being since 2016, and its possible impact on election results in 2019.

Will 2019 bring a national coalition government? Who might

constitute that government? What are the chances of the ANC and the Economic Freedom Fighters (EFF) teaming up? Or will the EFF and the DA, the odd couple of many municipal cooperative governments, join their fellow opposition parties in ganging up on the ANC?

Which policy issues could decide who the partners in government will be? What difference will the election of Cyril Ramaphosa as ANC leader and president make to the governing party's fortunes? And, perhaps most importantly, what will the public make of the potentially game-changing proposal Ramaphosa has up his sleeve to draw opposition parties into an ANC-led government?

Come 2019, the stakes will be incomparable to any election since 1994, and the political climate change from those days of relative political bonhomie will be complete. It will be a political battle royal with the ultimate reward on offer – the power to participate in the national government.

In essence, the national and provincial elections of 2019 will be fought between those voters who believe the ANC under Ramaphosa can rid itself of corruption and those who believe it cannot. Either way, the only party that can realistically aim for an absolute majority above 50% in South Africa's system of complete proportional representation at national and provincial level is the ANC.

But given the continued and unprecedented flow of support away from the ANC to various opposition parties, there is a definite possibility of the ANC dipping under 50%. If so, coalitions are the future of South African politics, on a provincial and probably a national level, as they already increasingly are on a municipal level. If the ANC does fall below 50% of the vote, then national or provincial coalitions or cooperative agreements will be a necessity whether the ANC wants them or not. It would no longer be the ANC's choice.

From 1994 onwards, the ANC became the behemoth of South African post-liberation democratic politics, with firm control over all provinces and metros outside the Western Cape (scoring overall majorities in KwaZulu-Natal since 2009). It was seemingly unshakable.

This led many a fashionable political commentator to state haughtily what I have always believed to be hogwash, namely that the only true power in South African politics, and at the same time the only true opposition to ANC excesses and misrule, resided within the ANC and its alliance partners, the South African Communist Party (SACP) and the Congress of South African Trade Unions (Cosatu) – in other words, that the only politics worth taking notice of was the politics inside the ruling alliance.

That notion – overwhelmingly popular as it was at one stage – blinded many in the political establishment to changes taking place in the national political psyche. These changes were evident in the word of mouth on the street, which is difficult to gauge beyond the anecdotal without a wide network of honest, non-self-serving contacts or a polling capacity. (Incidentally, I have found that the only organisations in South Africa with the capacity to poll accurately are the large political parties – certainly not the commercial polling companies, which are often very wide of the mark, for various reasons.) But the changes were even more obvious (and yet ignored – oh so wrongly and ever so often – by the many who peddle a narrative rather than being beholden to facts) if one were to analyse the changing patterns in by-election results and registration figures, which can reveal an accurate projection of expected results.

It is a core aim of this book to show how changing preferences, quality of governance, social and community activism, interparty relationships and quantitative statistical analysis can be used, without too much effort, by any South African interested in politics to arrive at a strong indication of the outcome of elections. In this way, one will not be unduly surprised by our election results, which helps one plan for the future.

If one realises that forecasting election results is to a large degree a statistically logical exercise, supported by tactical, strategic and/or policy-based decisions made by those whose job it is to make them, rather than following an analyst's emotional take on how he or she reads or feels about the national mood and voter preference, it allows one to avoid much of the bullshit that has left so many political analysts completely wide of the mark in their election predictions.

This was unmasked by columnist Gareth van Onselen in his usual devastatingly forthright and factual manner in his articles 'Why you should not trust a political analyst' for Business Day Live on 18 June 2013 and 'Why you should not trust a political analyst – Part 2' published by the same website on 6 November that year. Clearly, all of us are better served by applying our own, factually based analysis and projections.

Should one be so empirically inclined, one should not be as surprised by the 2016 election results or subsequent trends, as many analysts and other South Africans were – not least the still shell-shocked bigwigs of the ANC. I will tell the back story of how the apparently watershed 2016 election results and the subsequent coalitions and cooperative agreements came about. And I will show that it was possible to predict, or at least broadly project, the results beforehand – and, to a lesser degree, the machinations that subsequently took place between and within political parties – and that this was actually done and published, if one only knew to look in the right places.

If one follows the lessons learnt in 2016, any South African who is willing to make the effort, and possesses the required access to political sources and the ability to maintain an open mind, so that facts remain as untainted by political preference as possible, will be able to project future political outcomes. All the information is available: it is just a matter of using it correctly.

Much must still happen before the 2019 elections and anyone who wants to make predictions and projections before these things happen would be foolish. However, it is very possible to build a methodology and identify the most important trends that will make coalitions and cooperative agreements succeed or fail. In this way, one can be prepared rather than surprised.

Is the opposition's cooperative agreement merely a Bismarckian deal with the devil made between opportunistic opponents of the national democratic revolution, as the ANC would want us to believe? Or is it the art of the possible between patriotic South Africans willing to put aside individual and ideological differences in the national interest – to save the country from becoming a basket case, as the EFF's Julius Malema argued at a massively important but widely underestimated press conference in Johannesburg in February 2016?

Can the ANC correct itself and, if so, how? Should a coalition agreement post-2019 include or exclude the ANC? If so, which ANC factions? What was the effect of the December 2017 ANC leadership election process and outcome on the ANC, the national political power-relations picture and possible coalitions?

More importantly, beyond the vagaries of political power mathematics, the ebb and flow of individual power bases (the so-called politics of the big man or perhaps the big woman) and the identity of future governments, what will the effect of the future political landscape be on the lives of Joe and Joan Soap, those of us who are citizens of the beloved country and wish to make a future here for ourselves and our families?

Why does it matter, socially and economically?

What difference could it make?

Why should we care?

To attempt answers to these questions, we need to consider the nexus between power, self-interest, idealism, cynicism, political personality and policy. What are the options? What are the possibilities? What are the dynamics driving the main protagonists, and how will they have an impact on our politics, and therefore our personal lives, in the future South Africa?

All of these questions became topical after the remarkable 2016 local-government election results had shown that political change was possible in South Africa. The loss of support for the ANC in that election was unprecedented for any South African political party since 1910. It had fallen by a catastrophic nine percentage points in only two years to 53% support nationally.

Since then, by-elections in municipal wards have consistently shown a swing of between 12 and 16 percentage points away from the ANC in areas where the party has historically had a strong presence. This trend has been consistent across the many geographic and demographic boundaries of our diverse country's electorate.

Of course, there are major differences between results in national and local-government elections. For one thing, the percentage of people who vote in local government elections is much lower than the turnout in national and provincial elections.

Furthermore, it is a worldwide phenomenon that opposition parties tend to do better in local than national elections because a discontented voter is more likely to make the effort to vote than a satisfied voter – much like the problematic client who takes up much more time than the others, is impossible to please and often less profitable. Such is life!

This is especially true in proportional representation systems such as South Africa's – more so than in geographical, constituency-based first-past-the-post electoral systems, such as America and Britain's.

The reason for this is a phenomenon known as differential turnout. The concept is not as difficult to grasp as its highfalutin name would have it. Basically, it means that in a proportional-representation system, the key to success is mobilising your supporters to turn out to vote to a greater degree than your opponent can. The 'differential' is the difference between the percentage of your supporters who vote and the percentage of your opponents' voters. If the differential is in your favour (i.e. if the percentage of your voters is higher), you will perform better. Simply put: the more of your voters who turn out, the better you will do.

In a society where the governing party has overpromised, underdelivered and underperformed as much as the ANC has in South Africa, the potential differential dividend for the opposition is huge.

In essence, assuming that every political party believes its own supporters are the best, and its opponents represent the worst, for the ideal differential turnout in a proportional-representation system, one should turn the Irish poet WB Yeats's line from 'The Second Coming' on its head: 'The best lack all conviction, while the worst/ Are full of passionate intensity.' That is, one should ensure that the worst voters lack all conviction, while the best are filled with passionate intensity!

This was very true from an opposition perspective in the 2016 local-government elections, as the following table from the country's eight metros shows. Remember that every ward has roughly the same number of voters, so these figures show the relative success of opposition parties in driving up the differential turnout – in getting their voters to the polls.

Metro	Turnout: Opposition wards	Turnout: ANC wards	Average total turnout	Differential
Johannesburg	63.3%	51.3%	57.1%	12
Tshwane	68.7%	54.2%	59.2%	14.5
Ekurhuleni	64.5%	53.1%	58.0%	11.4
eThekwini	60.7%	59.2%	59.7%	1.5
Mangaung	63.7%	55.8%	57.7%	7.9
Buffalo City	67.7%	54.5%	55.9%	13.2
Nelson Mandela Bay	68.9%	59.9%	63.9%	9
Cape Town	69.9%	56.1%	64.2%	13.8

The differential turnout does not match the total turnout figure or the actual result because in Cape Town there are more opposition wards than ANC wards, and in the other seven metros there are more ANC wards than opposition wards. Therefore, differential turnout does not necessarily provide an overwhelming advantage. It only provides relative advantage. But in the metros of Johannesburg, Tshwane and Nelson Mandela Bay – and in a growing number of municipalities across the country – differential turnout meant the difference between victory and defeat, as an indication of the passionate intensity of many opposition voters to rid their local government of what they viewed as ANC mismanagement. It made the crucial difference between victory and defeat as ANC supporters saw the levels of their conviction drop while the liberation movement allowed its liberation dividend to be whittled away.

But whether the differential turnout provides the full or partial road map to victory in a proportional-representation system, the golden rule is that you have to register as many of your supporters as possible, and chase them through the polling booths on voting day like a dedicated farmer would push his sheep or cattle through a dip – the faster, and the greater the numbers, the better. To quote an old Afrikaans adage: Vote early, vote correctly, vote often!

Basically, you can't win if your voters aren't in the booths.

One of the many ways in which the emergence of the EFF since 2014 has changed South African politics is that it has changed the nature of the differential turnout. As one EFF source explained to me in the election centre as the landmark results of the 2016 election showed a greater advantage to the opposition than the differential turnout suggested: 'To date, the turnout differential was, to a large degree, racial in nature because the DA tended to win the wards where national racial minorities (white, coloured and Indian) are in the majority by lopsided margins, whereas the ANC did the same in areas where black African voters are in the majority. With the emergence of the EFF, that dynamic has changed, because our supporters weaken the ANC majorities in predominantly black African wards.'

That was a very good point, as the EFF unseated the ANC in several wards (and have done in a slowly growing number since then) where black African voters form the overwhelming majority.

But what this interpretation does not do justice to is the extent of the ANC's weakening in its former strongholds, where it underestimated what that formidable political brain, my friend and former colleague Mpumelelo Mkhabela, in the run-up to the election deftly predicted would be 'the splintering of the growing black opposition vote'. What this translated into was that various major opposition parties – especially the DA, IFP and United Democratic Movement (UDM) – saw a relative increase in their black support in 2016 as voters abandoned the ANC.

It saw the political resurrection of the IFP – long believed to be in slow but terminal decline – to the extent that it regained several rural KwaZulu-Natal municipalities and even beat the ANC in Zuma's bailiwick of Nkandla, where his homestead is. (That, incidentally, led to one of the funniest election examples of a political invention that South Africans have proved themselves to be great at: the meme. The unforgettable meme I refer to is a picture showing Zuma queuing with assorted smiling Zulu matriarchs at his local polling station in Nkandla municipality. The accompanying caption interprets those smiles not as subservient, as the casual passer-by might believe. It shows them to be knowing smiles: 'Queued with him. Didn't vote for him.')

But the real indication that the IFP was back from the political intensive-care unit was the by-election in the small Zululand hamlet of Nquthu on 24 May 2017. The 2016 result gave the combined opposition (IFP, DA and EFF) a majority of just one seat over the ANC. After some shenanigans by the local ANC and the KwaZulu-Natal Member of the Executive Council (MEC) for local government, the council was dissolved and new elections were called for.

Weeks of intense campaigning followed. The ANC rolled out all of its big guns against the ever cash-strapped IFP. Taxpayers' money and state largesse flowed into the ANC campaign. But, astoundingly, when the results came in, the IFP had grown from 45% to 58%, the ANC had dropped from 43% to 34% and the IFP's two cooperative partners, the DA and the EFF, had seen their fortunes remain largely the same, with minuscule support.

Journalist Nathi Oliphant compared the ANC's loss to 'taking a machine gun to a stick fight and still losing'. Since then, the IFP has not always sustained its growth. A month later, in the uPhongolo municipality, centred on the sugar-cane farming town of Pongola, the IFP failed to build on its momentum and take an ANC ward. Its decline in urban KwaZulu-Natal also continues unabated.

However, what held true for IFP growth in 2016 was even truer for the DA. It grew its black support in most provinces, and in some Western Cape township polling stations, notably in Khayelitsha (Cape Town) and Kayamandi (Stellenbosch), its support grew fivefold, albeit from a very low base.

Together with a strengthening of its support base among white, coloured and Indian voters, this ensured that the DA was again the major party that showed the largest growth in 2016. We shall examine the reasons for this, as well as the factors stifling DA growth.

This book sets out to map the possibilities of governance by cooperative agreement or coalition after the 2019 general election. But before we get to all that, let me take you behind the scenes of the 2016 coalition and cooperation deal that unseated the ANC and turned South African politics on its head.

Let's investigate how Jesus came to walk on the streets of Nelson Mandela Bay, Tshwane and Johannesburg, and what we can learn from this going into 2019. It is a tale of back-room dealings and double-crossed agreements offered, rejected and remade. It is nothing short of a political thriller. It was history in the making, history as it was made.

CHAPTER 2

Reading the tea leaves or, rather, the stats

On 21 August 2014, a tad more than three months after a general election that saw 25 of its number elected to the National Assembly, the EFF changed South African parliamentary politics forever. It managed to place Parliament at the centre of South African political discourse and elevated the parliamentary TV channel to one of the most popular in the country – outperforming in popularity the soap operas with which it came to share many characteristics.

The business of the day was presidential question time, until then an occasion as dour as the National Assembly itself, where ANC politicians would ask sweetheart non-questions and opposition leaders would direct hopelessly polite enquiries to President Zuma, who would laboriously stumble through, reading written non-replies (in extra-large text size for easier reading, one could see from the press gallery above his podium), cooked up on his behalf by government apparatchiks.

On that August afternoon, Zuma, who had not taken the time to prepare, was clearly struggling with the content of 'his' answers for the first time at the dais. In the process, he showed his presidential disdain for parliamentary question time, which should be a showcase of Westminster-style political cut-and-thrust politics.

Man, it was dire. But all this was about to change.

The next moment, the EFF leader, Julius Malema, asked Zuma when he was going to 'pay back the money' – the taxpayers' money spent on installing luxuries at his private homestead at Nkandla – as directed by then Public Protector Thuli Madonsela in her 'Secure in Comfort' report.

Of course, Zuma was never going to answer that question. He dodged it like he had so many times before, refusing to take responsibility, instead ducking and deflecting, as is his wont.

All of a sudden, the EFF contingent started chanting rhythmically, 'Pay back the money! Pay back the money!'

Their members started punching their benches with their fists. 'Pay back the money! Pay back the money!'

In no time, it became a primal scream that resonated with the South African public: 'Pay back the money!'

The EFF members refused to stop. The National Assembly speaker, Baleka Mbete (always biased in favour of the ANC and not objective, as the speaker should be) could do nothing to shut them up.

Other political parties could not be heard above the din. Eventually, Mbete adjourned proceedings. Only the EFF remained in the chamber, and four of us journalists in the press gallery.

At that point, parliamentary security officials attempted to clear us from the press gallery. We refused to leave. Our journalist colleagues outside the venue had noted the arrival of public-order police units, reportedly armed with canisters probably containing tear gas.

There were two main reasons why we refused to be removed. The first was that it is the primary duty of journalists to bear witness – to write a 'first rough draft of history', preferably from the position of eyewitness. The closer to the action, the better.

The second reason went deeper, and comes down to what William L Shirer, an American journalist and *Chicago Tribune* correspondent who was in Berlin during the build-up to the Third Reich, defined as the role of the journalist when confronted with the growth of evil. In his seminal work on that dark chapter of German history, *The Rise and Fall of the Third Reich*, Shirer preciously and, to my mind, correctly, argues that the role of journalists who are confronted by the clear and present danger of imminent evil is to report on it while opposing it.[1]

To my colleagues and me, it was clear that these EFF MPs were in imminent danger of being tear-gassed and assaulted. Such behaviour belonged to the old South Africa, and could never be repeated. We would not allow it – not on our watch. We would bear witness and oppose.

We refused to vacate and rallied our fellow parliamentary journalists to join us, noting that strength lies in numbers. In the end, proceedings were suspended for the day and the EFF MPs were not physically harmed. Given the intense violence later unleashed upon EFF MPs under Mbete's bloody and violent parliamentary reign, I believe we did the right thing.

The violent ejection of EFF members from the National Assembly to which they had been elected by the people became commonplace. It also became clear that the vast majority of ANC MPs enjoyed watching these thuggish assaults. I found it nauseating, particularly when female EFF MPs were assaulted and ANC leaders, including the president, could be seen and heard encouraging the violence against women, laughing out loud at the sight of their opponents being roughed up.

How uncouth and base these events were! How against everything our democratic constitutional order stands for.

In terms of future opposition cooperation, another very important event took place, this time on 13 November 2014, late at night, during a debate on, of all boring things, the Great Inga hydroelectric scheme in the Democratic Republic of Congo. Given the late hour, I was the only journalist in the parliamentary press gallery when 63-year-old EFF MP Reneilwe Mashabela rose to speak on the topic.

During her speech, she touched on the probability of corruption sullying the project, given the economic interests of the Zuma family holdings in the Congo. 'The president is a criminal! The president is a thief! The whole world knows the president of the ANC is the greatest thief in the world!' she screamed. She refused to withdraw her statement or leave the podium, as instructed.

It was an amazing speech. Watch it on YouTube if you haven't yet heard it.

Then, in an unprecedented move, the police entered to take her away. The police had last been seen on the floor of a parliamentary chamber in South Africa on 6 September 1966, when apartheid-era premier Hendrik Verwoerd was assassinated – but even that was not during a sitting.

The shock of seeing police in Parliament jolted even the oh-so-civilised DA into action. In scenes I have to admit I found rather inspiring, MPs from the DA, EFF and IFP clobbered the intruding cops into submission and threw them out of a chamber they should never have entered in the first place.

It was crude, but it was a turning point in opposition cooperation.

Never in their wildest dreams could the EFF have expected to see MPs, men and women, from the liberal DA and feudal IFP put their bodies on the line together, bleeding and spitting out teeth to the point of being hospitalised, to stop the ANC-directed thugs from beating up EFF members and undermining our constitutional democracy.

In the months and years that followed, this unacceptable violence became commonplace, reaching a low point in February 2015 during Zuma's state of the nation address. The white-shirted thugs specifically targeted Mashabela. They broke her jaw as the president looked on and laughed. She spent weeks recuperating but, as we will see, these chickens came home to roost when the EFF had to decide who to back when municipal coalitions and cooperative agreements had to be decided upon some 18 months later.

What goes around comes around, the ANC would learn.

As these events and other political developments were happening and the ANC became more and more mired in corruption, a low-key process was playing out far from the madding crowd.

In August 2014, I reliably understand, the EFF leadership asked an interlocutor whether the DA would be interested in cooperating with them politically. This request was repeated over the next months but, initially, the DA did not show much interest.

Then, towards the end of 2015, a few months before the 2016 local-government elections, the EFF roped in a second interlocutor too influential for even the complacent DA to ignore. The EFF intimated to this broker that it was willing to work together against ANC governance should the opportunity arise in the local-government elections

– with the proviso that the EFF had to keep the DA at arm's length in the interest of its own political growth prospects.

The message was delivered. This time, the DA took it seriously and reacted. Given how things developed, I'd say the EFF achieved its goal in the 2016 elections.

Although no formal meeting took place with the EFF, the DA's brains trust, notably Federal Executive Chairperson James Selfe, started working on possible coalition agreement wordings. The DA had to ask itself, and some outside the DA, an important political question: how could such political cooperation or coalition work with a party, specifically the EFF, with which it did not share much in the line of policy or political principle?

The answer it came up with was twofold. First, sometimes distrust can be a very good foundation for political cooperation because it keeps all partners honest. Secondly, the major issues where the DA differed from the EFF – such as land, nationalisation and non-racialism – did not primarily affect the kind of municipal service-delivery and clean-governance issues upon which local-government elections turn.

The DA also realised that it would need a corps of well-trained party members to take up key municipal management positions should these municipalities fall to the opposition. So they started training such individuals, which was an excellent move. The only problem was that they ended up not training enough – they were surprised by and unprepared for their own success, winning many more municipalities than they had ever anticipated.

Malema made an important move at a press conference in Johannesburg in February 2016 where he coined the term 'Zupta' to reflect the confluence of the nefarious interests of the Zuma and Gupta families. He was at his quotable best when he said he would not allow South Africa to be 'sold for a pot of curry'. Malema also indicated that the EFF was willing to work with anyone to ensure that South Africa did not become the next African failure.

A few months before Malema's statement, my suspicions had been raised that coalition talks may be afoot. Having watched the hatching entente for a while, the February 2016 EFF press conference was the point when I realised that an unlikely opposition cooperative agreement was indeed on the cards. When I checked with reliable EFF and DA sources, my impression was confirmed – off the record, of course. This was big news and I decided to monitor developments closely.

The impression that the electoral tide was turning against the ANC and the realisation that the opposition could make great strides in the 2016 local-government elections was confirmed by the registration figures for the first voter-registration weekend at the beginning of 2016.

It was not widely realised, but, as I wrote in the *Sunday Times* almost three months before the election, 'Opposition strongholds registered more new voters than the bastions of ANC support in metros where the ruling party is vulnerable – but the ANC did spectacularly well in KwaZulu-Natal.'

To me, this was an early and strong indication that differential turnout could be decisive in 2016. And it was. I continued:

> When analysed, the wealth of data for the 22 617 polling stations across the country provides the strongest pointer yet to the election outcome. Because of their divided past, South Africans tend to vote in geographical blocs determined largely by race and, increasingly, by class. Very few metropolitan municipal wards are diverse

enough to be closely contested, which gives analysts the luxury of using data showing where people registered, to project how these areas are likely to vote.[2]

I also wrote that factors to watch in Johannesburg specifically would be 'whether the three main parties can motivate their supporters to turn out and vote, and whether allegiance will switch between the ANC and EFF in either direction. Another crucial consideration will be whether, if the ANC misses 50%, the DA and the EFF can find each other to create a coalition government.'[3]

Furthermore, I pointed out that about 12 000 new DA voters had registered in Nelson Mandela Bay, against about 5 000 new ANC voters and fewer than 1 000 new EFF voters. 'This is a net gain of about 7 000 for the DA, which is still about 13 000 short of a majority, but would also ensure that the ANC does not achieve 50%. A hung council – where no single party has more than 46% of the vote – thus becomes a strong possibility.'[4]

In an apparent foreboding of things to come in this troublesome metro, I noted that '[s]uch a city government could be unstable and hard to manage, with the larger parties at the mercy of the smaller groupings'.[5]

In KwaZulu-Natal, however, the ANC outregistered its main rivals by a factor of almost six to one.

This trend of higher registration in opposition-supporting wards of key metros – and, more remarkably, of a decrease in the number of voters registered in ANC strongholds in those same metros was confirmed once more during the second voters' registration weekend. The August 2016 election results were not hard to predict or interpret if you transposed the number of new voters per ward onto the voting history of each ward.

This is an important and easy skill to acquire for anyone wishing to make a fast buck betting on South African election results. Personally, I don't bet on politics, but some of my friends made handsome amounts using this method to extrapolate and project probable election results. One of the ways to do so is to note the decrease in voters registering in wards where the ANC had traditionally held huge majorities, as I did in an article published in the *Rand Daily Mail* on 7 July 2016, about a month before the election:

> Registration figures released by the Electoral Commission show growth in integrated suburban areas, and a decline in the number of voters in many township wards, with some losing as many as 2 000 voters over the last two years. ... [S]everal ANC township strongholds in Cape Town show much fewer voters have registered than in 2014, with Nonqubela (ward 89) now having 2 211 fewer voters than in 2014. In the Port Elizabeth-based Nelson Mandela Bay metro, KwaDwesi has lost the most voters (1 929), and in Johannesburg the ANC-supporting Naledi in Soweto has 1 038 fewer voters.[6]

This decline in registration figures was reflected in the election results.

This method of projecting or predicting results rests on three imperfect pillars of assumption. The first assumption relies on the findings in countless marketing surveys, according to which South Africans are generally accepted as being among the most brand-conservative people in the world. (Note how we refer to Five Roses when ordering Ceylon tea in restaurants, how we refer to all dishwashing liquid as Sunlight, how we rarely change washing-powder brands and how many South Africans regard 'remaining true' to their political party brand as a source of pride – even when their party has not specifically remained true to their interests or principles.)

The second assumption is that because of the enduring relics of ethnic thinking and apartheid spatial planning in communities, they do not easily shift their political allegiances.

Thirdly, and especially, the growing body of historical voting data showing voter preference trends and percentage polls per polling station makes ever more accurate projections of election results possible.

It is a very basic process. One takes the trends in the ward for the previous four election cycles, and then extrapolates these trends to the current cycle, taking into account the number of voters added or lost in the specific ward, and allocating them to political parties according to trends seen in the results of previous election cycles.

Of course, this system is far from watertight, mainly because it presupposes the brand conservatism to which I just referred, and does not always take note of unexpected developments, like the growth of a new informal housing area/squatter camp in the middle of a wealthy and established residential area, or an unexpected event, such as the death of a charismatic or ineffective party leader.

The trick is to investigate and understand these trends, as well as the demographic shifts in the few areas where huge variations in voter numbers occur. But, mostly, the extrapolation method I have just explained provides an excellent rule of thumb for projecting and, if you're feeling bold, even predicting election results.

It can be a lonely, time-consuming pastime. But, luckily, I am not the only political nerd in town, and I have friends who are ready, willing and able to check and respond to my calculations and conclusions, and point out my mistakes. In the end, the two voter-registration weekends for 2016 provided astounding and confounding statistics, all pointing to a probable rise in opposition votes and a decline in ANC votes.

Not many South African political pundits have the appetite, inclination or patience to work out these extrapolations. They take a long time and you need to keep your data bank up to date, so I was largely out on a limb.

But, as my friend and mentor Ryan Coetzee taught me years ago, in political punditry you must develop your method to a point where you trust it, and then you must be prepared to stick your neck out – not arrogantly, but with some degree of confidence, explaining all the while how you reached your conclusions – and be prepared to learn from your mistakes, wipe the egg off your face and dust yourself off should your method prove a failure.

So, I decided to trust my extrapolation method, especially as it chimed with the anecdotal information I was getting from trusted political sources in the ANC, DA, EFF and IFP based on their feedback from interactions with voters canvassed in many varied communities across the country.

With all the signs indicating the possibility of strong opposition growth and corresponding ANC decline, the stage was set for possible opposition coalitions, unseating the ANC in key metros and municipalities. So, the logical next step was to find out who was in charge of possible coalition talks in the different opposition parties and whether they would prefer coalitions with the ANC or with other opposition parties, and under which terms. This was done in the understanding that preferences might well change as circumstances or the nature of deals offered changed, in the event of the different coalition possibilities the extrapolation method pointed to.

I set about calling the people in charge of coalition talks in the seven leading opposition parties, to let them speak for themselves. What astounded me at the time was how prepared most opposition parties were to state their preference – on the record – to work with fellow opposition parties rather than with the ANC. Although this echoed the detente I could see was emerging between opposition MPs of different ideological perspectives, I was still surprised by the frankness with which I was able to report on probable coalition and cooperation tendencies about a month before the election.

For example, the IFP's chief whip, Narend Singh, told me that his party's national council would meet after the election to discuss possible coalitions, should the possibility arise. 'Although we have worked with the ANC on a provincial level, we prefer not to work with them on a local government level. Parties who have done that, have shown suicidal tendencies,' Singh said, adding that the IFP was not ruling out any party as a potential partner.[7]

DA representatives told me that the party had been in informal talks with 'several opposition groupings – notably the EFF, the UDM, ACDP [African Christian Democratic Party], COPE [Congress of the People] and – in the hotly contested Nelson Mandela Bay where a hung council and much horse-trading is expected – with the union-aligned United Front. Nothing formal has been decided yet, though, with potential partners clearly holding out to get the best deal and the most power possible.'

UDM chief whip Nqabayomzi Kwankwa said that although they would not rule out any party as a coalition partner, they would gauge the support of their 'sister opposition parties' – mainly because they would be their preferred partners in Nelson Mandela Bay. Senior ACDP MP Steve Swart said there was no reason to change 'a very healthy relationship' with the DA and that his party would find it very difficult to work with the ANC. 'It would be suicide. In fact, it is an absolute no-no,' Swart said.

The one party that didn't want to go on the record about possible coalitions, however, was the EFF. They have become known for playing their cards close to their chest in this and other matters.

Nevertheless, I was able to come to the conclusion that the major opposition parties were generally loath to enter into coalition agreements with the ANC, preferring to look for partners who also oppose the ruling party. The only two opposition parties leaving any doubt about that were the EFF and the Freedom Front Plus (at the extreme left and extreme right), but for different reasons.

As we shall see later, this refusal to be pinned down early is part of the EFF's strategy to get its prospective partners to agree with as many as possible of its policies. In the case of the Freedom Front Plus, it was more a question of speaking with forked tongue, or maybe just a lack of strategic coordination (maybe there are good reasons why small parties remain small).

It transpired that Anton Alberts, a politically ambitious Freedom Front Plus MP from Johannesburg, had issued a pamphlet that was widely distributed in Afrikaner communities in the north of the country claiming that the Freedom Front Plus differed from the DA in that it would never work with the EFF.

READING THE TEA LEAVES OR, RATHER, THE STATS

Corné Mulder, a more astute political operator and one of the foremost political brains of the Freedom Front Plus since its inception in 1994, knew that this was folly and kept a back door open in his interview with me for my *Rand Daily Mail* article. Never say 'never' in politics. And, when push came to shove, the Freedom Front Plus did in fact enter into cooperative agreements with the EFF. Alberts and his opportunist election-time promises were nowhere to be seen.

With that, we political reporters continued covering the daily to and fro of the South African election silly season as we awaited the voters' verdict.

CHAPTER 3

How the 2016 opposition deal was done – the back story

South Africans always vote on a Wednesday, and it is always given as a public holiday to ensure that as many citizens as possible can take part in this democratic process.

At 9 pm, the polls close, except where there are abnormal circumstances, and the counting begins. Each vote is counted in the room where it was cast, and the ballot can be queried by party agents – every political party has the right to this in every counting station to ensure that all its votes are counted.

Once the counting is finalised to everybody's satisfaction, the result slip for that polling station is signed by each party agent, and they are permitted to photograph it to send it to their party, which counter-checks it against the results announced by the IEC, to avoid any fraud or skulduggery regarding the results. A copy of the result slip is sent to the IEC and another copy is displayed on the outside of each polling station.

All of this makes committing voter fraud during the counting process in South African elections very, very difficult because the system is simple (if a trifle time-consuming) and decentralised and there are many checks and balances.

Long may it remain unchanged, and long may South Africa resist efforts to switch to the type of electronic and other voting systems that have led to the sometimes violent contesting of election results in democracies as far apart as the United States and Kenya.

From the moment the polls close, the national focus shifts to a remarkable South African invention called the election results centre. Situated in a cavernous exhibition hall at the showgrounds in Pretoria West (known rather swankily these days as the Tshwane Events Centre), for about four days after each election the place becomes an object of national fixation as the election results are displayed as they trickle in from every corner of the country.

For a politics junkie, the results centre is heaven – a playpen of statistics and real-time history being made dramatically as the verdict from every polling station arrives – the product of millions of South Africans waking up and queuing in rain or shine, heat or cold to vote their hopes and fears.

The hall is laid out on two levels. The lower floor has tables and chairs where each major party participating in the poll can gather and examine the results on the computers provided. It also means journalists can buttonhole leading politicians for opinions and interviews, and study the interactions of those representing the political parties as the results picture becomes clearer – especially in the small hours of the night, when their guard is down and their true nature shines through.

Also on the lower level is a type of glass cage, known colloquially as the fish bowl, in which the multi-party liaison committee meets. Every major political party is represented on this committee, whose job is to deal with voting and counting issues as they arise. These individuals meet regularly, also outside of the election cycle, and form the basic bonds of trust, decency and personal kinship that help ensure that some small hiccup does not derail the whole election process, and that rumours of shenanigans are dealt with before they cause a major disruption.

The fish bowl – brain child of Judge Johann Kriegler, the first IEC chairman – also symbolises transparency, because although the discussions between political parties are held behind closed doors, the transparency afforded by the glass walls means everybody can see exactly what is going on – nothing is hidden from view.

The lower level contains seats for the auditors who check and officially verify the results from across the country. There is also an area for the press conferences the IEC hosts every four hours to update the media on election-related news.

One entire wall of the lower level is taken up by ten huge scoreboards that show the number of votes for each party in the national ballot and in each province at that moment in time – and the percentage of polling stations where the votes remain to be counted.

The upper level consists of temporary offices for media houses that have accredited their journalists for the event. There are views over the lower level, where the action takes place. From here, television news channels broadcast 24/7 to those glued to their screens at home waiting to find out what the immediate political future will hold.

Also on the upper level is a dining room where food is served to accredited journalists, politicians, IEC staff and auditors. This is a great meeting place for comparing notes and sharing insights into how to read the tea leaves, for discussing how the political dice are falling and to find out what your media competitors know.

The upper level also features a bar, where tongues become loosened and opinions less guarded as hour follows sleep-deprived hour, and liquor acts as lubricant to ease the passage of opinion over the conventional impediments, such as judgement, so that many an individual suddenly feels emboldened to share a candid view or insight that would normally remain unsaid.

But the best thing about the election results centre — and this is the reason why it is my favourite place and why there is nowhere in the world I would rather be during those four days after elections — is the nooks and crannies where the deals are done between the politicians.

If you know your politics, your politicians and your election results statistics, and if you have good contacts and keep your eyes open, much can be garnered from who speaks to whom and in what way, and what their body language indicates. Much can be learnt by observing who vanishes with whom behind the black curtains skirting the venue for private talks, perhaps laying the foundations for a possible political deal that will ultimately have an impact on every South African.

It was in the election results centre where much of the formal mating dance that led to the forging of the opposition alliances in the wake of the 2016 local-government elections took place, although there was a preamble in Parliament stretching back all the way to 2014, as we have seen.

Having voted at my polling station in Sea Point, Cape Town, at 7 am on 3 August 2016 (vote *early*, vote correctly, vote often!), I took a flight to OR Tambo International Airport and went to the election results centre.

Information I received from sources around the country seemed to favour the opposition in key metros. In the Nelson Mandela Bay area, a massive storm had led to flash flooding in low-lying ANC-supporting areas, while in opposition areas voters were voting like there was no tomorrow, sensing possible victory. By 11 am, the opposition had built up a turnout differential[1] that the ANC could not counter, despite their best efforts later in the day.

At 6.30 am, my cousin had sent me a photo from their polling station in the stoically DA stronghold of Lynnwood in Pretoria's wealthy eastern suburbs. It showed hundreds of voters already queuing in the bitter cold of the Pretoria winter daybreak, half an hour before the polls had opened. If that was the picture in Pretoria's eastern suburbs, it would be replicated in the southern and northern parts, which are rock-ribbed DA heartland.

Were the EFF to do the same in its strongest areas to the far north of the city, Tshwane Metro was in play for the opposition. It would take a massive effort from the divided ANC in Tshwane to match such a turnout in its strongholds, the established majority black African townships to the immediate west, east and north of the city – townships like Mamelodi, Atteridgeville and Mabopane.

As luck would have it, the first person I bumped into upon entering the election results centre was the EFF's ultra-intelligent live wire of a national spokesperson, Mbuyiseni Ndlozi, whose easy-going likeability has earned him the nickname 'the people's bae'. (In case you didn't know, 'bae' means boyfriend.)

Ndlozi was in charge of the EFF campaign in Tshwane and was chipper: their supporters were turning out en masse in their strongholds in the extreme north of the city. He also – quite correctly – tipped me off to watch the results in Rustenburg and the Metsimaholo municipality, which is centred on the northern Free State industrial hub of Sasolburg. Their supporters were coming out in numbers, Ndlozi said – much more so than they had anticipated. Yet he made the completely mistaken prediction that the EFF would sweep Polokwane, the provincial capital of Limpopo, where the party's leader resides.

Allowing, as ever, for the fact that optimistic politicians tend to overstate their expectations on election day in the hope that positive reportage on the day might encourage their supporters to vote, the glum feedback from ANC sources I contacted across the country and the excitement slowly mounting among opposition politicians did nevertheless confirm that the tide was flowing away from the governing party.

I have always believed the key to good Sunday newspaper political reporting is to identify trends, and the key people taking the decisions necessitated by those trends, early, and to open – and keep open – communication channels before competitors spot those trends.

What was clear as day to me after doing the rounds in the election results centre that watershed election day of Wednesday 3 August 2016 was that two political possibilities were taking shape that would determine the news agenda by the weekend. One was that the ANC would scrape home in the metros outside of the DA heartland in Cape Town and the storm-affected Nelson Mandela Bay. The other was that no one would win overall majorities in many municipalities, opening the door to coalition or cooperation agreements.

Questions put to leading figures in the DA, including James Selfe, who would become the party's chief coalition negotiator, revealed that under no circumstances would the DA be interested in coalitions or cooperation with the ANC. In the case of this big decision the DA kept to its word, with one exception – the Kannaland municipality centred on the Western Cape town of Ladismith, where local DA leaders decided to work with the ANC (a decision that was, to my mind, correct). In so doing, they jointly relieved the municipality of the deeply flawed leadership of Icosa's[2] Jeffrey Donson, a local strongman of rather uncertain virtue.

But, in all other cases, ANC–DA cooperation agreements were out of the question. Given this, the position of the EFF as the third largest party would be the deal maker. The question to be put by the weekend would be the classic conundrum faced by third largest parties the world over in situations where no party holds an overall majority: which would they back – the governing party or the opposition?

What, in the words of Vladimir Lenin, was to be done? Go with the ANC, go with the opposition or go it alone, leaving unstable minority governments in charge? The eventual decision could make or break the EFF. It was crunch time for the feisty men and women in the red overalls.

The first thing to find out was the process the EFF would follow to reach a decision, and who would be the main coalition/cooperation negotiator on the party's behalf. That designated person was the EFF secretary general, the friendly and capable Godrich Gardee, an MP and former municipal manager from Mpumalanga.

The great thing about the election results centre is that everybody who is anybody in South African politics is present and available, including, at that point, Gardee. And the great thing about Godrich Gardee is that he is an unequivocal, straight-shooting politician who understands process.

Gardee explained that his party's process would be, first, to hear what the various potential coalition partners offered, then to see what the EFF could negotiate to implement the policy pillars of its constitution (more on this in Chapter 5), and then for its top leaders to make a decision. Such a decision would be binding on the EFF structures within all municipalities, in keeping with the EFF principle of democratic centralism, explained Gardee.

For a journalist, this was extremely important information, because it meant one did not have to gauge the specific preference of EFF structures in every municipality. The central decision would be binding.

My next step was to corner as many of the key political leaders as possible in the EFF executive (the body that would make the binding central decision) to find out their preferences regarding coalition or cooperative partners before the results upped the stakes and fellow journalists started pestering them. That is what I focused on for the next few days.

By Friday afternoon, I had contacted enough key players in the EFF to conclude that there was very little desire for a general working agreement with the ANC. It was clear what the EFF would not do. What was fuzzier was what they *would* do.

Within the EFF leadership, four initial options started to crystallise. First, they could work with the ANC in all municipalities without overall majorities (so-called 'hung councils'). But there was very little appetite in the party for this option because of the thuggish and violent behaviour shown by the ANC towards EFF supporters in places where the media seldom venture, and of course in Parliament. As one EFF insider put it to me at the time: 'Fuck them, fuck them, fuck them and fuck them. The ANC should have thought about this possibility [a coalition] before they broke the jaw of our member on the floor of Parliament.'

The ANC was to be haunted by its own thuggery now that it needed friends. The doors it had shut so callously remained shut. The chickens had come home to roost. No one of any substance in opposition ranks would answer when the ANC came courting for coalition partners.

But this still lay in the future. On to the EFF's second option, favoured at the time, some said, by Malema, namely to work with the largest party in each municipality. Although that would have been rather politically unprincipled, it would have held the massive advantage that the EFF would not be beholden to a single coalition or cooperative partner as a junior appendix nationally.

As we shall see, protecting its political independence weighed heavily on the EFF – to put it plainly, it would not be anybody's political bitch. That was never going to happen.

Which brings us to the third EFF option, namely to work with other opposition parties, notably the DA and the IFP. The advantage of such an approach was that it placed clear blue water between the EFF and the ANC, from which pond the EFF will have to fish for future supporters. It could prove that it could govern better than the ANC, thereby luring its supporters over time, as the DA has done.

But the big negative for the EFF with this third option lay in how the results panned out. In no municipality did the EFF achieve an overall majority, and in every hung municipality bar one (Rustenburg, which includes the EFF stronghold of Marikana), the EFF was beaten by either the liberal DA or the traditionalist, feudal IFP.

This meant that the EFF would always play second fiddle to (or be the bitch of, if you prefer forthright imagery) political parties with

HOW THE 2016 OPPOSITION DEAL WAS DONE – THE BACK STORY

which it had very little policy overlap. Nowhere would it be able to implement its radical policies unfettered.

The fourth and final option open to the EFF was to go it alone. This option, with its echoes of Bikoist Black Consciousness ideology, had much appeal in EFF circles, purportedly from its influential deputy president, Floyd Shivambu, among others.

As the results trickled in that Thursday and the EFF kingmakers pondered their options, the courting and waving of carrots began. I was flabbergasted when, from my conversations with politicians from different parties, I realised that no one knew who to speak to or who to negotiate with in any other political party. At this point there had been no formal meetings between the parties.

Former leader of the official opposition Tony Leon has often decried the silos in which South African political parties operate – politicians' friendships rarely transcend party-political boundaries in the way they do in many other democracies. In the end, intermediaries had to point the politicians to their prospective negotiating partners. Once that had been done, the political mating dance could begin.

Then ANC secretary general and all-round Mr Nice Guy, the incorruptible and charismatic straight shooter Gwede Mantashe, started circulating among the opposition parties, but his beguiling efforts at winning friends and influencing people were utterly hampered by the presence of two of the ANC's most unpopular and unpleasant cadres: his deputy, Jessie Duarte (personal note to Ms Duarte: it is immensely counterproductive to throw zap signs to people you need to ask to be your partners some hours later) and the ANC Women's

League (ANCWL) president, Bathabile Dlamini, the guardian of the ANC's 'smallanyana skeletons', whom most opposition members view as uncouth. With these two as his accomplices, failure would follow Mantashe's efforts as surely as night follows day.

At one point, the EFF's Gardee and the DA's Selfe vanished for a while. It transpired later that this was a most fortuitous meeting between two of the country's finest politicians – both play a straight bat, understand structures and respect process. These two would manage to steer the DA–EFF cooperative partnerships through many a white-water rapid and trouble spot for long afterwards. The IFP, which had scored a marked improvement in its support in KwaZulu-Natal, and other opposition parties soon started hunting for partners as well.

Within the DA, not everyone was convinced that working with the EFF was viable or preferable, given, as mentioned, EFF policies, and the race-tinged statements made by too many in its leadership, which tended to be very disparaging of vulnerable minorities. Sentiments in this regard were often expressed in colourful language: 'This is potentially a "we will not invade Poland" moment,' said one DA MP, raising a Nazi spectre. 'In the end, I fear they want to kill all of us with their machetes,' claimed another, echoing imagery from the Mau Mau uprising in 1950s Kenya.

These were exceptions to the rule, but somewhat more progressive DA sources revealed two further concerns, hidden but real, and honestly expressed. The first was that EFF councillors may be of the same high quality as EFF MPs, and run rings around inexperienced DA councillors facing the burdens and confines of government for the first time. The second was that the DA and the EFF would soon be at each other's throats, driving the EFF into the arms of the ANC, to the future detriment of the country from a DA point of view.

The answer to these two concerns also provided the solution to the EFF's distaste for being seen as the DA's bitch. This consisted of the DA offering coalition spots not only to the EFF, but to all willing opposition parties in hung municipalities. This proved to be the silver bullet to success for three distinct reasons.

First, it reduced the ANC and those small opposition groupings in its awe and in its orbit (such as the Patriotic Alliance in some predominantly coloured communities, Durban's Indian-focused Truly Alliance, the Khoisan Revolution in the Northern Cape and Muslim group Al Jama-ah) to what they actually were: an impediment to the true opposition parties.

Secondly, it allowed smaller opposition parties, such as the UDM, ACDP, Freedom Front Plus and COPE, and small, single-municipality parties to punch way above their weight and make a potentially positive contribution to governance.

Thirdly, these smaller coalition partners would widen the coalition or cooperative mandate and act as buffers, so that every divisive issue did not become a DA–EFF fight or a zero-sum game.

But, first, the EFF had to execute its battle plan. It had to see whether it could get a better deal to have its policies implemented and its strategic goals realised.

The ANC proceeded to do its best to try to win over the EFF. It used the tried-and-trusted method that had always served it so well in the past – a combination of old ties, the race card and tempting the potential partner with gold and silver.

EFF sources spoke of crudely racist attempts to align the EFF with the

ANC against the supposedly white supremacist DA. They told of bribes and positions being offered. They also told of former comrades from the days before the EFF leadership's expulsion from the ANC Youth League suddenly calling up, all buddy-like, to recall the good old days.

But EFF leaders were not going to succumb easily to these kinds of machinations. Its preference remained to go it alone or to go against the ANC. One of the non-negotiables from an EFF perspective was its insistence that all corrupt politicians and officials must be prosecuted. Given how deep the ANC had sunk into the swamp of maladministration and what became known as state capture, it was a low bar that proved just too high for the governing party, a once proud liberation movement. After all, Zuma, its leader, who had been elected by a 75% margin by the ANC rank and file at its 2012 elective conference in Mangaung, was potentially facing at least 783 counts of corruption.

Maybe the ANC realised it was on a hiding second to none, but it was always going to put up its best fight not to lose the glittering Gauteng metro prizes of Johannesburg, Tshwane and Ekurhuleni, all of which had returned ANC tallies of lower than 50%, as had Cape Town and Nelson Mandela Bay.

So, to some panic in opposition circles, the ANC wheeled out its big gun, Winnie Madikizela-Mandela, to prevail upon Malema, to whom she is personally very close, to help the ANC in its hour of need.

EFF members who did not support working with the ANC were adamant the ploy would not work. 'Imagine how deep they are in trouble if they play their best card this early. They underestimate us. They think we are unsophisticated, but they are wrong. They must accede to all our demands or we will not work with them,' said an EFF source, in a reading that proved to be correct.

But the EFF was not going to be timid in how it approached the DA either. During a typically robust EFF media conference held in the fish bowl on Friday 5 August, two days after the election, Malema showed that he knew that he would be the kingmaker.

'We are proud to have won our home ward,' he crowed about the EFF victory in the Seshego ward in Polokwane, where he lives and votes. It was a cruel and effective jibe, pointing out that the country's president was now alone among the leaders of the four largest parties living in a ward his party had not won, following the IFP's victory in Nkandla.

The DA scored a huge win in the home ward of its leader, Mmusi Maimane, in Roodepoort, Johannesburg; the EFF had gained Malema's Seshego base from the ANC; and the IFP leader, Mangosuthu Buthelezi, saw his party romp to an easy victory in the Ekudubekeni area of Ulundi municipality, where he lives.

Malema showed himself to be his own man, taunting the ANC while making the DA sweat. He seemed very positive about the option of supporting government by the biggest party in each municipality, meaning, for instance, that the EFF would support the DA in Tshwane but the ANC in Johannesburg. His media conference left the ANC and the DA equally uncomfortable and perplexed.

In reality, however, the EFF's position was not as enviable or powerful as Malema would have one believe. The deep divisions within its ranks were evidenced in the results of a snap internal survey conducted the next day – the Saturday after the election. This showed that about two-thirds of its supporters favoured a working relationship with the opposition, and a third favoured working with the ANC.

Even more enlightening was the tone and content of the discussion (some would plainly say the disagreement or even the fight) about the EFF's future path playing out on the party's social-media platforms, notably its website and Facebook page.

The arguments showed the EFF's imminent choice to be a painful, important and unpalatable one. The tone of the social-media discussion was wild and negative – listing reasons why the party should work against the ANC or the DA, rather than why it should cooperate with either.

The DA, worried that it might well miss the unexpected opportunity to rule more widely than it had ever believed possible due to preferences within the EFF, did what it could to unite the stronger opposition groupings against the ANC.

If the major opposition parties were to club together, the opposition could control 28 out of the Western Cape's 30 municipalities, Kouga (Humansdorp) and Nelson Mandela Bay in the Eastern Cape, Kgatelopele municipality centred on the town of Danielskuil in the Northern Cape, Midvaal, Mogale City (Krugersdorp), Tshwane and Johannesburg in Gauteng, Metsimaholo (Sasolburg) in the Free State, Modimolle (Nylstroom) in Limpopo and several rural municipalities in KwaZulu-Natal.

The IFP, ACDP, Freedom Front Plus (abandoning Alberts's thoughtless promises), COPE and several small groupings in the Western Cape's Central Karoo District were keen to keep out the ANC.

Bantu Holomisa's UDM, internally divided and uncertain about its future path, was widely reported to be playing both sides – the ANC and the opposition – waiting to see how the cookie would crumble. This tallied with what I had been told at the time by some within the UDM ranks, even though it was later denied.

HOW THE 2016 OPPOSITION DEAL WAS DONE – THE BACK STORY

As Friday became Saturday, certain ANC elements, especially within the party's Gauteng leadership, showed themselves yet again to be masters at political skulduggery, lying and subterfuge. Realising the uncertainty about a mutual cooperation between the DA and the EFF, these ANC figures tried to, and almost succeeded in, selling a ruse to the media. They claimed that a deal was about to be struck (and had already been agreed upon informally) between the ANC and the EFF, according to which control of hung municipalities would be divided up between the two parties, with the ANC retaining Johannesburg and the EFF being given Tshwane to rule, in return.

Many in the media, lacking sources in the EFF and maybe trusting instead long-standing sources in the ANC, swallowed this lie hook, line and sinker. This was despite Gardee making a show of telling journalists at the election results centre, accompanied by hilarious gestures for all to see, that it was nonsense: 'What is this? [pretends to lose his footing] ... It is an elephant stumbling. The elephant is the ANC. And who will make it stumble? The EFF will make it stumble!'

The DA had its own demons to tame. If its young leader didn't yet know the truth of the saying 'uneasy lies the head that wears the crown', he was about to learn it. In the midst of the delicate negotiations that were to eventually bring about an entirely unlikely cooperative agreement between two ideological poles, the DA and the EFF, Maimane had to fly to Port Elizabeth to douse a fire started by his party's political bulldog and national chairman, Athol Trollip, who thought it appropriate to boast that he could rule Nelson Mandela Bay with or without the EFF – that is, that he did not need them.

Given the negotiations that were about to get under way upcountry, this statement was unwise. Hence, Maimane had to explain to Trollip 'that there was a world outside Nelson Mandela Bay', as one DA insider put it to me.

Within the DA, for many different reasons, there was a fatalistic belief that, when push came to shove, the EFF would side with the ANC. This is because, so the argument went, firstly, the EFF came from the ANC, and would be more likely than not to return to where it came from. Secondly, as the ruling party, the ANC could offer the EFF much more by way of largesse and policy compromise than the DA could. Thirdly, the EFF is closer to the ANC in ideology than it is to the DA. There were also personal friendships between individuals in the ANC and the EFF going back decades, which could be leveraged in times of crisis. None such existed between people in the DA and the EFF. And, lastly, it was well known that the ANC in government had turned the country's criminal-justice system into its personal fiefdom, with prosecution without fear or favour increasingly being honoured only in the breach. The legal challenges faced by leading individuals within the EFF – notably Malema – could be made to disappear quite easily in this corrupt set-up, it was felt.

Quite frankly, the DA and the ANC underestimated the resolve of the EFF's senior ranks, and their disgust at the extent of state capture and municipal maladministration, not to mention corruption. This had been voiced strongly by Malema at the media conference in February 2016 where he coined the term 'Zupta', but clearly not enough people had taken the EFF leader at his word. Those who had not were to be proven wrong.

That night, South Africans were treated by means of a violent spectacle to yet another vivid indication of the level of distrust between the ANC and the EFF. It is customary for the head of state to deliver a speech at the election results centre to mark the announcement by the

HOW THE 2016 OPPOSITION DEAL WAS DONE – THE BACK STORY

IEC of the final results after every election. When Zuma stepped up to the podium to read the speech prepared for him, broadcast live on television, he was not the only one to rise. Four young women stood up in silent protest and took up positions in front of the president, obscuring him from the audience in the hall and television viewers alike.

They stood, serenely, holding placards bearing the phrases 'Khanga',[3] '10 years later', 'I am 1 in 3' and 'Remember Khwezi'. They were references to the 2006 court case in which Zuma was found not guilty of raping a young woman, the daughter of a close friend of his. In court she had been referred to as 'Khwezi' to protect her true identity.

After a while, all hell broke loose. Bathabile Dlamini again showed her rough side by rushing up to the stage, shoving the young women off their feet and ripping apart their placards. To no one's great surprise, Dlamini showed a stunned audience in the hall and watching at home exactly how far her commitment to decency, civilised behaviour and respect for the right to peaceful protest guaranteed in the Constitution extended – and that is not very far.

Security heavies then arrived on the scene and removed the young women with unnecessary levels of violence. The screaming women were removed backstage and whisked away in police vans.

Those women who had been manhandled so roughly were members of the EFF, it turned out, the same party that the ANC was now courting as a partner, the party with which some of its Gauteng top brass falsely claimed a deal had been struck.

A fascinating ten days followed the official declaration of results by the IEC as negotiations took place between leaders of the EFF, the DA and the ANC. At the conclusion of these talks, Selfe and Ndlozi agreed to grant me on-the-record interviews that unravelled, for the historical record, how the deals were done.[4]

Ndlozi told me the EFF were involved in six formal meetings – three with the ANC and three with the DA. 'Although there were informal conversations between individuals before the local-government elections, things only really started happening after the EFF commander-in-chief, Julius Malema, held his press conference, at which he said no one had contacted the EFF yet, and until it was clear that there would be so many councils where no single party would hold a majority,' he said.

Then, Ndlozi continued, suddenly, the calls started coming in from everybody, asking if they could meet with the EFF. First up was the ANC in the form of ANC Gauteng provincial leaders Paul Mashatile, Hope Papo and David Makhura. They asked for formal talks. 'We as the EFF said we will listen to you, but it must be your national leadership,' said Ndlozi. A meeting was agreed upon for 7 August in Johannesburg, and not Midrand, as some have claimed.

Then the DA wrote to the EFF under James Selfe's letterhead, also asking for a meeting. 'We agreed to a meeting on Sunday, 7 August, also in Johannesburg.'

The ANC delegation arrived, consisting of a core team of Mantashe, Duarte, Zweli Mkhize, Jeff Radebe, Andries Nel and Papo. In later meetings, Ayanda Dlodlo joined them.

'Because they had come to us, we asked them to put their case forward. They said that they would like to go into coalition with us, and gave us the option of either sharing power with them in municipalities, or to trade control of some municipalities in exchange for control of other municipalities.

HOW THE 2016 OPPOSITION DEAL WAS DONE — THE BACK STORY

'As the EFF, we told them that we took exception to their offer, because it was based on careerism. We told them that any coalition would have to be based on shared ideology and policy, or else it would collapse anyway,' said Ndlozi.

The EFF then put their demands, which included:
- the nationalisation of the mines;
- the nationalisation of banks;
- expropriation of land without compensation;
- dropping *'Die Stem'* from the national anthem;
- no nuclear deal with the Russians;
- a commission of inquiry into state capture by the Gupta family;
- free education; and
- the removal of Zuma as president.

Ndlozi explained: 'The ANC delegation said they had to discuss matters with their organisation, that they had to consult. Their national working committee was meeting the next day, Monday 8 August, and they would revert back to us.'

On 8 August, the EFF's central command team also met, and the party leaders obtained a mandate to continue with formal negotiations.

At the second meeting, the ANC delegation said it was in a difficult position. It was ready to move on all the policy questions the EFF had raised, but 'the removal of Zuma was a no-no'. They said it would be like asking for a meeting with the EFF, but without Malema.

'As the EFF, we said this was not good enough. The ANC had to focus on issues of substance.' At issue, explained Ndlozi, was the kleptocracy the country had become, and the findings of the Constitutional Court — that the president had essentially broken his oath of office

– not some personality issue with Zuma. 'We asked them: What do you say to that?'

Dodging the question, the ANC replied to the effect that the president could issue a proclamation to change the national anthem, but only after a process of public consultation. 'As the EFF, we were not happy with that.' On the nationalisation of mines, the ANC proposed a state mining company, and on the nationalisation of banks, the ANC proposed a state bank. On the matter of expropriation, the ANC said there could be negotiations, and on the nuclear deal, the ANC said there was no deal with the Russians.

'Regarding the Guptas, the ANC was prepared to institute a commission of inquiry into state capture, but not into the Guptas as such. We as the EFF said that was not good enough; state capture started with Jan van Riebeeck and included Madiba staying in (mining mogul) Clive Menell's house. It was too broad – it had to focus on the Guptas.'

The EFF told the ANC that their proposals were not good enough. 'We would need to see a fundamental shift by them if they wanted to work with us,' said Ndlozi. So, the ANC said they would go back to their organisation to consult.

'After the meeting of the ANC NEC the following weekend, the ANC delegation came back to us with even weaker proposals than before. On free education, they were wishy-washy, making it subject to the findings of the presidential higher education task team. They were now zigzagging on expropriation without compensation, saying they were for expropriation with compensation as detailed in the new Expropriation Bill, which complied with Section 25 of the Constitution [the property clause].

'We as the EFF again offered them our votes in Parliament to obtain a two-thirds majority and change Section 25 of the Constitution, but that was not accepted.'

The ANC also reiterated that the removal of Zuma was a non-starter. That meant, explained Ndlozi, that the EFF would not have the chance during these negotiations to state its case regarding the removal of Cyril Ramaphosa, Baleka Mbete, Nathi Mthethwa and Susan Shabangu. That discussion never even came up, because of the Zuma proposal.

'The talks with the ANC thus ended in failure, the ANC having shown a complete lack of creativity, and no drive to act on the Marikana massacre,' concluded Ndlozi.

The EFF also had three meetings with the DA. These were shorter than those with the ANC. 'From the first meeting, on Sunday 7 August, it was clear that the DA could not think outside the box. They were mostly interested in coalitions. For us as the EFF, coalitions were always secondary, because coalitions had to rest on policy conditions. To be in coalition with the EFF, you have to rule and govern according to EFF policy,' said Ndlozi.

The DA told the EFF that its demands hinged on matters of national policy, and that they wanted to limit the discussions to municipal matters, because these were municipal elections, and the DA was not in a position to implement policy on national issues anyway because they were in opposition.

'We ... told them that we understood their position, but that we wanted their support and votes in Parliament for our national policies, especially as these municipal elections were mostly decided on national issues. 'Take corruption, for instance. Parks Tau (the unseated ANC mayor of Johannesburg) is not a corrupt person, yet the corruption issue was central in the Johannesburg contest.'

At the third meeting with the DA, no one talked much. 'We had taken note of their letter in which they set out how they would govern municipalities – what they would practically do. We agreed that we would support their candidates because it was better than the ANC, but that we did not agree with their policies and therefore could not go in coalition with them.'

For Ndlozi, what was disappointing about the negotiations with both the ANC and the DA was that both those parties thought the EFF was up to some trick. Both those parties wanted, first and foremost, to talk about positions of power in councils.

'We ... kept telling them: "You are speaking to the wrong people. We take exception to your approach. We are not here to talk about careerism. We are here to have a revolution."'

In the end, the EFF chose to support the DA candidates in an effort to create an opposition voting bloc. 'In this regard, our experience of the success of opposition voting blocs in Parliament was central. Central to our thinking was that we have to create a vibrant, creative political environment where change is possible.

'As we have always maintained, this is not possible in the political one-party dominant environment the ANC has created. In one-party dominant systems, dispersing of patronage becomes paramount. That meant we could never agree to cooperate with the ANC as it is. This we have always maintained, consistently.'

Ndlozi said that the ANC's problem is that it is rotten to its core, and it refuses to deal with it. 'Nowhere is this clearer than in its undermining of the rule of law. The rule of law is central in any functioning state. The tragedy of the ANC is not that it contains corrupt individuals. All organisations have that. The tragedy of the ANC is that it fails to act against those individuals. When the people's money is stolen, nothing happens.'

As for the DA, Ndlozi said that one of the EFF's great disappointments was Maimane's inability to frame thoughts and solutions in a political context. 'It was left to James Selfe and Patricia de Lille to do that – to tell us what their policies meant. Selfe and De Lille were the only ones in the DA delegation with that ability.'

Maimane would talk for a long time, said Ndlozi, 'but say nothing. Afterwards, we ... would look at each other not knowing what this guy actually meant. We were unsure of his position on most issues. Maimane also failed to understand that these were negotiations: give and take. The issue of Herman Mashaba as mayor of Johannesburg is an example. Maimane kept asking: "What do you want from us?" He did not seem to understand that we were interested in policy, not positions or personalities,' said Ndlozi.

Regarding the EFF's refusal to take up the mayoralty of Rustenburg and control that big hung council, where they had beaten the DA, in coalition with other opposition parties, Ndlozi explained that the decision was based on the premise that you can't have revolution through coalition.

'For a revolution, you need an unequivocal popular mandate. The EFF wants state power to implement its policy pillars. That's that.'

On the way forward, especially the passing of municipal budgets and integrated development plans (IDPs), Ndlozi said the EFF would negotiate the best possible service-delivery deal for its core constituency, the marginalised black poor. He said that the party was aware of the current laws governing municipalities and that it respected the rule of law. 'We will see to it that in Tshwane, for instance, a non-corrupt budget shifts so that the poor of Hammanskraal and Soshanguve [townships to the north of the city, close to the Limpopo border] are the main beneficiaries, and that the burden of rates and taxes are spread fairly. Otherwise, we will not support the budget and the IDP.'

In his version of events, Selfe said no formal coalition or cooperation talks had taken place with any political parties before the trends in the election results had become known.

'The first discussions took place on the floor of the election results centre in Tshwane, once the arithmetic showed the centrality of the EFF and the smaller opposition parties. I first made contact with Floyd Shivambu, and we discussed the situation regarding hung councils.'

The DA knew that an agreement with the smaller parties was going to be very important, so Selfe also had discussions with the ACDP, COPE and the Freedom Front Plus at the election results centre. 'We let it be known that we were open for business, and by the time we left the election results centre, all of us had a loose understanding of what we were dealing with.'

The DA had set up a coalition negotiations reference group, consisting of De Lille, Patricia Kopane, Thomas Walters and Selfe, and they set about planning. On 7 August, they met the EFF in Johannesburg. 'The EFF decided to involve their top six leaders and asked that we do the same, so we obliged,' said Selfe. 'At that meeting, the EFF raised its issues. These were issues of national rather than municipal policy, such as leaving *'Die Stem'* out of the national anthem, expropriation without compensation, nationalisation of mines and so forth. They invited our response, which we agreed to give.'

HOW THE 2016 OPPOSITION DEAL WAS DONE – THE BACK STORY

The DA was now involved in three parallel negotiation processes – one with the EFF, a second with the IFP and a third with the smaller opposition parties. 'With the IFP, we agreed to support their candidates for executive office in KwaZulu-Natal hung councils, and they agreed to support our executive candidates in Gauteng. That agreement stands.

'Also on Sunday [7 August], we met with the smaller parties. It was a meeting where throats were cleared. They were very angry with us about an election SMS where we had asked voters not to waste their vote on smaller parties, and also about the way they felt we had treated them before.

'We took it on the chin, and we decided to implement the will of the people and thus to co-govern, and proceeded to edit a draft agreement on co-governance – a process of change and editing which continued for the next few days.'

On 10 August the DA had its second meeting with the EFF. 'We again raised the issue that they wanted to discuss matters which fell outside the realm of municipal governance. We said we were happy to have those discussions, but that municipal governance was actually about roads, sewerage and the like.

'The EFF said that they understood our position. We undertook to engage with them on their issues of national concern, noting that mines were almost nationalised already, given all the taxes and levies payable by the mining sector!'

During that second meeting, the EFF also raised for the first time that they did not want to co-govern with the DA. 'They said that they were in parallel discussions with the ANC, and were considering supporting our candidates for executive office,' said Selfe. They set a date for a third meeting – 15 August.

During that meeting, continued Selfe, 'They informed us that they would support our candidates as the lesser of two evils when compared to the ANC. They confirmed that they wanted no executive responsibility. We then set about discussing the modalities of how this would work. The EFF understood that we could not be elected to govern, and then be emasculated.'

Regarding the passing of budgets and IDPs, Selfe said they would require support of 50% plus one. The understanding was that each party would put forward its preferences, and that everybody would try their best to reach a consensus. If no consensus could be reached, it would be escalated to a dispute-resolution committee, including Selfe and Gardee.

In that meeting, Julius Malema raised for the first time the EFF's unhappiness with the candidature of Herman Mashaba of the DA as mayor of Johannesburg. 'We said we would think about it. It was discussed by the DA leadership on Wednesday 17 August, and the party decided to stand by its candidate.'

Meanwhile, the content of coalition agreements with the smaller parties was finalised and signed on the evening of 16 August.

Selfe denied that there was a difference of opinion between him and Maimane on whether Mashaba should remain the DA's Johannesburg mayoral candidate. They discussed it and agreed much was at stake in Johannesburg, 'where there will have to be very close political management. The EFF has agreed that the Mashaba issue is not a deal breaker, so he will be mayor,' said Selfe.

The EFF, through Ndlozi, confirmed that the EFF would vote for Mashaba despite their misgivings, if he remained the DA candidate.

Selfe said that the DA, which had quietly trained 150 people before the election to help run municipalities the party gained, was aware of concerns that it would not have the capacity to run all the municipalities it had so unexpectedly won quite as well as its brand demanded.

Selfe said that they would start interacting with the new mayors and councillors the following week, with the help of people who had gained experience in the councils they had governed before. They would also send officials for training with the South African Local Government Association and the National Treasury. They would monitor these municipalities very closely and intervene as required. This would include providing training on how to handle the situations in multi-party governance, 'where one has to be humble, attentive and always count your words,' he said.

Selfe said he had had several weird experiences during the negotiations, but none stranger than his meeting with Patriotic Alliance leader, Gayton McKenzie, in a parking garage in Braamfontein.

'We wanted the PA's cooperation in Ekurhuleni. The only place we could meet Mr McKenzie was in the parking garage. He said that he was ready to talk about coalitions, but that he had already signed with the ANC. As if he was some sort of soccer star. It was a short and unsatisfactory meeting,' said Selfe.

CHAPTER 4

Cyril Ramaphosa's impact on coalition politics

The ANC has governed South Africa since the country's democratisation. Since 1994 the party has won every national election – and every provincial election outside the Western Cape and KwaZulu-Natal (a province that it has controlled since 2004, and where it gained an overall majority in 2009 and 2014).

As the leading light in the anti-apartheid struggle, the ANC has in the past operated from the moral high ground. In the eyes of its supporters, the ANC brought freedom to South Africans and can therefore rightly claim the title of a 'people's party'. As with most liberation movements turned ruling party, its core supporters are fiercely loyal.

However, in recent years the ANC monolith has started to crumble. The party has lost so much support since 2014 that even its leaders fear it might not achieve a majority in the 2019 elections.

To understand how the ANC ended up in this position and what the different options are that it will consider going into the 2019 elections, it is important to understand the party's history and what it stands for.

Of all political parties in South Africa, the ANC has the longest history. It was founded as the South African Native National Congress in Bloemfontein in 1912, changing its name to the African National Congress in 1923. Initially it was an elite organisation led by people in the professions, often in the legal and medical field. But during World War II, a period that saw South Africa's urbanisation and industrialisation grow rapidly, a younger and more progressive leadership group radicalised the ANC, especially after the founding of the ANC Youth League in 1943. Many of these young leaders would become legendary: Nelson Mandela, OR Tambo, Walter Sisulu, Anton Lembede (who died young but provided a very clear intellectual vision) and the like.

In the 1950s, the ANC became a mass liberation movement of the people, organising protests on issues directly concerning the downtrodden and those denied the vote under apartheid. The defiance campaign against apartheid legislation, boycotts against bus fee increases, the potato boycott against labour conditions on potato farms and protests against the pass system regulating the movement of black people, all cemented loyalty towards the ANC into the very being of many South Africans.

In 1960 the ANC announced that it would organise a massive anti-pass boycott in March that year. However, this was overtaken by events on 21 March at Sharpeville in the Vaal Triangle region of what is today Gauteng when the police shot dead 69 people at an anti-pass protest that had been organised by the Pan Africanist Congress (PAC).

In April that year, the apartheid government then banned both the ANC and PAC, which meant neither could operate legally inside the country. After much discussion and debate, the ANC leaders decided to engage in an armed struggle and continued to operate illegally inside the country, all the while isolating the apartheid government by making the case for democracy worldwide.

It was an uphill struggle in which many lives were lost. In 1964 Mandela and eight others were sentenced to life imprisonment. In the 1960s and early 1970s, the apartheid state seemed more in control, but underneath the surface, the Black Consciousness Movement was reigniting the flame of freedom.

It all exploded on 16 June 1976 when schoolchildren across Soweto rioted against the education system that imposed Afrikaans as the language of instruction. The security establishment struggled to bring the situation under control and a large number of new recruits crossed the border to join the freedom movement in exile.

Back home, the apartheid government slowly but surely started to lose control. In 1983 the United Democratic Front (UDF), an amalgam of community-based organisations, was founded and in 1985 a giant new trade-union federation, Cosatu, was formed. Both these mass organisations made it hard for the apartheid state to govern. Violent and repressive measures were taken by the state in what became a cycle of violence.

Nowhere was this violence more terrible than in present-day KwaZulu-Natal, where the Inkatha homeland government faced violent resistance from ANC- and UDF-aligned opposition in areas designated black, especially south of the Thukela River. The security forces responded with ever stricter oppression. Thousands died there and in Gauteng.

By the beginning of 1990, something had to give. On 2 February 1990, President FW de Klerk unbanned the ANC, PAC, Communist Party and several other organisations and Mandela was released. In

1991 the ANC elected Mandela as its leader. The first democratic elections were held in 1994, with the ANC winning in seven provinces (all except the Western Cape and KwaZulu-Natal) and gaining 62.6% of the national vote. Mandela formed a Government of National Unity with the National Party and the IFP.

The ANC won again in 1999 and 2004 under Thabo Mbeki, increasing its share of the vote every time. Storm clouds were gathering, though. For one, Mbeki's denialist stance on antiretrovirals (ARVs) to treat the country's HIV/AIDS pandemic had deathly consequences as thousands lost their lives because the state would not procure the ARVs needed for them to survive. The arms procurement deal of R77 billion, the first major corruption scandal to rock the ANC government, also whittled away at the immense moral high ground the party had occupied since it had come to power in 1994.

Below the seemingly calm ANC political surface, unease was mounting and ready to boil over. The trouble started in 2005, after the KwaZulu-Natal High Court found Schabir Shaik, financial advisor to Mbeki's deputy, Zuma, guilty on corruption-related charges. So closely was Shaik associated with Zuma, and so thoroughly was Zuma implicated in Shaik's actions, that Mbeki fired Zuma.

That truly set the cat among the pigeons in the ANC. Enemies of the high-handed Mbeki coalesced around Zuma, who was cast as a man of the people – a role the populist Zuma could play with gusto. Anger at Mbeki's callous stance on HIV/AIDS and frustration with his market-driven macroeconomic policy, which resulted in growth without concomitant job creation, fuelled anti-Mbeki sentiment.

At the ANC's elective conference in Polokwane in 2007, it all blew up when Mbeki was soundly thumped by his deputy. It was a tale of a victory of the everyman over the elite, of passion over reason, of practical politics over theory, and of the wounded over the politically exalted.

Nine months later, Mbeki was recalled as president by the new Zuma-aligned ANC. Kgalema Motlanthe took over as caretaker president of the country until the 2009 general elections, when Zuma became president of South Africa.

The Zuma presidency is probably best described by the title of a Justice Malala book: *We Have Now Begun our Descent*.[1] Zuma became enmeshed in the affairs of the wealthy Gupta family, whose influence in his government was so strong and so dubious that a term coined by the World Bank, 'state capture', entered into the general South African political vocabulary. Under Zuma, the ANC became closely associated with corruption and maladministration. In his mid-2017 organisational report, the party's secretary general, Gwede Mantashe, admitted that corruption and vote buying had even permeated to branch level.

The ANC also suffered splits of varied sizes, with Holomisa's UDM, Mosiuoa Lekota's COPE and Malema's EFF all crossing to the opposition benches.

Electoral decline quickly followed, and this became clearly evident in 2016, when the ANC lost its majority in a further three metros outside Cape Town – Tshwane, Johannesburg and Nelson Mandela Bay – and in about 30 municipalities. Although the ANC parliamentary chief whip, Jackson Mthembu, had vowed that the 2016 local-government election results would lead to self-reflection and self-correction, 2017 saw even worse infighting than before in the ANC as supporters of ANC leadership contenders jousted with each other.

Preparing for 2019 under Ramaphosa

In December 2017, about 5 000 ANC delegates descended on the Nasrec facility south of Johannesburg, and elected Cyril Ramaphosa as the party's president by 2 440 votes to 2 261 for his opponent, Nkosazana Dlamini-Zuma. Mpumalanga premier David Mabuza was elected deputy president, Mantashe won the race for national chairman, Free State premier Ace Magashule became secretary general, Gauteng ANC leader Paul Mashatile became treasurer general and Jessie Duarte won the race to be Magashule's deputy.

According to discussions I had with the Ramaphosa grouping before and after the elective conference, the result and the margin of their candidate's victory did not surprise them at all. In fact, their prior calculations were out by only about 20 votes.

They have had to admit – some more grudgingly than others – that Mabuza was the kingmaker, the puppet master and the big winner at Nasrec. Mpumalanga's delegates had made the difference, and the way Mabuza directed those votes showed him to be a master tactician.

Ramaphosa had employed a dual strategy to deal with Mabuza in the run-up to the conference. Publicly, he placed clear blue water between himself and Mabuza, whose premiership and leadership of the ANC in Mpumalanga have shown him not to be a choir boy. In fact, Ramaphosa took the step of announcing the squeaky-clean science and technology minister, Naledi Pandor, as his preferred candidate for the ANC deputy presidency five weeks before the conference. In the end she did not even make it onto the ballot, and many observers commented, probably correctly, that the bulk of Ramaphosa's supporters seemed to back Minister of Human Settlements Lindiwe Sisulu against Mabuza.

What opened the door for Mabuza's victory was the Mpumalanga premier's stance of endorsing ANC unity, which he discussed with other provincial chairpersons of the ANC. In the end, 'unity' came to mean that the ANC top six should be balanced between historical supporters and historical critics of Zuma. That was indeed how it panned out. Ramaphosa, Mantashe and Mashatile have been more critical of Zuma, while Mabuza, Magashule and Duarte have been known to be Zuma supporters.

From Ramaphosa's side, the important mover and shaker here was Gauteng ANC chair Paul Mashatile, a staunch Ramaphosa ally and member of his inner circle. Mashatile attended meetings with a firm mandate from Ramaphosa's people to lobby Mabuza to support Ramaphosa's bid, I've been told.

Mabuza's 'unity' view had two basic underlying tactical points. First, he realised the main fear of many a compromised ANC public representative, namely that a divided ANC was sure to lose the 2019 general election, which would have calamitous consequences for those with their snouts in the trough. Not only would they stand to lose lucrative positions, but they might also be held to account by regimes run by their opponents from other parties, who would have a huge appetite to see them accept responsibility and make them pay for any mistakes made or laws and regulations flouted during their tenure.

Secondly, and this was a point made informally by Mabuza to journalists for months before the conference, no matter who won the ANC presidency, he, David Mabuza, wanted to be the deputy president.

If we therefore understand Mabuza's goals to have been to minimise the risk of a 2019 ANC defeat by engineering that the candidate most likely to minimise ANC losses (i.e. Ramaphosa) won, and to ensure a balance between the two opposing internal ANC camps so as to minimise the risk of an ANC split by installing himself as deputy president, then he succeeded admirably. The key to his success in the race between the two opposing slates, headed by Ramaphosa and Dlamini-Zuma, was his control of the votes of some 200 Mpumalanga delegates, who provided the bulk of the victory margin in every race.

The odd race, as the figures would show, was the one for secretary general, which Free State premier Ace Magashule won by only 24 votes against the Ramaphosa campaign's favourite, Senzo Mchunu. This was a nasty surprise for the Ramaphosa camp. Afterwards, some Ramaphosa backers claimed Mabuza had been unclear to his acolytes that he no longer backed Magashule. That sounds rather unlikely. An MP, who is a close confidante of Mabuza and who predicted every result in the top six correctly on the day before voting, claimed later that 'we [the Mabuza supporters] have done our work well'. Either way, Mabuza achieved one of his dual goals, namely to balance the result 3-3 between the Ramaphosa slate and the Dlamini-Zuma slate.

This caused mayhem among Dlamini-Zuma's supporters, and mass desertion of her cause as many politicians sought new horizons. Those ministers who knew that their time was up as ethically compromised Zuma supporters, started lobbying for ambassadorial positions immediately. Clearly, to lose your place on the gravy train is a calamity once you're used to its plush seating.

Although some initial media estimates put the number of Ramaphosa supporters at just over half of the newly elected 86 NEC members, Ramaphosa supporters told me on the day after the election that they could count on 54 outspoken supporters. Ten days later, they had adjusted that number to 56 out of 86 as people set their career sails to the prevailing wind.

That said, the fact remained that Mabuza, who was appointed deputy president two months later, had shown that he looks after himself first, and emerged from the conference as the ANC's master kingmaker. This is fine for Ramaphosa – until, perhaps, one day Mabuza turns on Ramaphosa in his own interest.

Ramaphosa, having proved himself to be a master of patience and strategy, is sure to have a plan in place in case his deputy turns on him. If this were to happen, some of his supporters claim he may turn to the ANCWL for support. Hell hath no fury like a Women's League scorned, as was evident when the ANCWL made it very clear that after their candidate, Dlamini-Zuma, had lost to Ramaphosa, their anger was aimed specifically at Mabuza (and Magashule, for that matter), who, they believed – correctly or not, but they believed it vehemently – had deceived them into believing he backed Dlamini-Zuma while actually crafting the Ramaphosa victory. They are therefore potentially a vitriolic asset arraigned against Mabuza in the NEC.

So, why did Mabuza turn on Dlamini-Zuma? Obviously it is hard, maybe impossible, to read anyone's mind conclusively, and on matters like these rumours abound, but one of the stories being peddled seems more likely than the others in nailing the main reason. It is said that, in the build-up to the conference, the Dlamini-Zuma camp (which, of course, included her former husband who, as head of state, held sway over the security forces) realised they would need Mabuza's support and influence at the conference. In an attempt to coerce him into providing this support, they therefore had the Mpumalanga police compile a dossier of Mabuza's alleged wrongdoings and planned to put him under pressure with the content. But Mabuza got wind of it and, being the strongman that he is, he refused to be held to ransom, knowing that giving in to blackmail leaves you powerless.

During this time of hope and candour preceding, during and following Ramaphosa's election, two of his key backers, both senior and trusted politicians, independently provided me with information on what he planned to do once he was president of the ANC and eventually the country. These insights provide a valuable checklist of his initial ideas upon election as ANC president. Many of these steps were implemented with remarkable speed, especially after his election as president of the country in February 2018. Some initial plans were changed, as plans often are when opinions, priorities, circumstances and information change.

It is a truth universally acknowledged that a politician is more candid before being elected to a position of power than after being elected to a position of power. It is also true that situations, circumstances and possibilities change with the passage of time, and that what was once true and possible may be neither true nor possible just a few weeks later. A week, after all, is a long time in politics, is it not?

But let's take a step back to the heady days of late December 2017 and see what the Ramaphosa camp's intentions were. Time would tell whether they would be realised or frustrated in the ever-changing ebb and flow of South African politics.

In the wake of their victory, the triumphant Ramaphosa camp claimed there were three strikes that assured Dlamini-Zuma's demise as a candidate and, with it, Zuma's demise as president of the country, as ratified by the NEC in January 2018. The first was that her supporters were too confident of victory, and were out of touch with grass-roots feelings in ANC branches (ironically, the same mistake Mbeki had made with

Zuma ten years before). The second was that they had underestimated Mabuza's influence and had misread him. The third was that they had underestimated the negative effect that Zuma's various misadventures in court had had on the Zuma name. The courts literally seemed irritated with Zuma in the run-up to the elective conference. The Zuma supporters had failed to take into account the effect that the judiciary's apparent anger at and frustration with Zuma had had on the general population, Ramaphosa supporters claimed.

They seemed vindicated on this last point when, just nine days after the conference on 29 December 2017, the Constitutional Court (albeit in a remarkably bitterly divided judgment) ordered Parliament to start impeachment procedures against Zuma. This suited Ramaphosa supporters to a tee, and they had expected it. It placed them in a position to be able to keep their promise of replacing Zuma as president by January 2018, and giving him the option to depart gracefully by resigning quietly (and keeping his pension) or face impeachment (and losing that pension).

Ramaphosa's backers also had their candidate ready to step in as caretaker president in the event that Zuma resigned and Ramaphosa became president. It would have been National Assembly speaker and former ANC national chairperson Baleka Mbete.

Mabuza's supporters pointed out that, as ANC deputy president, he had every expectation to fill the resulting vacancy as deputy president in the national government. Only time will tell whether it would not have been wiser for Ramaphosa to have waited a while before becoming president.

Had he waited, he could have had a compliant caretaker and enough time to investigate everything his deputy had done in Mpumalanga. He would also have been able to manage what Parliament calls 'government business' from within a cabinet compiled, to some degree, of people who may not have been his first choice but whom he had to keep on in the interests of party unity and to keep party factions on board.

Examples are Bathabile Dlamini, who was not dropped but shifted to become Minister of Women, Children and People with Disabilities, and Nkosazana Dlamini-Zuma, who was made Minister in the Presidency (keep your friends close but your political enemies closer?). But the worst compromise was Malusi Gigaba, who was removed from the finance ministry, but made Minister of Home Affairs despite a court finding that he had lied under oath as a minister!

That said, in his first cabinet reshuffle Ramaphosa removed much of the worst Zuma rot. Gone were ministers deeply implicated in state capture, like Des van Rooyen (once Minister of Finance for a weekend), Mosebenzi Zwane (mineral resources), David Mahlobo (the energy minister who championed an expensive nuclear deal), Faith Muthambi and the dangerous state security minister, Bongani Bongo. He made some great improvements: Nhlanhla Nene back at finance, Pravin Gordhan moved to public enterprises and – thank goodness – the Department of Energy was placed in the safe hands of Jeff Radebe.

Politics is often a messy choice between compromises. Clearly, Ramaphosa faced many of these. He did not fare badly, but he may still come to regret some of his choices.

Ramaphosa was also faced with the problem of how to deal with the divided top six ANC officials and the Zuma cabinet. As we have seen, Ramaphosa could count on his own, Mantashe's and Mashatile's support. Furthermore, straight after the election of the ANC top six, Mabuza and Duarte started making very reconciliatory noises. Magashule remained the odd one out.

A strategy was devised to deal with Magashule. A thorough investigation into corruption at all levels of government would be instituted. At provincial level, many questions would have to be asked of the former premier, Magashule, not least about a massive dairy farm project benefiting the Guptas. That could place the new ANC secretary general under pressure, as we shall see below.

As for the Zuma cabinet, the Ramaphosa grouping could not just have it reshuffled wholesale without the risk of splitting the ANC. To deal with this, he and his team also had a strategy drawn up before his victory at the conference. It would pivot on his position as leader of government business, and on the knowledge that true power in cabinet resides in whoever chairs the committees that cabinet is divided into. The strategy would therefore be to remove Zuma's allies from these cabinet committee chairs and replace them with Ramaphosa's people.

'First to fall will be Nathi Mthethwa, you'll see!' a well-placed Ramaphosa supporter told me. Mthethwa, Minister of Arts and Culture at the time of the Nasrec conference, had earlier become infamous as the police minister who ran to Zuma's bidding by declaring all the upgrades to the Zuma homestead at Nkandla to be security upgrades, and then playing an unintentionally hilarious video to the assembled parliamentary press corps to try to make his point.

The same process would unfold in the NEC's committees, I was told, and I was warned to look out specifically for the return of former finance minister Pravin Gordhan as Minister of Public Enterprises to turn struggling state-owned enterprises (SOEs) around. Gordhan would take charge of cabinet committees dealing with economics, and the likes of former Reserve Bank governor Tito Mboweni would fulfil the same role on the NEC, I was told.

'Cyril realises that you need money in the state's kitty to transform society. The liquid assets currently held by private companies must also be turned into investments for the economy to thrive,' I was tipped off.

The Nasrec conference's decision on land expropriation without compensation caused the most concern among investors, especially after many in the media hyped it up by not adding the caveat that such a decision would only be considered after a feasibility study had been done to ensure that it would not endanger the economy or food security.

'The kind of blanket expropriation without compensation which the EFF wants is not going to happen on Ramaphosa's watch,' I was told. 'The feasibility study will take a long time. We realise that South Africa needs to retain its position as a bread basket of food security, and we realise how many job opportunities are reliant on successful commercial agriculture.'

The Ramaphosa grouping's ideal for land expropriation, which I have to admit I find noble but somewhat unrealistic, is to follow the Chinese example and focus on food security and the creation of rural growth points to slow down urbanisation.

In February 2018, Ramaphosa's headaches increased when the National Assembly passed an EFF motion that called for the parliamentary constitutional review committee to finalise the modalities of land expropriation without compensation by August 2018. It was a massive policy victory for the EFF. The party immediately promised the three metros where the EFF is kingmaker to the ANC as reward.

However, it will not be possible to finalise such a process before the studies on the effect this will have on the economy and food security have been concluded. Therefore there is a possibility that the economy could be held to ransom by an ANC/EFF political power play.

The most important tip-off I received during the conference was that Ramaphosa's preferred main strategy for the 2019 general election could be, in a way, to turn the clock back to 1994. He could possibly run on a ticket of a Government of National Unity. That is, he could offer opposition parties the chance to join a Government of National Unity after the election – irrespective of the result. Ramaphosa may therefore offer opposition parties positions in the cabinet even if the ANC receives more than 50% of the vote and is in a position to govern by itself.

He could also pursue a Government of National Unity if the ANC were to fall below 50% in the 2019 general election. To my mind, this is a brilliant strategy for a number of reasons:

- ❏ It turns the ANC from the mean spoiler party it became after the Mandela regime back to the party of reconciliation. It will go a long way to start restoring the moral high ground the ANC has lost since 1994.
- ❏ It gives the political initiative back to the ANC.
- ❏ It will maximise ANC turnout because many voters who have come to regard the ANC as self-interested, corrupt bullies will react positively to the idea of an ANC whose rough edges will be blunted by an opposition presence to curb its power.
- ❏ It would divide the opposition completely. From the beginning, those within the ANC who hatched the strategy believed that

it would divide the DA on what to do, leave the EFF out in the cold with the image of an embittered opposition and bring almost all other opposition parties within the ANC's area of influence. Their gut feeling has been proved correct by subsequent events within and between parties.

❏ It will go a long way towards creating the political certainty that local and international investors have long been waiting for.

❏ It will give South Africa the opportunity to go back to the 1994 drawing board, but older and wiser, and with lessons learnt since then.

❏ It is the best opportunity to turn the National Development Plan (NDP), which Ramaphosa co-authored, from a political fig leaf and excuse into an actual possibility.

'We believe that a new Government of National Unity will give us the chance to deal with opportunities which fell through the cracks in 1994. This will be the ultimate expression of the social cohesion Ramaphosa wants to create, in bringing the Constitution to fruition, implementing the NDP and giving practical effect to non-racialism,' I was informed.

Now, of course, these ideals would be wonderful, if they could be realised. I have to admit – and I'd be only too happy to be proven wrong – it smacks a little of naive optimism after a political victory, such as the one Ramaphosa achieved at Nasrec. But if Ramaphosa and his supporters in the ANC could actually follow through on it – and depending on how the voters and other political parties react to it of course – this could be a political game changer. And it could be quite a political vote winner, if managed honestly and correctly.

What gave credence to the indications from the Ramaphosa camp that they would campaign on a Government of National Unity ticket was that they were not shy to point out the numerous strategic reasons for doing so. Firstly, they said, the ANC had failed to attain victories in four metros in the 2016 local elections, and the Ramaphosa grouping viewed a Government of National Unity as the best way for the ANC to win back these economic heartlands in 2021. Secondly, the disunity and inflammatory divisions in the country had cost it internationally – as the unexpected loss to France and Ireland of the right to host the 2023 Rugby World Cup, and many other examples, have shown.

Thirdly, South Africa was facing too many fundamental challenges, which could not be tackled unless everyone worked together in a united manner (or risk becoming a failed state and letting down the promise of the 1994 democratic transition). Furthermore, the Ramaphosa grouping believes an annual economic growth rate of up to 7% is possible if agreement to a social compact could be found between government, labour, business and society at large. Finally, it is seen as the only way of giving the NDP (to which Ramaphosa is deeply committed) any chance of success.

As the views of Dr Kraai van Niekerk, a veteran of the 1994 Government of National Unity, and current leading figures in opposition parties show (for more, see Chapter 11), the jury is very much out on whether an ANC strategy of campaigning on a Government of National Unity ticket in 2019 will succeed, and whether a Government of National Unity after 2019 would succeed in obtaining all the lofty goals Ramaphosa supporters have set for themselves. It might also be stillborn if major opposition parties shoot it out of the water, or it may be shelved to avoid allowing opposition parties the luxury of refusing Ramaphosa. But in the days before, during and directly after Nasrec, that was the ideal.

Only time will tell. Nevertheless, whether South Africans think a Government of National Unity is a good idea or not, many would agree that it is a step in the right direction. At least, one could argue, the ANC was starting to think idealistically, with higher purpose and constructively, and that it is good for them to regard opposition parties as opponents – or even potential partners – rather than as mortal enemies. At the very least, it could make for a more civil kind of politics in South Africa.

Another important goal of the Ramaphosa camp following its Nasrec 2017 conference was to upskill ANC councillors in municipal governments. The expectation was – and one has to bear in mind that this expectation was formulated in the idealistic days just after Ramaphosa's victory – that at some point in the near future, all serving ANC municipal councillors would have to have at least a matric qualification, so that they can be confident in their handling of the issues that their positions require them to engage with.

This might sound like a good plan, but as always in politics, every decision comes at a price. If this decision was implemented, it would disqualify community leaders, including an older generation of ANC activists who had to forego schooling because of poverty, from being elected as councillors.

The plan was also to send a very strong signal against corruption and maladministration by appointing former finance minister Pravin

Gordhan as Minister of Public Enterprises. The mandate given to Gordhan, who is a qualified pharmacist, would be to give the right medicine to the money-gobbling, ineffective state enterprises. That would put the politician who became the most respected victim of Zuma's wrath for diligently opposing state capture back at the political coalface with an important portfolio where he could make a huge difference. This was indeed how it happened.

A probe of corruption at provincial level would have to start somewhere and after Nasrec it was thought strategically wise to start such an inquiry in the Free State, where tales of alleged corruption have abounded. This also just happens to be the province where the problematic newly elected ANC secretary general, Magashule, was premier. In the event that everything in the Free State was found to have been largely above reproach (and this was thought highly unlikely), Magashule would have proven his detractors wrong and be ready to be a very strong secretary general. If, however, the persistent rumours about the state of his province were proven to be largely true, it would be his undoing.

In addition, the ANC secretary general has to deal closely with provincial ANC secretaries. The secretaries of ANC provinces loyal to and supportive of Ramaphosa could be used to make sure any wayward Magashule tendencies are kept in check.

After their Nasrec triumph, the Ramaphosa grouping was aware that the structure of the ANC would present problem man Magashule with his own very difficult challenge once a decision was made with regards to Zuma. 'If you wonder why Ace has been looking so pale and grim, a Ramaphosa insider told me, 'it is because the decision by the ANC to recall Zuma as president will have to be communicated to him by the ANC secretary general. Ace will have to face the old man and tell him that he has to go.'

In the end, this was exactly how it transpired. Magashule had to tell Zuma that he was being recalled.

A master clause in the Ramaphosa grouping's plan to tackle corruption after Nasrec was to make a call on ANC branches to set the example and take the lead in exposing corruption locally, provincially and nationally, so that the ANC becomes the party that fights corruption. That would serve the dual purpose of improving the ANC's image with voters and handing ANC branch-level members a mandate and an incentive to act against the corrupt, even those in their own midst. But it carried the risk that the ANC had to be careful what it wished for – if the anti-corruption drive were to expose a rot that ran too deep, voters might decide to dump the ANC, and Bathabile Dlamini's threatening comment about 'smallanyana skeletons' (i.e. don't blow the whistle unless you want your own skeletons in the cupboard to be discovered) may be proven correct!

A further double word of caution, at this point, would not be out of place. Many have tried to topple Magashule and have failed. Also, at some stage such a probe would have to focus on Mpumalanga under the premiership of Mabuza. How would the kingmaker and newly minted master strategist react to that? What would such a probe unearth and what would the consequences be in the run-up to 2019?

After Nasrec, the Ramaphosa grouping's plan was to place immediate focus on the financial black hole called public enterprises, which would be placed, as mentioned, under the leadership of Gordhan. Freeing up the money wasted there for more deserving causes, such as uplifting the poor, was identified as crucial to South Africa moving forward. This was one of the first steps he took in January 2018, when he purged the leadership of power utility Eskom.

Very importantly, it was realised that, however unpalatable such a step would be to the ANC as a disciplined force of the Left, the public enterprises would have to be run as public–private partnerships, which would unlock money and lead to greater effectiveness. The correct balance would be crucial, and Gordhan was best positioned to strike that balance.

But actions would certainly not be limited to the Department of Public Enterprises. Other government departments – and, in fact, the whole of the public service – would be tackled, guided by the reports of the Auditor-General, which are thorough and freely available.

At all times, so the Ramaphosa grouping argued, economic growth would be a primary focus, among other things because it would increase tax revenue, thereby creating more opportunity for social spending and the upliftment of the poor.

Trade unions would be asked to become part of a South African version of the Marshall Plan and increase productivity, so that the economy could grow at the requisite rate. (This was a reference to the plan enacted by the US Congress effective from 1948 and named after the then American secretary of state, George Marshall, to help recover Western European economies from the devastation of World War II.) During the Ramaphosa grouping's discussions, it was said that the term was used because it implied acting in the national interest, drew attention to the extent of the damage caused by the Zuma era rot and put country before self in an exacting effort to do the best for South Africa. The state would set the example by using the Auditor-General's reports as a guide to root out maladministration. It would then expect labour, business and the citizenry to follow course.

For this to happen, a cabinet reshuffle would be necessary, for which Zuma's recall would offer a perfect opportunity, I was briefed. The cabinet has of course been reshuffled.

A matter that Ramaphosa could not deal with immediately after his election as ANC president, but something he and his supporters feel very strongly about, is reducing the size of Zuma's bloated cabinet. Under Zuma, South Africa had more than 35 cabinet ministers. Together with the deputy ministers, the executive numbered 74. Ramaphosa's preference, it was communicated to me, would be to reduce the size of cabinet, specifically after the 2019 elections, when he plans to still be president, to something approaching its 1994 size – about 25 ministers and 15 deputies. After all, what was good enough for President Mandela should be good enough for President Ramaphosa.

A smaller, more streamlined cabinet represents a huge improvement because the Zuma model proved ineffective for several reasons. Firstly, the exact role and responsibility of every minister was unclear and overlapped with the portfolios and responsibilities assigned to several others. There were simply more people in cabinet than was necessary – they got in each other's way, making the whole construct unwieldy and unresponsive. Secondly, they cost the taxpayer a lot of money. For every ministry, a separate and often repetitive structure had to be created, with offices, secretaries, expensive cars, official residences, spokespersons, advisors and the like. What a waste! And this sent a message to the public that, at the highest level, government was not serious about saving money and being frugal. This has led to much public cynicism towards politicians, their perks and their reasons for going into public office, and has weakened government's right and ability to criticise the excesses of the private sector. It also made a laughing stock of any claim by the ANC that it is a political liberation movement of the Left focused on alleviating the plight of the poor.

Yet, at the same time, Ramaphosa might find it very hard to implement his no doubt noble intention to cut the size of cabinet to the extent he wants to. Two reasons could be advanced to raise such doubts. The needs of the country may not be quite the same as they were in 1994. Secondly, and this is as important practically as it is ignoble morally, it may place his efforts to build a Government of National Unity and keep the ANC intact under huge stress. Politicians choose politics as their career, and career politicians want to advance – in seniority, stature and income. When they are not given a position, and even more so when they lose a position they once held, as a rule they take it personally, they do not act gracefully and they look to exact revenge. Put plainly, if Ramaphosa decides to reduce cabinet to anything approaching 25 ministers, and if he appoints 15 deputy ministers in a proposed Government of National Unity, where will he find positions for everybody in the ANC and opposition parties who believe it is their due? And how will he deal with the fallout?

Another very strong sign of how clean the new Ramaphosa broom intended to sweep would be the announcement, I was told, that the proposed Russian nuclear deal, a contract that is estimated at a cost of a trillion rands – which the country absolutely cannot afford and which would bankrupt it – was off. The focus would henceforth be increased use of renewable energy, for which South Africa has huge potential.

This was one of the very first key decisions taken by Ramaphosa as ANC leader. Its importance and positive impact can hardly be overstated. It does not mean that nuclear should not be part of the South African energy mix. But Ramaphosa's decision delivered the antidote to what was maybe the most dangerous, and potentially lethal, of the toxins Zuma had tried to introduce into the South African economy, and one of the most imperative reasons why he and his henchmen (and henchwomen) had to be stopped, in the national interest.

The threat and danger of the Russian nuclear deal was real and enormous. It is something that I have spent much of my time and energy focusing on since 2014. The problem with the nuclear deal is that it has never been publicly acknowledged and that those with direct personal knowledge of it either became very co-opted, or very, very scared and do not want to go public. It boils down to the basic point that many very powerful Russians, who – to make the understatement of the century – do not play nice at all, believe that Zuma and some in his inner circle gave an undertaking to them on which they bargain that South Africa would sign a nuclear new-build contract with Russia to the tune of the sum explained above. It is very widely alleged that vast amounts of money were paid to certain individuals, and it is understood by at least two sources I spoke to that if that deal is not signed, some extremely angry and, to put it mildly, frustrated Russian heavies will require utterly uncomfortable answers and explanations from said individuals.

I would not want to be those South African individuals.

It is my clear understanding that two consecutive Zuma energy ministers, Tina Joemat-Pettersson and Mmamoloko Kubayi, baulked at signing the proposed deal and that Kubayi, during a visit to her

Russian energy counterpart, was told in no uncertain terms that there was an expectation that she must sign this contract on behalf of South Africa. She could not bring herself to do it. Shortly afterwards, she was replaced by David Mahlobo, whom Zuma had plucked from obscurity in the Mpumalanga provincial bureaucracy in 2014 to head the shadowy cabinet portfolio of state security (a story told bravely and against much powerful opposition by Jacques Pauw in his best-seller *The President's Keepers*, leaving no need to revisit it here).

Mahlobo, who seems on the surface to be friendly and approachable, had been trained in Russia and had visited the country often in Zuma's company. Upon his appointment as minister of energy (a field in which there was no indication that he had any expertise), he gave every indication through his actions and his statements to the Parliamentary Portfolio Committee on Energy that he intended to fast-track the process. Ramaphosa sacked Mahlobo in February 2018.

Ramaphosa needed to make these Russians understand that if they had been led to believe that South Africa would agree to such a nuclear deal, then they had been conned by the Zuma grouping. One hopes that all concerned will be brought to book by the South African law-enforcement authorities. Given the alternative of Russian heavies, those concerned might well prefer such an arrangement.

On the day of Helen Zille's election as DA leader at the DA federal congress in Midrand in May 2007, her predecessor Tony Leon offered the new leader some sage advice. He said to Zille: 'Enjoy your victory. This is the height of your stature and political capital. From here on, it diminishes.'

CYRIL RAMAPHOSA'S IMPACT ON COALITION POLITICS

He was proven right, and Cyril Ramaphosa may very well find that the same advice holds true for him in the run-up to and after the 2019 elections.

CHAPTER 5

The two biggest opposition parties and their options for 2019

Democratic Alliance

The DA is a child of coalition politics. It was founded in 2000 after a successful coalition government in the Western Cape between the New National Party (which was actually very much the old National Party with some added coloured support) and the Democratic Party. The latter had carried, under various different names, the liberal torch in South African politics since 1959.

Although they came from very different backgrounds, the Democratic Party and the New National Party had found common cause against the ANC, and in their wish to provide an alternative to ANC governance based on strong, well-functioning bureaucracies and opposition to corruption. It was a formula that galvanised opposition voters, and in 2000 the two parties merged with a small grouping called the Federal Alliance to form the DA.

But the two main partners had been at each other's throats for decades, and it soon turned into the marriage from hell, as former DA leader Tony Leon dubbed it in his political memoir, *On the Contrary*.[1]

Bickering, drama and infighting characterised the early years of the DA. Infighting is one thing opposition voters detest, and the ANC soon

THE TWO BIGGEST OPPOSITION PARTIES AND THEIR OPTIONS

capitalised on the power struggle between former Democratic Party leader Leon and the deputy leader of the DA, former New National Party leader Marthinus van Schalkwyk.

Following secret talks between the ANC and the Van Schalkwyk grouping, the former New National Party leadership walked out of the DA and formed a cooperation agreement with the ANC. The Van Schalkwyk breakaway group had enough support to form coalition governments with the ANC in the Western Cape provincial government and several local governments countrywide. This set the DA back in the 2004 general elections but did not bode well for the New National Party either, which folded into the ANC in 2005.

The 2006 local-government elections proved a watershed moment for the DA. The party won back several municipalities and grabbed the opportunity to form a coalition government with six other parties in Cape Town, which became its flagship project in providing an alternative to the ANC.

It was a rickety coalition, which nevertheless ruled well. The coalition became stable after the Independent Democrats, a small party with firm support in the Western Cape and a feisty leader called Patricia de Lille, joined the coalition.

This paved the way for the Independent Democrats to fold into the DA, and for De Lille to become first the Western Cape's MEC for social development, then mayor of Cape Town and eventually Western Cape leader of the DA.

Although the 2006 coalition was a boon for the DA, in that it transformed the party in the public eye from an opposition grouping (a relatively negative view) to a capable alternative government option (a more positive view), it also left a sour taste in the mouth, which lingers to this day, for the six coalition partners – the ACDP, Freedom Front Plus, UDM, the United Independent Front, the African Muslim Party and the Universal Party – all of which the DA dumped in favour of working with the Independent Democrats.

In an interview for this book, James Selfe, who, as mentioned, is the DA's greatest institutional knowledge resource, agreed that the party's conduct towards some of the smaller parties that had initially kept it in power before it dumped them for the Independent Democrats was 'cavalier'.

He was specifically referring to the ACDP, but in interviews for this book, UDM leader Holomisa and the Freedom Front Plus leader, Groenewald, both said their parties did not regard the DA as a completely trustworthy ally.

Nevertheless, building on its Cape Town success, the DA came to power in the Western Cape in 2009 with an overall majority and held the province in 2014 against all comers by an increased majority. It also held Cape Town by an increased majority in the 2011 local-government poll, increasing its majority in the metro to almost two-thirds in 2016, and controlling 28 out of 30 Western Cape municipalities, several through coalition and cooperation agreements.

The big bonus for the DA in 2016, however, was the large number of municipalities in all provinces (except Mpumalanga) where the ANC fell below 50% support and the DA could join municipal governments through coalition and cooperative agreements with a number of opposition parties. Of these, the metros of Johannesburg, Tshwane and Nelson Mandela Bay (as discussed earlier) were the sweetest prizes, as well as large municipalities such as Mogale City (Krugersdorp), Metsimaholo (Sasolburg) (subsequently lost to an ANC–SACP coalition in a by-election), Thabazimbi and Modimolle.

THE TWO BIGGEST OPPOSITION PARTIES AND THEIR OPTIONS

Although the DA is much admired by potential coalition and cooperative partners for the way it runs its party machinery, it is simply not trusted in the way other political parties are. Many of its partners view the DA as dishonest. Other opposition parties also dislike the DA for what they term its 'arrogance' – a weird superiority complex rooted in its superior polling and technical systems. On the rare occasions that the DA has reflected critically on how other parties view it, it has, over the years, struggled to understand why other parties find it arrogant but acknowledges their view nevertheless.

Specific examples and events aside, maybe the best way to explain this is the analogy with America, and why so many citizens of other countries detest the US as crass and base – rightly or wrongly. Perhaps American humourist PJ O'Rourke explains it best in his hilarious book *Holidays in Hell*, where he points out that the massive numbers of people protesting in front of American embassies worldwide is eclipsed only by the massive number of people queuing for visas at American embassies worldwide.[2] People just love to hate the DA.

The DA is also resented by its partners for its annoying habit of repeatedly and unfailingly reminding everyone that it is the largest opposition party (as if anyone with more than three brain cells hadn't already realised) and that it is the largest party in just about all coalition and cooperative-governance municipal governments outside KwaZulu-Natal.

If the DA were to, just for once, actually truly listen to what its coalition and cooperative partners are unhappy about, it would, for instance, ban the phrase 'DA-led coalitions' and replace it with 'opposition coalitions'. But maybe that is just a bridge too far for those making the calls in the DA.

Going into 2019, the DA has strong views on the role of coalitions and wants to realise its goal of being in the national and provincial governments. But, with no current realistic chance of winning a national majority by itself, the DA's main hope for 2019 is that the ANC is forced below 50% of the vote, nationally and in provinces like Gauteng and the Northern Cape. This will place it in a position to form a governing coalition with other opposition parties – or with the ANC.

Maimane and Selfe granted separate, candid interviews for this book in November 2017, which provided much insight into DA thinking on coalitions.

I met Maimane in a room adjacent to his huge corner office on the second floor of the Marks Building in Cape Town's parliamentary precinct. He is an extremely likeable fellow with a ready smile, especially when he allows his impish and sometimes risqué sense of humour to shine through. As ever, he was immaculately dressed and well prepared for the interview. When he becomes animated, he leans forward and uses big hand gestures to persuade you.

Maimane is an excellent and unrushed listener – a rare trait among politicians. Maybe it can be explained by his years as a pastor, when he must have been called upon to comfort many a congregant. I once confided in him about a personal problem. The caring way in which he dealt with it is something I appreciated very deeply and will never forget. It was, to me, the measure of the man, not just the politician.

When history catapulted him into the hot seat as DA leader in 2015, many of us thought he was very inconclusive on important matters of principle and policy. Suffice it to say he has grown enormously in stature and confidence, and has led the DA to its best election results ever.

THE TWO BIGGEST OPPOSITION PARTIES AND THEIR OPTIONS

Regarding 2019, Maimane said the DA is very much in favour of coalitions. It is also on record that the DA will not work with the ANC, as it is currently configured, even in local government.

'The ANC does not have the people, the capability or the policy to succeed. Politics is like a game of golf, where the player, the clubs, the course and the weather all play a part in success,' said Maimane. The player is the politician, the clubs represent the political party, the course is the country and the weather is the changing political circumstances outside the party's control.

'We will only work in coalitions where the spirit of 1994 is present. After all, what the DA brings to the coalition – and as long as I am DA leader that will be a non-negotiable – is the ability to bring multiple races together. We do not bring ultra-espousers of ideology', as he put it, 'to the table.'

When the option of cooperating with the ANC was put to him, Maimane left very little room for doubt: 'We will only consider working with a breakaway ANC grouping. I will never work with people like former Free State premier and currently ANC Secretary General Ace Magashule, North West Premier Supra Mahumapelo and other kleptocrats, who have made a mockery of the trusted position of provincial premier. It would also be hard to work with certain trade-union federations as long as they are exclusively focused on the interests of the employed to the detriment of all else.'

But what if the Ramaphosa grouping offers the DA a position in a Government of National Unity?

'Regarding Ramaphosa, if the ANC holds, the question is whether to fold or to keep the opposition. I will not dismantle the opposition – the role of the opposition is too important. In Africa, a Government of National Unity has too often been used to kill off the opposition,' answers Maimane.

'The DA will only work with Ramaphosa if he is not with the ANC – otherwise we would be incapacitated by continuous internal warfare in government. We will not become ANC lite. If Cyril wants to be DA lite, that's his choice.

'Mr Ramaphosa should rather not make that offer. He must not undermine the importance of the opposition. A strong opposition is important,' said Maimane.

Maimane's opinions on how to make a coalition work offer much insight for anyone who may be part of a future coalition in which the DA will be a partner.

'It is important not to rush into a coalition,' he cautions, 'and to remember that dispute-resolution mechanisms are important. There is the time pressure to create coalitions, but to do away with such time pressures you need a capable state and civil service which can keep things going while negotiations are held. In South Africa we do not have that luxury,' Maimane said. 'However, during the negotiation stage, you must give yourself as much time and space as possible to think.'

He also believes coalition partners should be constantly engaged in negotiations and especially once coalitions are agreed upon. 'For coalitions to succeed, they must not be about positions or who gets the best car. It must be about policy to ensure better basic service delivery, especially to the poor, who are the majority,' Maimane said, before adding ruefully: 'Parties to the left often want the state to become their main source of income. That's not great.'

Maimane is very aware of the policy issues he would have to traverse should the DA be able to form a national government with other opposition groupings in 2019. 'The most important policy issue is the country's future economic framework. Policy discussions will need to be confined by reality, not decided by ideology. Nationalisation, for instance, did not work very well for Venezuela, did it?' he asks naughtily.

'Land will be another hot policy issue. Without a two-thirds majority, no change to Section 25 of the Constitution can happen.

'In policy discussions, we should ask ourselves, "What are the country's main problems?" The main problems are poverty, unemployment and inequality, all of which contribute to other problems, like crime. From that departure point, your main policy question – in fact the underlying basis to any policy question – is, how will it benefit the poor?'

According to Maimane, economic policy is the deal breaker, given our high unemployment figure and the great divide between rich and poor. 'Labour reforms must be prioritised so that they do not just favour the employed, but also the unemployed.'

Apart from land and the economic system, he lists fighting corruption, promoting business confidence and investment, tax-income issues and resultant fiscal restraint as red-flag issues. 'We must make the state smaller and better by attracting the best people into the civil service. Also, there must be no presidential appointments – we must strip away presidential powers.'

Maimane firmly believes that, in all policy discussions, the DA should ask itself one guiding question first: how does policy benefit the poor? 'This country is divided between the connected and the unconnected. We must bridge that divide. On job creation, we must ask,

"What would work for the poor?" A system which would make it easy to create job opportunities. On the land issue, we should ask, "What would work for the poor?" Surely not more power for the chiefs.

'We should ask the questions: why does money buy you the best medical and educational services? Why is TB such a killer among blacks, but is almost unknown among whites? It speaks to the divide we must bridge,' said Maimane.

Selfe echoed these sentiments. He is convinced there would be complicated policy issues for future coalitions to contend with. 'There will have to be tough discussions on almost all policies because of the grim economic realities we face. We must decrease the power and cost of the state, which means the defence force and the civil service would have to be downsized. These steps will be unpopular. We will have to increase welfare grants. There will have to be targeted interventions to create opportunity for those who do not have opportunities. This must include targeted education interventions.

'Essentially, we must take money from entities like the SANDF [South African National Defence Force] and spend it on opportunities for the young,' said Selfe.

In our interview, Selfe, who has been primarily tasked with handling the often grimy nitty-gritty of coalition and governance management for the DA, elaborated on the party's views. Selfe is perhaps the most courteous of the current crop of South African politicians. His office is a treasure trove of memorabilia from his three decades in the trenches fighting for the parties variously carrying the torch for the South African liberal ideal – the Progressive Federal Party, which merged with the National Democratic Movement and the Independent Party to form the Democratic Party in 1989, and finally the DA from 2000.

THE TWO BIGGEST OPPOSITION PARTIES AND THEIR OPTIONS

He is meticulous and hard-working, and one of the few parliamentarians of whom it can be said that he is universally respected across party lines. He has what is called the ear of the House: when he speaks, everyone in the National Assembly listens.

Selfe is widely read and is much beloved by all true political journalists because he always answers his phone, always calls back when he says he will, always acts like a professional gentleman to strained journalists and is knowledgeable, quotable, consistent and measured, but armed with a barbed sense of humour, which is very close to my own. He loves a glass of good wine in the afternoon and is not shy to share it with you when you visit his office and the time is right.

On coalitions, Selfe has strong views: 'One has to be realistic in one's expectations about coalitions. Don't expect seismic shifts where there are none. It is, for instance, very unlikely that the DA will get an absolute majority in 2019, so if it wants to be part of government, coalitions are the only way. The question now is with whom can the DA go into government and how close can the DA come to implementing its policy in such a coalition?'

Another option is to go it alone. He referred to the Social Democratic Party in Germany, which recently decided not to join a governing coalition. This came after it had been part of the ruling coalition with the Christian Democratic Union and the Christian Social Union on a federal level since December 2013.

'The key to a strong coalition is the ability to give and take – within reason,' Selfe remarked. 'We are reasonably open to working with anyone – except the ANC in the way it is currently constituted. If we have enough in common with an ANC breakaway group to govern with them, like the commitment we share with the EFF to root out corruption, we can talk about it. But is Mr Ramaphosa truly serious about rooting out corruption?

'There are other possibilities to consider. What if we have no suitors? To some extent, it would not bother us – we are used to being in opposition. But it will set back the democratic process.'

Selfe is sceptical of the DA participating in a Government of National Unity. If the ANC takes above 50% and proposes a Government of National Unity, he doesn't believe the DA should be part of it. 'Contestation is needed in politics. That was the decision the Democratic Party took in 1995, and it was the right decision. Surely it was harder to turn down Nelson Mandela than it is to turn down Cyril Ramaphosa?'

He points out that in an alliance, ideological incoherence could become an issue. 'You can live with it if you are in charge, but as a junior partner you are blamed for the failures while not getting any credit for the successes. As a junior partner, it is tough to hold the senior partner to account, as we saw with the Liberal Democrats in Britain.

'All of this was in play in the 2016 elections, where we were faced with a duality of possibilities. On the one hand, we planned to win outright in as many municipalities as possible. On the other hand, we planned for a number of coalition scenarios.

'We had discussions on what was possible and what was not, but we did not publicise these, because we did not want DA staff, supporters or candidates to take their foot off the accelerator during the election process. In fact, we discounted public talks of coalition in the run-up to 2016.'

Selfe believes staying true to principle is the mainstay of successful coalition formation. 'We cannot just take power for power's sake.

THE TWO BIGGEST OPPOSITION PARTIES AND THEIR OPTIONS

We must be in a position to do what we were elected to do, or back off. That is why we did not work with the Khoisan Revolution in Springbok's Nama Khoi council.' (In the 2016 provincial election, the Khoisan Revolution was the kingmaker in this Namaqualand council and apparently offered its allegiance to whichever party would give its sole councillor a lucrative position.)

'We cannot be like the Patriotic Alliance, which really is only interested in positions.' (The Patriotic Alliance was started in 2013 by one-time convicted criminal Gayton McKenzie. In the 2016 local election, the party won seats in several councils, potentially being kingmakers in Nelson Mandela Bay and Ekurhuleni.)

Selfe believes coalitions can only really work if they take a party in the direction it wants to go. 'We have told the public that coalitions were not the preferred outcome because of ideological confusion, and that they should vote for the party they would prefer to rule them and has a reasonable chance of winning. If they do so, they will create strong blocs of support rather than lots of small parties that hold you to ransom, like the UDM did to us on the Bobani matter in Nelson Mandela Bay. [The UDM pulled out of the governing coalition in this council after the DA had UDM member Mongameli Bobani removed as deputy mayor.]

'In South Africa, voters are energised by the possibility of government change. It is a fine line to tread, but change is possible through coalitions, especially if you drive up voter turnout,' said Selfe.

One of the great conundrums for politicians involved in coalition talks is how much to tell the public, who, after all, elected them and are usually very keen to find out what is going on.

'One should tell the public very little while negotiations are on the go. Public discourse is often a temptation to slag off opponents, which could poison the environment if shared concerns are to be addressed. One has only 14 days to put together a coalition. It is best not to take part in media speculation,' said Selfe.

At that moment he sat back in the chair of his office and did a fine imitation of Don Corleone in *The Godfather*: 'Never talk in front of the family.'

He insists that for coalition talks to be successful, a political party's team must be carefully briefed and must stick closely to the agreed-upon script. 'There must be complete solidarity. Never differ in public.'

Selfe says the DA is unlikely to start detailed negotiations before the voters have cast their ballots. 'In 2016, accurate internal polling helped us to project results very early, especially in Johannesburg and Tshwane. Negotiations could therefore start early.'

According to him, negotiations with the ACDP and COPE are always easy for the DA. In the case of the EFF, it is more complicated. 'There are two ways [to negotiate]: either beforehand, in principle, as we have already started doing in the run-up to 2019, or, alternatively, on the floor of the results centre with polling projections, as EFF deputy president Floyd Shivambu and I did in 2016.

'In this regard, it is very important to know what you are prepared to negotiate on and what you are not prepared to negotiate on.'

So, the results are in and coalitions are a possibility. Now, who makes the first move?

Selfe smiled, stretched back in his chair and placed his hands behind his head. 'Don't you know? Whoever is more in love will make the first move!'

Then he became more deadpan. 'It is always best to make the first move and to cast your bread on the water lest anyone else is faster. In Cape Town in 2006 we moved especially rapidly. At the time, the then Western Cape ANC chairperson, Mcebisi Skwatsha, said that Helen Zille would never be mayor of Cape Town. Twenty-four hours later, she was.'

The DA has a tried-and-tested way of dealing with coalition and cooperation possibilities. Once the results are out, it holds a federal executive (fedex) meeting. 'By then, some discussions have happened internally and with other parties. Fedex then has to decide how to proceed,' Selfe said.

'After discussion, we rank the level of acceptability of potential partners. A decision is taken and the mandate is executed. Telecons take place daily to keep leaders abreast of developments. Provinces are included if they are affected and the most important aspect is always the national interest.

'Fedex consults with the provincial leadership on the identity of local executive position holders, because the DA rule is that anyone who stands to benefit from the filling of a specific position is not allowed in the negotiating team.'

According to Selfe, no local, provincial or national deals can be concluded without fedex agreement. As mentioned, in 2016 local DA and ANC leaders concluded a deal in the Kannaland municipality to oust the sitting mayor, Jeffrey Donson. The local DA structures went rogue and combined with the ANC to vote Donson out, to much local support. However, the actions of the Kannaland DA caused much distress in the normally disciplined DA, and Selfe had to handle the fallout. 'Although we felt much understanding for the Kannaland situation, it has not worked out well locally,' Selfe said, referring to several practical governance problems encountered since.

Once the coalition or cooperation deal has been agreed to, it has to be put in writing and rectified by each participating party. Having learnt by trial and error over many years, Selfe has firm views on how these agreements should be reached.

'I believe in written agreements, especially in complex coalitions, so that you can understand what you have agreed to. In the case of our cooperative agreement with the EFF, we agreed to combat cronyism and corruption, and to improve service delivery. A written agreement is a compass to steer by, although it is not binding.

'Conflict-resolution mechanisms are also important. Currently, our conflict-resolution mechanisms do not work very well – they are too complicated. ... We will simplify them to make them more accessible. They need to be understood by the local politicians, who must implement them. They can be negotiated nationally, but must be explained and understood locally.

'If you build a rhythm locally, events like the problems between the DA and the UDM in Nelson Mandela Bay would not happen. Local leaders must ensure observation of agreements. Only if that fails should it be escalated to the provincial, and eventually the national level.'

He prefers it straight and simple: 'It is better to have fewer parties in a coalition. It is much easier to manage. But our cooperative partner, the EFF, does not prefer it that way, for understandable reasons,' said Selfe, with reference to the fact that the presence of more partners

THE TWO BIGGEST OPPOSITION PARTIES AND THEIR OPTIONS

would prevent every disagreement from becoming a zero-sum showdown between the larger DA and the smaller EFF.

So, which parties would the DA prefer to work with as coalition partners?

'We worked with the ANC in coalitions after 2006, but it was never particularly successful,' remarked Selfe candidly. 'It failed for the same reason the Government of National Unity failed: it was always their people against our people. We decided against attempting to work with them again after 2016.'

He claimed the EFF is a different matter altogether. 'Working with the EFF is complex for obvious ideological reasons. But we like working with them because they stick to the deal and speak openly. That is good enough for me, personally.

'I don't always get the feeling that the EFF national structures are quite as in control of the local members as they would like to be, so we often have to take local conflict resolution to a higher level. In especially Nelson Mandela Bay and Modimolle municipalities, the understanding on a national level did not always seep through to the local level.'

According to Selfe, the IFP is a partner with a will of its own.

'The IFP is a complex partner. According to its manifesto, there should be a close ideological overlap and there is much commonality between some individuals in the DA and IFP. I got on very well, for instance, with former IFP MP Musa Zondi and was very sad when he left. However, the Coalition for Change [a reference to when the DA and the IFP joined forces against the ANC in KwaZulu-Natal in a 2004 election cooperative effort that flopped rather spectacularly] showed up the practical difficulties between the two parties. We found vestiges of tribalism and sexism in the IFP, which we did not agree with. This found expression mostly in views on traditional leadership and ownership of communal land. Because these are expressed more in what the IFP does than what it says, it makes coalitions with them quite difficult.

'The Coalition for Change was mainly based on the election arithmetic leading up to 2004, which is no longer valid. We found there was only so much we could coalesce around without holding public power,' Selfe said.

Nevertheless, where the DA and IFP have worked together, as they currently do in several municipalities in KwaZulu-Natal and Gauteng, they have tended to remain together – even though tensions between the two parties are not unknown.

Selfe conceded that working with the smaller parties has been a mixed bag for the DA to contend with. 'Working with the UDM has been interesting, with its leader, Bantu Holomisa, reinventing himself as a reconciler. We have at times found it hard to de-escalate their expectations. The UDM needs to accept that it is not the only party which has been around the block.

'The party is often easier to deal with than Holomisa is. Having built his reputation on his anti-corruption stance, we could never understand his focus on protecting former Nelson Mandela Bay deputy mayor Mongameli Bobani.'

As far as the ACDP goes, Selfe admits the relationship was unnecessarily soured by the fact that the DA dropped the party from the Cape Town coalition after 2006. 'We treated them in a cavalier way. It was wrong of the DA not to stick by its friend. They have every right to be peeved. The DA has much to atone for. Outside of Cape Town, that problem has been overcome. The ACDP is a party of great integrity that buys into the opposition project.'

According to Selfe, COPE is the closest to the DA in terms of ideology. 'The only issue is how to accommodate its leadership given its low support. COPE claims to attract people who would not vote DA. It is a small pool. COPE would really be better off within the DA.'

The Freedom Front Plus and the DA have had their problems in the past, and Selfe was curt and clipped in discussing their relationship. 'They are very opposed to the ANC and are skilful in government. We have found the Freedom Front Plus to be an easy partner, because we do not compete for the same constituency. People who support them should not vote for us.'

When asked what makes for successful coalition or cooperation negotiations, and what makes a coalition or cooperation agreement work, Selfe rapidly provided a handy list:

❏ Don't ever be arrogant.
❏ Show humility.
❏ Treat your negotiating partner as an esteemed equal.
❏ Listen carefully.
❏ Engage honestly.

Economic Freedom Fighters

Founded in 2013, the EFF has been led since its inception by Malema, whose hard-core views have earned him the nickname Kidi Amin. Malema was a charismatic leader of the ANC Youth League before he was booted out of the organisation for a series of misdeeds and harsh utterances. The last straw was his criticism of Botswana's president, Ian Khama, a key ally of South Africa.

WHO WILL RULE IN 2019?

When the EFF was founded as the wild child of South African politics, the mainstream parties did not take them very seriously. They were regarded as just the next flash in the pan for the 250 000 or so South African political nomads who vote for parties that are the new kids on the block. These are the types of voters who have had enough of the party-political status quo – the likes who voted for the UDM in 1999, Patricia de Lille's erstwhile Independent Democrats in 2004 and Lekota's COPE in 2009, only to change their vote in every election. They represent a true floating vote.

But the EFF turned out to be a different kettle of fish altogether. Like other major South African newbie parties, the EFF had a successful first outing, gaining 1.16 million votes in the 2014 general election, which amounted to 25 seats in the National Assembly – five seats fewer than COPE had achieved in its first general election in 2009.

However, the EFF has bucked the trend of other newbie parties by increasing its vote to more than 8% of the total (this during the 2016 local-government elections), proving itself to be anything but the flash in the pan its political opponents had hoped it would be.

Its success has much to do with the clarity and purpose of the EFF's economic vision, as well as the nature of those at its helm. Malema is impossible to ignore. His unpredictability and gift of the gab, with which he is abundantly endowed, ensure a spellbound audience wherever he speaks and through whichever medium he chooses to communicate.

The EFF core leadership is made up of charismatic, very intelligent and articulate individuals. Deputy President Floyd Shivambu is an intellectual, widely acknowledged to have a fine grasp of economics, while Secretary General Godrich Gardee is a very able administrator

THE TWO BIGGEST OPPOSITION PARTIES AND THEIR OPTIONS

with a ready sense of humour and much experience of municipal management. National Chairman Dali Mpofu is one of the country's most prominent legal practitioners; Deputy Secretary General Hlengiwe Hlophe has become a leading parliamentarian; the party's national spokesperson, Dr Mbuyiseni Ndlozi, is many a South African's favourite political communicator.

After much negotiation, the EFF did not make a senior member available to be interviewed for this book, but their policy documents, their evolving track record and the many discussions I've had with them enable a thorough analysis of their policies, negotiating tactics and political strategy (the interpretation of which I take full responsibility for).

Unlike many other major South African political parties, the EFF has very clear and defined policies. It is also the only major player that wants to change rather than tweak the way the constitutional order has prevailed in South Africa since democratisation in 1994. It is therefore worth examining how exactly the EFF wants to change the basic tenets of South African society were they ever to assume power, and the practical implications of some of its policies.

On the issue of land, the EFF believes in expropriation without compensation, so that the land can be equitably redistributed. According to its policy documents, all land should be transferred to the ownership and custodianship of the state – in the same way that all mineral and petroleum resources were transferred to the state through the Mineral and Petroleum Resources Development Act. The state would then administer and use land for sustainable-development purposes. This transfer should happen without compensation, and should apply to all South Africans, black and white, the EFF states.

Then, once the state is in control of land, those who had been using it, or who intend to use it, would have to apply for land-use licences, which would be granted only when there is a specific, stated purpose for which the land would be used.

Those applying for licences would be granted them for a maximum of 25 years, renewable on the basis that the land is used as planned. The state should, within this context, hold the right to withdraw the licence and reallocate the land for public purposes.

'Under this legislation, no one should be allowed to own land forever, because those who have money can, over time, buy huge plots of land and use them for counter-developmental private purposes, such as using land as game farms,' an EFF policy document explains. The state will retain the right to again expropriate the land without compensation where the land is not being used for the purpose applied for.

The EFF believes the state should also provide equipment and services to help those who farm the land to use it productively.

'Furthermore, the state's procurement of food should prioritise small-scale farmers so that small-scale farming becomes a sustainable economic activity. The state must buy more than 50% of the food for hospitals, prisons and schools from small-scale farmers in order to develop small-scale agriculture,' EFF policy documents envision.

Controversially, the EFF believes such a state-led system will create sustainable economic activity and inspire many young people to go into food production because there will be income and financial benefits. 'The economy of food production needs well-structured protection mechanisms and subsidies in order to protect jobs and safeguard food security. Most developed and developing nations are doing the same,' the policy document claims.

THE TWO BIGGEST OPPOSITION PARTIES AND THEIR OPTIONS

Then, it gets to the nub of the issue: 'This will, of course, require land reform to be expedited and water supplies to be guaranteed for the sustainability of this important sector of the economy,' the land policy document concludes.

Another issue on which the EFF is far to the left of other major South African political role players is nationalisation. It believes in the nationalisation of mines, banks and other strategic sectors of the economy. On this issue, it believes state ownership and control of strategic sectors of the economy should be the foundation for addressing the country's poverty and inequality crisis. Doing so without transfer of wealth from those who currently own it to the people as a whole is illusory, its policy document states: 'The transfer of wealth from the minority should include minerals, metals, banks, energy production and telecommunications, and [the state should] retain the ownership of central transport and logistics modes such as Transnet, Sasol, Mittal Steel, Eskom, Telkom and all harbours and airports. ...

'The ownership of mineral wealth should be considered through various means, firstly through the expropriation of the current minerals-production processes in South Africa and the commencement of extraction, processing and trade on new land,' it continues, arguing for the cancellation of private ownership in the production of mineral wealth in South Africa through various means, including the creation of an efficient and impactful state-owned mining company.

Importantly, the EFF believes 'nationalised mineral wealth will constitute a firm base for the beneficiation of these products in both heavy and light industrial processes in South Africa, which could be left to industrial and manufacturing entrepreneurs, co-operatives and small and medium enterprises.'

Instead of relying on what it calls 'neoliberal mechanisms' to attract industrial and manufacturing investments to South Africa, such as a narrow fiscal stability and decreased labour costs, the EFF believes the state, as owner of mineral wealth and metals, could provide incentives to reduce prices for primary and raw commodities, which will be industrialised and beneficiated in South Africa.

Such a beneficiation scheme – which EFF economic fundis love to refer to – 'will constitute a sustainable and labour-absorptive industrial process, which will feature both import-substituting and export-led industrialisation,' states its policy.

Showing a refreshing, non-dogmatic pragmatism, the EFF believes industrial and manufacturing entrepreneurs, cooperatives, and small and medium-sized enterprises from outside and inside South Africa should be allowed to industrialise the South African economy. They should be given guaranteed rights, regulated through transformation charters, which will lead to skills transfer at all levels of corporations' structures, coupled with an effective skills development, training and education strategy, feeding into the industrial and manufacturing process.

The EFF deals with the expected – and surely well founded – criticism of its nationalisation policies by predicting that 'the nationalisation of minerals and metals might ignite international condemnation by global imperialists, institutionalised in the World Bank, International Monetary Fund, and, notably, the World Trade Organization.'

It then asks that 'a broader mass movement should be mobilised in South Africa in defence of these massive economic reforms, because they constitute the core of our economic emancipation programme'.

Mass campaigns to garner support from the people as a whole are foreseen.

Very contentiously, the EFF believes that nationalising strategic sectors of the economy will lead to an increased fiscus, and therefore more resources for education, housing, healthcare, infrastructure development, safety and security, and sustainable livelihoods.

The creation of a state bank and the nationalisation of the Reserve Bank are also on the EFF's agenda. They want to transform the financial sector as a whole, particularly banking and insurance industry practices and norms.

The EFF 'wants to limit foreign ownership of strategic sectors in order to protect South Africa's sovereignty and to limit the repatriation of profits'.

Quite what an impact such a policy will have on foreign investment is not spelt out in the EFF policies. Regarding the strengthening of the state's capacity, the EFF believes an inspired, skilled and well-compensated public service is required, monitored by strong anti-corruption measures.

The EFF wants to abolish all tenders because 'the state's dependence on tenders often reduces the quality of work provided because of corruption and the corruptibility of the whole tendering system.

'In addition, the reliance on tenders limits the capacity of the state to directly industrialise the country by deliberately building value chains through direct state procurement,' the EFF argues.

In line with its headline-grabbing 'pay back the money' antics in Parliament, EFF policy documents place great emphasis on fighting corruption and criminality within the state.

'The fight against corruption should not be a side issue, but a fundamental component of the state apparatus in order to increase public confidence in the state,' the party declares.

Whether its solution to the state corruption scourge – namely, 'to place a premium on strengthening the revolutionary trade union movement in the public sector, which should establish a practical and immediate bridge through which the working class exercises its power over the state apparatus' – will work is open to much debate, given the poor performance, violence and corruption to which the largest public-sector trade union, the South African Democratic Teachers' Union, is linked.

Regarding the dismal state of the country's SOEs, like Eskom, South African Airways (SAA) and others, EFF policies state that 'it can never be correct that the state operates only with the hope that the still colonial and foreign-owned, and thus unpatriotic, private sector, in particular, will voluntarily underwrite its developmental agenda and pursue the agenda of job creation, poverty reduction and sustainable development with the same vigour that should define government'.

Therefore, the EFF proposes a series of state-owned and state-run companies: a state housing construction company, a state road construction company, a state cement company, a state pharmaceutical company, a state-owned mining company and a state food-stocking company (the latter to regulate prices of basic foodstuffs and guarantee food security).

It believes state companies 'will be buttressed by state ownership of critical parts of the value chains in which these companies operate, such as petrochemicals and steel, so that they produce essential inputs into the economy on a non-profit-maximisation basis'.

Therefore, if the EFF had its way, the state will employ engineers, quantity surveyors, project managers and builders for sustainable tasks, such as the construction of houses, roads, bridges, sports facilities, dams, sewerage systems and such.

THE TWO BIGGEST OPPOSITION PARTIES AND THEIR OPTIONS

The EFF explains how its vision for these companies will differ from the approach of the current disastrously managed SOEs: 'State-owned companies will not be driven by principles of profit maximisation, but by the need to provide cheap and affordable services to the people and the economy at large.'

Despite South Africa's dire economic state, the EFF promises free quality education, healthcare services, housing and sanitation. What the costing involves and how all this will be paid for are not explained in EFF documents.

The EFF education policy includes a welcome focus on vocational training, but also includes a strange fixation on the need to provide Cuban training for South Africans, despite the embarrassment that South African medical students studying in Cuba have become.

On healthcare, the EFF wants state regulation of medicine prices and a state pharmaceutical company to produce medicine. In a populist flourish, the EFF claims all house repossessions should be illegal. On the subject of unemployment, and sticking to its deeply contestable vision of state-powered economic growth, the EFF envisions a solution to the South African unemployment crisis in what it calls 'massive protected industrial development to create millions of sustainable jobs' and a strict system of minimum wages.

Local beneficiation and industrialisation rather than the export of South African raw materials form the mainstays of the EFF's industrialisation policies.

The EFF wants to abolish labour brokers (organisations that hire casual labour for part-time work on behalf of others) and to focus on changing the work environment of, specifically, mineworkers, farmworkers, private security guards, domestic workers, cleaners, petrol attendants, waiters and waitresses, and retail store workers. No particulars are given, but a great many of South Africa's voters are employed in these categories of work!

In another bow to populism, the EFF promises to narrow the wage gap between top managers and ordinary workers. This the EFF wants to achieve by regulating the pay of chief executive officers, directors, chief financial officers and managers in all sectors of the economy, and by stipulating that executive pay should not exceed a certain proportion of the wages of the lowest paid workers. No plan to combat the resulting managerial brain drain is provided.

The EFF places much emphasis on the development of the African continental economy, which it believes is inextricably linked with that of South Africa. In a policy move sure to attract much criticism, the EFF calls for 'the regulation and abolishment of foreign control and ownership of strategic sectors of the economy in South Africa and the African continent to discontinue foreign control in order to take ownership of African economic resources within the context of providing assistance where there is difficulty'.

Finally, as one of its policy pillars, the EFF takes a specifically strong stance against corruption and misuse of state agencies. It states that 'all political parties should be obliged by law to publicly disclose their sources of funds in order to avoid political coup d'états financed by greedy multinational corporations and criminal associations that seek to have access to South Africa's resources.

'If political parties are interested in managing so many mineral resources and so much wealth in South Africa, they should be interested in disclosing their sources of funding,' the EFF argues.

Clearly reacting against the state capture so entrenched in the Zuma

THE TWO BIGGEST OPPOSITION PARTIES AND THEIR OPTIONS

presidency, the EFF argues that state agencies should have relative autonomy, which will rid them of micromanagement and manipulation by politicians.

In particular, 'The head of the National Prosecuting Authority, the Public Protector, the national police commissioner and all Chapter 9 institutions should be appointed by a joint merit-based process that involves the executive, parliament and judiciary, and cannot be appointed by a president who can use his or her capacity to appoint in order to manipulate those appointed,' the EFF argues.

Its policy document ends on a bang, arguing for referendums to be held every time the country is called upon to go to war.

After the 2016 local elections, the EFF faced the classic conundrum of being the third largest party in a coalition situation – whether to throw its lot in with the ruling party, with other opposition parties or whether to go it alone. It really is a Hobson's choice – a no-win situation.

In the end, the EFF decided to stick with the opposition and vote the ANC out of power, but to maintain its independence of thought and action by not joining any coalition. It lends its vote to the other opposition parties against the ANC on an issue-by-issue basis.

It has shown itself to be a trusty and disciplined ally, sticking with its fellow opposition parties when the going gets tough, and expelling EFF councillors who have not done the same. At the same time, it has not been a pushover, with Shivambu warning the DA in a fiery parliamentary speech not to take the EFF's vote for granted.

That warning came to pass when the EFF served notice on the DA that it would vote to remove DA national chairperson Athol Trollip as mayor of Nelson Mandela Bay and replace him with an ANC mayor if the ANC could put up a non-corrupt candidate. Clearly, the EFF was continuing its 2016 efforts to use its position as local government king-maker to try to extract policy concessions from the ANC at a national level. That could prove a risky strategy for the EFF, since it could cause the party to lose the trust and goodwill of other parties.

CHAPTER 6

The smaller opposition parties and their options for 2019

Inkatha Freedom Party

Inkatha was founded in 1975 as a cultural-political movement under the leadership of Prince Mangosuthu Buthelezi. In 1990 it became a fully fledged political party under its current name, the Inkatha Freedom Party. Although strongly influenced by some aspects of Black Consciousness thinking, it was also in certain ways a reincarnation of the Inkatha movement, which had been started by royalists and traditionalists as a reaction to the growth of trade unionism in what is today KwaZulu-Natal in the 1920s and 1930s.

In that part of the country, the popularity of the Industrial and Commercial Workers' Union under the energetic leadership of Clements Kadalie nationally and AWG Champion, provincially, threatened the traditional Zulu hierarchy by preaching equality. That first Inkatha movement became moribund as the Industrial and Commercial Workers' Union floundered and Inkatha traditionalists found it unnecessary to maintain a counterweight.

Generally, two binary views of the IFP prevail. Those broadly sympathetic to it see the IFP and Buthelezi as a necessary counterbalance to the ANC, and its supporters view it as having contributed to the liberation struggle by preaching a policy of black self-reliance and opposing independence for the KwaZulu bantustan, which it ruled, thereby thwarting the ideals of grand apartheid.

Its opponents, on the other hand, insist that Inkatha's participation in the bantustan system made it a willing accomplice to apartheid, and characterise Buthelezi as a blood-thirsty stooge of that system. They do not place Inkatha on the side of the liberation forces.

Much of the bitterness and polarised nature of the debate around Inkatha reside in the violent conflicts of the 1980s and early 1990s in KwaZulu-Natal and Gauteng, when thousands died. These conflicts featured Inkatha supporters on the one hand and people broadly supportive of the ANC and its allies, such as the UDF, on the other, in what was one of the bloodiest power struggles in South African history.

Inkatha supporters claim that they had to defend themselves against violent efforts by the ANC and its allies to impose ANC political hegemony by force and take away people's freedom to choose in an attempt to turn the country into a de facto one-party dominant state.

On the other hand, opponents of Inkatha claim that the IFP and its forerunners fought the liberation movement and spilt much blood in cahoots with and on behalf of the apartheid government and its security forces, and the party will therefore always remain tainted and beyond the pale.

In the run-up to the first democratic elections in 1994, the IFP's brinkmanship about whether it would take part had many fearing there would be no free-and-fair election. In the end, just a week before polling day, the IFP decided to take part. Ballot papers had already been printed without the IFP as a choice, but in a remarkable effort,

THE SMALLER OPPOSITION PARTIES AND THEIR OPTIONS

the electoral commission ordered stickers with the IFP name and logo on them, and added the party to the ballot papers.

The IFP won KwaZulu-Natal with an outright majority in 1994 but that was the high-water mark of its support. In 1999 it lost its overall majority, but remained the biggest party in the province. It formed a coalition government, first only with the ANC, but later adding the DA.

In 2004 the ANC beat the IFP in KwaZulu-Natal, but did not attain an overall majority. It formed a rocky coalition with the IFP and Amichand Rajbansi's Minority Front, supported by the UDM.

In 2009 the IFP slipped further and the ANC took control of KwaZulu-Natal with an overall majority. The IFP slide was mirrored in the local-government elections of 2000, 2006 and 2011. In the general election of 2014, the IFP was overtaken by the DA in its KwaZulu-Natal heartland, falling to third place in the province and garnering only 2.5% of support nationally – a big decline from its 1994 high point of 10.5%.

But then, just as almost everyone was ready to write off the IFP, they made a comeback in the 2016 local elections, governing 14 municipalities in KwaZulu-Natal, some with the support of the DA and the EFF. The IFP scored a specifically sweet victory in Nkandla when it won the ward in which Zuma has his homestead. The party showed that this was no fluke result by increasing its vote when the municipal council of Nquthu was dissolved in 2017. This time, the IFP held the municipality by an overall majority. It has shown a growth trajectory in rural northern KwaZulu-Natal ever since.

I had the rare opportunity to ask the IFP's leader, Buthelezi, about his views on coalitions during an interview in his office in Cape Town.

Speaking to him, I always remind myself that I'm in the presence of a colossus of the South African political scene. Love him or loathe him, no one can deny his massive influence, which has spanned my whole life and much longer, especially in KwaZulu-Natal, the province where I grew up.

More than any current South African politician, Buthelezi oozes old-world charm and manners. His humour and laughter are infectious, and the sheer range of his political experience is awe-inspiring. One has to sit close and speak loudly and clearly. (And I am not ashamed to admit that I have asked him to speak as loudly and clearly to me in turn, so that I would be sure to catch his every word.)

The interview I had with him in November 2017 focused on other matters but I was able to slip in a question on potential cooperation between the IFP and other political parties. 'I am very enthusiastic about coalitions. They work well in many well-governed countries. I will do anything to make the current coalitions succeed,' said Buthelezi, whose behind-the-scenes role in keeping things together when the post-2016 coalition and cooperative agreements have threatened to come unstuck has been immense, if not widely publicised.

'We are doing our utmost to make coalitions and cooperative agreements work. If everybody gives it their best, there is no reason why we shall not succeed,' Buthelezi opined.

Does he think the opposition should include the ANC in coalitions, or would he even perhaps opt for a Government of National Unity, like the one he was part of after 1994? 'I can't see why not. We must put our country first and be prepared to work with everyone,' said Buthelezi.

The IFP's chief negotiator when it comes to coalitions is the party's chief whip in the National Assembly, Narend Singh. One of the political heavyweights in Parliament, Singh is highly regarded for his thorough knowledge, his forthright manner, his unwillingness to become involved in trivial political spats and his friendliness. I have had the honour to get to know him quite well professionally, and this has added to my life in a very positive way.

Singh entered Parliament in 1989 as MP for the Umzinto constituency in the tricameral system. He was elected on the ticket of a party called Solidarity, which no longer exists and which focused on serving the interests of South Africans of Indian descent. In 1993 he joined the IFP and is currently its treasurer general. In 1994 he was elected as an IFP MP in the first democratic Parliament. In 1996 the IFP moved him to the KwaZulu-Natal provincial legislature, serving as MEC in various portfolios. He joined the National Assembly as an IFP MP in August 2007, and was elected its chief whip in 2014.

Interviewed for this book, Singh was as courteous as ever, even though it was late in the evening after a particularly long day in Parliament. He pointed out that the IFP had been involved in the Government of National Unity and the KwaZulu-Natal government of provincial unity from 1994 to 1999, as mandated by the 1993 interim constitution.

'From 1999 to 2009, no political party had an absolute majority in KwaZulu-Natal, so we co-governed with the ANC, without an agreement but on the understanding that the period 1994 to 1999 had provided a sound basis for cooperation,' he recalled.

'From 1999, we found it very difficult to work with the ANC. There was much undermining by the ANC of the IFP-led government. We realised that ANC MECs were trying to use their positions to take power. They used the largesse afforded them by their provincial ministries to campaign for the ANC. In this, they were supported by their even more cash-flush colleagues in national government.

'A mistake we made in 1999 was that there was no agreement to hold the ANC to. Our premier, the late Lionel Mtshali, found the way the ANC undermined him so extreme that he fired two ANC members of the provincial cabinet, Mike Mabuyakhulu and Dumisani Makhaye, and replaced them with the DA's Roger Burrows and Wilson Ngcobo.

'That meant that the provincial cabinet consisted of six IFP, two ANC and two DA members. This increased ANC efforts to oust the IFP in KwaZulu-Natal.

'We found that our relationship with the DA was less frosty than our relations with the ANC, so from 2004 we campaigned with the DA in a construct called the Coalition for Change, which saw the IFP and the DA contest the 2004 provincial and national elections as partners.

'Unfortunately, that did not work out too well. It stranded on two issues. Firstly, the IFP and DA differed on where the provincial capital should be situated, with the DA favouring Pietermaritzburg and us favouring Ulundi. Secondly, both parties felt during and after the campaign that they would have done better among their base without the presence of the other.

'In the end, we had a different constituency from the DA. The DA, at the time, was largely white. It was uncomfortable, as the two big rallies at West Ridge Park and on the East Rand showed. It was oil and water – the two just did not mix,' explained Singh.

'As it happened, the ANC replaced us as the majority party in KwaZulu-Natal after the 2004 elections. We remained in the provincial government until 2007, and have been in opposition since.'

Singh added that municipal coalitions and cooperative agreements between the IFP and the DA worked better in the years after the failed experiment of the Coalition for Change.

When asked what makes coalitions work well, Singh said that a coalition has to rest on concrete policy proposals, given the understanding that no coalition can agree on everything. 'Therefore, the principle of give and take is important. It is important that the leaders of the party put the will and needs of the people before their own and the party's needs, that it can compromise on anything but principle. Often, the negotiating requires politicians to put the interests of the party above their own interests. This could become quite a big problem, because every politician wants to be a leader,' he warned.

'One must understand that leadership, trust and personal relationships play a big role. No coalition is legally binding; the sanction is to pull out. Therefore, similarity in ideology is helpful even if it is not an exact fit. For instance, the IFP and the EFF disagree on the land issue, but we agree on many other matters. The IFP and the DA do not agree on traditional leadership, but agree on other matters. Cool heads are important,' Singh reflects, with the wisdom of accumulated practical experience.

'It is absolutely imperative that coalition partners must abide by what is agreed. Individuals cannot be allowed to rock the boat, especially not people who want to take up executive positions.'

So, what cannot work for the IFP in a coalition?

'It would not work for the IFP to go into coalition with the far left or the far right. It has to be natural, as is the case with the Christian Democratic Union and the Christian Social Union in Germany,' Singh answered.

He shares the sentiments expressed by the DA's James Selfe when he says there must not be too many parties in a coalition, because it then becomes unmanageable. 'Also, box in your division – know your weight. The tail cannot wag the dog.'

However, on the point of how much of the negotiations should be communicated to voters, the IFP has a different view from that of the DA: 'As much as possible in the negotiating process must be shared with the public, so that the voter is not surprised.'

I asked Singh what the state of play is in post-2016 coalition and cooperative agreements. 'Currently, there are broad guidelines rather than exact rules,' he said. 'The rules are not completely binding and are not legally enforceable. Similar ideology plays a role, although the agreements and differences between the IFP, EFF and DA have at times been problematic. Joint opinion on clean governance – as opposed to the ANC way – is important.

'Each party stays in its lane [by which Singh seems to mean its geographical area of primary influence]. For instance, in KwaZulu-Natal the DA stays out of executive positions, even in eDumbe [Paulpietersburg] and Endumeni [Dundee], where they have more seats than us.'

Singh laughs when I confront him with a tale doing the rounds in political circles – that the IFP had told the DA not to campaign too hard in IFP areas. He denies that his party had ever done such a thing.

Regarding the coalition and cooperation mating dance once the votes are in and the results are known, Singh seems to be of the school of thought that smaller parties are like blushing maidens waiting to be courted: 'The largest party in every locality or sphere of government must make the first move; the smaller parties must be wooed. The smaller parties tend to play hard to get, because they are important

THE SMALLER OPPOSITION PARTIES AND THEIR OPTIONS

enough to do so and because they want the best deal for the ideals of their voters.

'Sometimes, preferences differ in a party. In 2016 the Gauteng structures of the IFP favoured working with the ANC, but the party as a whole was swayed by the better offer from the DA over KwaZulu-Natal, and the Gauteng IFP structures had to fall in line.

'As in any relationship, history also plays a role. For instance, after the 2016 elections, the IFP negotiated long and hard with the ANC, with which it shares a similar constituency, common purpose and several similar policies.

'The offer from the ANC was that whoever had the most seats between the IFP and ANC in a council should govern that council. However, we in the IFP remembered how the ANC chose the National Freedom Party [started in 2011 by former IFP chairperson Zanele kaMagwaza-Msibi] above us when they had the chance in 2011. That came back to bite them in 2016; we knew they were not a reliable partner.

'Both Jeff Radebe and Cyril Ramaphosa came to speak to the IFP, but the KwaZulu-Natal ANC was less keen to work with the IFP than the national ANC was. On the other hand, IFP structures felt that the IFP had been hurt when it worked with the DA.'

As for the 2019 elections, Singh says the IFP is open for business as far as coalitions are concerned: 'The IFP certainly believes that coalitions are the future. The 2016 election can be used as a springboard to that future. We have learnt from our mistakes. The IFP started its upward curve in 2016, and continued it when it took the Nquthu municipality away from the ANC in 2017.'

He maintained that the most important policy issues for the IFP going forward to 2019 would be resolving uncertainty over land policy, with much emphasis on maintaining and strengthening the system of communal land tenure, the future economic system (focusing on self-help and redress without nationalisation) and safeguarding the role and position of traditional leaders.

United Democratic Movement

The UDM was founded in 1998 and has had only one leader since its inception – General Bantu Holomisa. Before 1994 Holomisa ruled the roost as an ANC-aligned leader in the former Transkei homeland in the Eastern Cape, having come to power there by means of a military coup.

After 1994 he became an ANC MP and deputy minister of environmental affairs in the Mandela cabinet, but soon fell out with the ANC establishment after he accused an ANC minister, Stella Sigcau, of corruption when she was ruling the Transkei (Sigcau had been Holomisa's predecessor as Transkei leader, whom he deposed in his coup).

Holomisa resigned from the ANC and formed the UDM. He was joined by former National Party chief negotiator in the democratisation process, Roelf Meyer, and for a while Holomisa played the ebony to Meyer's ivory in the UDM political melody – a multiracial duo that preached racial harmony. The dual act split up, though, when Meyer left to become an ANC supporter.

In the 1999 general elections, the UDM took about 3.5% of the vote, which enabled it to have 14 MPs in Parliament. It also became the official opposition in the Eastern Cape legislature. Since then, its support

THE SMALLER OPPOSITION PARTIES AND THEIR OPTIONS

has slipped, however, and in 2004, 2009 and 2014 it had just four MPs elected to Parliament each time.

In the 2000 local-government elections, the UDM won the important King Sabata Dalindyebo municipality, centred on the former Transkei capital, Mthatha, which now falls in the Eastern Cape province. The UDM found it hard to govern the municipality, and claimed that the ANC in the national and provincial governments, as well as in the local district council, was undermining it by not providing due financial means. If this was the case, the ANC could claim success, as it won an overall majority in King Sabata Dalindyebo in 2006, and held it in the 2011 and 2016 local elections.

Strategically, the UDM has over the years joined up with a number of political partners, believing that governments need to change periodically to prevent corruption from settling in. The UDM helped the ANC secure a working majority in the KwaZulu-Natal legislature in 2004. The party contributed a deputy minister, Ntopile Kganyago, to the Mbeki, Motlanthe and Zuma cabinets, before Kganyago's death in 2012.

In 2016 the UDM chose to side with the opposition in Nelson Mandela Bay, where its two councillors (out of a council of 120 members) were pivotal in securing the DA's Athol Trollip as mayor, helped by COPE and the ACDP with one councillor each. The UDM's Mongameli Bobani was installed as Trollip's deputy.

Subsequently, Trollip and Bobani had such big differences that the UDM no longer supported Trollip and the position of deputy mayor has been abolished in Nelson Mandela Bay. Since November 2017, Trollip has been dependent on the support of the EFF, the ACDP and COPE for his survival as mayor. The UDM remained supportive of fellow national opposition parties' governments in councils elsewhere.

The UDM finds its strongest support in the former Transkei region of the Eastern Cape, and has pockets of support in the mining areas of North West, western Gauteng and the northern Free State, where many from the Transkei work as migrant labour. The party also enjoys some support in the Limpopo Bible belt around Polokwane. The party has the potential to provide a political home to voters who are disenchanted with ANC corruption and do not feel comfortable voting for the DA or the EFF.

Policywise, the UDM has placed itself to the left of the ANC and to the right of the EFF; the party takes a strong stance against corruption and firmly favours state-led growth.

When I met Holomisa in his Cape Town office to conduct the interview for this book, he cut a dapper figure, as ever. The interesting thing about Holomisa is that he may have left the military, but the military has certainly not left him! He has retained his upright military bearing and that certain clipped, forthright way of speaking that often characterises military men, which makes him one of my favourite politicians to interview. Holomisa has the ability that only gifted intellectuals possess to cut to the chase and focus on the core of the matter in a logical way that is rooted in causality.

In the interview, Holomisa characterised the UDM as architects of coalitions. 'In 2004 we helped the ANC in KwaZulu-Natal, and in 2006 we helped the DA in Cape Town. We believe that one-party dominance breeds corruption. Coalition governments provide checks and balances.

'I have said before that we need coalition guidelines nationally, like Germany and New Zealand have. In Germany you have three months after an election to negotiate coalitions.

THE SMALLER OPPOSITION PARTIES AND THEIR OPTIONS

'We support coalitions, especially given the situation in South Africa, where we must accommodate diversity. Some parties really represent interest groups, like Azapo [the Azanian People's Organisation], the Freedom Front Plus and the PAC. Azapo has many very well-educated people who can make a contribution. The Freedom Front Plus is not just a bunch of old white guys. They can contribute. There is so much intellectual capacity in Azapo and the PAC but no directors general or chief directors come from there.

'Madiba and FW de Klerk started very well with the Government of National Unity, but now the political and economic power is in different hands. If the wealthy have no confidence in government, they take their money out.'

Holomisa believes no coalition talks should take place before the final results are in. Coalition and cooperation discussions should start only after elections, because negotiations depend on election outcomes. 'There must be a common strategic goal. Therefore, policy talks are important – they make coalitions doable,' he said, in his clipped, military delivery.

Holomisa believes coalition and cooperation agreements should be negotiated behind closed doors, before an agreement is signed and made public, as he did in 2004. After that election, the UDM gave its vote to the ANC in KwaZulu-Natal, enabling it to enjoy a provincial majority there for the first time. The then UDM deputy leader, Ntopile Kganyago, was made a deputy minister in Mbeki's national cabinet. Holomisa did not get a position.

'After the 2004 elections, President Thabo Mbeki called me for support. It was important – and it remains important – not to think what is in it for me. In metros after the 2016 local-government elections, the

UDM listed which issues should be prioritised rather than which positions we wanted. That document was signed and made public, and the public has bought into it.'

Regarding the coalition mating dance, like the IFP, Holomisa believes the biggest party should make the first move, and look at who could make them top up to a majority. 'There is also a gap for small kingmakers. I initiated a meeting in Midrand after the 2016 elections for COPE, the DA, the UDM, the United Front of the Eastern Cape trade-union movement and the EFF.

'EFF commander-in-chief Julius Malema wanted free education, land, the resignation of President Jacob Zuma and several other issues to be addressed. I called him to order and said, "Hey, Chief, not so fast! This election was for municipal councils." Opposition parties cannot decide national issues.

'A while after the meeting, ANC Secretary General Gwede Mantashe called about possible coalitions. Referring to Malema, I told him that Juju held the keys to the cities, not me. In the end, the EFF demand that Zuma must go was too much for the ANC, so it did not materialise.

'Then the DA came and we decided to help. I'm sorry that they are often too immature to make it work. Also, there are still elements of *baasskap* in their party,' Holomisa maintains – in clear reference to the conflict between the UDM and the DA in Nelson Mandela Bay since 2016.

He then listed his dos and don'ts when it comes to coalition agreements. 'One of the great challenges in South African coalitions is a Big Brother mentality, as we have experienced with the DA in Nelson Mandela Bay.' Holomisa believes, like the DA, that a written agreement is important, as are dispute-resolution mechanisms with escalation possibilities. 'As coalition partners you must handle things locally if

THE SMALLER OPPOSITION PARTIES AND THEIR OPTIONS

you can, and must always follow the Public Finance Management Act, which all councillors must honour and know well.

'Carry your mandate, focusing on service delivery, with the focus always on caring for the poor. There must be comradeship in a coalition, which should be easier than it sometimes is, despite policy and priority differences.

'I firmly believe that coalition partners should also interact informally – for instance, at a Friday braai – where issues can be discussed informally, like the military does in the officers' mess. This solves an issue before it becomes a problem.'

Regarding potential UDM partnerships, Holomisa's ideal for South Africa after the 2019 general elections, as he has often stated, is a Government of National Unity, like South Africa had after 1994.

'The UDM would support a Government of National Unity. It would be better for service delivery, because a Government of National Unity looks after all interest groups,' he said, opening up the real possibility of finding common ground with the Ramaphosa grouping in the ANC.

'Actually, all parties are the same as partners. It is only in Nelson Mandela Bay where we have problems. We work with the DA in Johannesburg, where we chair Scopa [the Standing Committee on Public Accounts]. I don't struggle with coordinating relationships between parties,' mused Holomisa.

He says that, for the UDM, the most important policy issues to be discussed for a successful 2019 national coalition to take place would be the shape of the economy, land distribution, addressing backlogs and imbalances in housing, healthcare and several other services, the review of laws that do not have the desired effects, and issues of good governance, like combating corruption.

'The nature and content of the discussion on land and property have narrowed its scope. It needs to be de-escalated and the discussion should be restarted between all role players, so that it is not a zero-sum game.'

On many policy issues, he believes, the problem is mostly with implementation. As far as labour is concerned, the UDM is for the minimum wage and against worker exploitation. On nationalisation, the only question is a matter of the extent – every nation does it – even the US bails out problematic sectors.

'The government must do more, but that presupposes a capable state,' Holomisa concludes.

Freedom Front Plus

The Freedom Front was founded on the eve of the first democratic elections in 1994. It added the 'Plus' to its name later, as will become evident. The party's founder was ex-defence force chief General Constand Viljoen, whose leadership added the weight of his considerable reputation among a grouping focused on achieving their own 'country' – a *volkstaat* (people's state) for Afrikaners (specifically white Afrikaans-speaking South Africans who wish to classify themselves as such).

In the period between the 1990 unbanning of the ANC and the 1994 general elections, right-wing groupings like the Conservative Party – the party with the second most white support after the ruling National Party – and the paramilitary Afrikaner-Weerstandsbeweging boycotted the negotiations that would lead eventually to a democratic election and the writing of a new Constitution. Instead, they held protest meetings and some turned to violence.

THE SMALLER OPPOSITION PARTIES AND THEIR OPTIONS

Some of these right-wing leaders came to understand that they were painting themselves into a corner. Whereas the Conservative Party continued to refuse to participate in non-racial elections (they preached a racially based separate development – grand apartheid – to the bitter end) and refused to negotiate with 'terrorists' (as they continued to refer to the ANC), others realised they were going to miss the train that was leaving the station of the present for the politics of the future.

Those right-wing leaders who did want to be part of the politics of the future needed a vehicle that would enable them to be part of the new political trend, which is how the Freedom Front came about. In Viljoen the party had a leader of stature with a simple message – a vote for the Freedom Front is a vote for an Afrikaner *volkstaat* separate from the rest of South Africa. Viljoen went so far as to say that the 1994 general elections would be considered a referendum on a *volkstaat* – every vote cast for the Freedom Front would be considered a vote for a *volkstaat*.

The problems with the viability of the *volkstaat* idea were manifold. First, no one could agree where it should be situated, as there is nowhere in the country where Afrikaners make up anything approaching a majority. Secondly, such separatist development and secession would fly in the face of the unitary state South Africa had become. Thirdly, the *volkstaat* would have to be negotiated from a position of weakness because the government was unsympathetic – in fact diametrically opposed to – the idea of separatism, which was actually a euphemism for apartheid. And, fourthly, most South Africans of all races simply thought the idea was batty – it was never taken seriously except by a core group of true believers.

Based on the results achieved by the Conservative Party in previous whites-only elections, the Freedom Front had every reason to believe it could garner at least a million votes. In the event, it managed only 424 555, or 2.2% of the overall votes, translating to nine seats in the National Assembly. Although this was a deeply disappointing result for those hoping for a *volkstaat*, it was nevertheless the highest level of support for a right-wing party in democratic South Africa.

Many wonder what the meaning of the 'Plus' in the Freedom Front Plus is, and where it comes from. It derives from a decision made in 2003 among the remnants of the Conservative Party – which had continued to exist and hold on to its substantial material assets but had not contested elections – to acknowledge reality and merge with the Freedom Front, thereby creating the Freedom Front Plus.

After Viljoen retired from politics in 2001, Dr Pieter Mulder took over as leader of the Freedom Front Plus. The party has consistently won around 1% of the national vote and four seats in the National Assembly in the 2004, 2009 and 2014 elections. This means it receives around 15% of the Afrikaner vote. In other words, about 85% of Afrikaners cast their votes elsewhere, mostly for the DA.

In coalition situations, the party has continually used its public representatives to keep the ANC out of power, and is seen as an honest dealer by its fellow opposition parties. Its policy is to work together with opposition parties against the ANC in any political set-up where the ANC has less than 50% support.

An interesting interregnum to this trend occurred in the period between 2009 and 2014 when Zuma – ever ready to spot a gap – saw and seized upon the obvious gap in the Freedom Front Plus coalition policy: how about the Freedom Front Plus working with the ANC in an area where the ANC has more than 50% support, like the national government? Zuma reasoned.

THE SMALLER OPPOSITION PARTIES AND THEIR OPTIONS

So Zuma offered Mulder the position of Deputy Minister of Agriculture, Forestry and Fisheries – a particularly enticing offer because Afrikaners are strongly represented in the agricultural sector, especially in commercial farming and food production. The top structures of the Party were divided on whether Mulder should join the ANC-led government. But, after much infighting and arguing, it was decided that he should accept Zuma's offer.

This led to the resignation of several top Freedom Front Plus members, including youth leader Cornelius van Rensburg and the party's youngest MP, Willie Spies. Its voter support levels, however, were largely unaffected, as subsequent election results show. Mulder continued as leader until 2017, when he resigned. He was succeeded by Dr Pieter Groenewald.

Groenewald entered the tricameral Parliament in 1989 as the pro-apartheid Conservative Party's MP for the Stilfontein constituency. After 1994 he served variously as member of the North West provincial legislature and the National Assembly. Groenewald holds a doctorate in political science and is well versed in the martial arts.

With his booming voice, he is also one of the better orators in Parliament and one of the very few members who generally speak off the cuff when at the podium. Politically not one to be trifled with and certainly a tougher customer than his utterly polite predecessor, Mulder, I have nevertheless always found Groenewald the easier of the two to engage with because he plays such a straight bat. He is also a great conversationist with a remarkably ready and wicked sense of humour for such a conservative fellow. He is always up for a chat, and is likeable and gregarious – whether you agree with his politics or not.

Groenewald told me he believes that Mulder's decision to join the

ANC-dominated government was the right one. 'When the ANC contacted us about Dr Mulder going into government, we made it very clear that our policy remained not to cooperate with the ANC where the ANC received less than 50% of the vote. If the voters voted the ANC out of a majority, we would not restore that ANC majority.

'I believe we did the right thing when we decided that Dr Mulder should accept President Jacob Zuma's offer. But we did not take that decision by ourselves. We consulted with Solidarity, the Afrikanerbond, AgriSA and the Transvaal Agricultural Union. They were all in favour of Dr Mulder's joining the government. In fact, they would have been peeved if we had not done so.

'It is true that there were differences of opinion about the issue on the executive level of the Freedom Front Plus. But we set certain preconditions for joining government, one of which was that Lulu Xingwana, who served as minister of agriculture at that stage, had to be replaced. And she was replaced.

'Amongst the farming community, the overwhelming feeling was that an opportunity to gain access to national government could not be passed up. And we delivered: the agricultural unions got to meet with the new agriculture minister, Tina Joemat-Pettersson, every month during Dr Mulder's tenure as deputy minister.'

Regarding the 2016 negotiations, Groenewald was just as candid: 'As the election results trickled in, it became clear that as the Freedom Front Plus, we were going to hold the balance of power in a number of municipalities. James Selfe, chairman of the DA federal executive, came to me on the floor of the election results centre to ask whether we would cooperate with them in coalitions. I told him that we were not very happy with how the DA kept repeating the lie during every election that a vote cast for a smaller party was a wasted vote, but we did not shut the door on them.

'After the election results were finalised, North West premier Supra Mahumapelo contacted me about the Freedom Front Plus being part of an ANC-centred coalition in Rustenburg, where no one had an overall majority. I said these things had to be negotiated at a national level.

'ANC Secretary General Gwede Mantashe then called Dr Pieter Mulder, who was then still our leader,' Groenewald continued, 'and he and I met Mantashe and ANC Treasurer General Zweli Mkhize at a hotel. The ANC wanted to conclude a coalition agreement with the Freedom Front Plus for the three municipalities where we held the balance of power, namely Modimolle and Thabazimbi, both in Limpopo, and the Western Cape municipality of Hessequa, centred on the town of Riversdale.

'The two ANC representatives cast the net wider, asking us what we wanted in return, and offered us a possible seat in national government in 2019. We informed them again of the Freedom Front Plus policy of helping the opposition where the ANC achieved less than 50% of the vote, and left it at that.

'We then met the DA, the UDM and the ACDP in Midrand. We could see that the EFF was around and probably also meeting potential partners, but we did not meet with the EFF.

'Just as we had done with the ANC, we reminded the DA, UDM and ACDP that the Freedom Front policy was cooperation with the opposition where the ANC scored below 50% of the vote, and the talks were on,' Groenewald said.

He still does not rate at all highly the DA's conduct as a coalition partner. 'Our partnerships with them are for strictly political reasons.

They are not to be trusted. They do not understand the nature of coalitions. The point is that strength of numbers is very important during negotiations for executive positions, such as mayor, speaker and the like. After that, all partners need each other for the coalition to survive, so in a sense everyone is equal.

'Coalition politics requires strong, responsible and accountable government. At times it seems not all parties are equal to the task,' said Groenewald (clearly another jibe at the DA).

He added that the Freedom Front Plus was not comfortable entering into a coalition with the EFF, and had in fact not done so. 'We would rather cooperate with them or not on an individual issue-by-issue basis, in the way they have cooperated with other opposition parties since 2016,' he said.

The Freedom Front Plus leader has strong views on the dos and don'ts of coalition politics:

- ❏ The strongest partner cannot play the numbers game with the smaller partners after the coalition is agreed upon. Smaller partners must not be pushed aside.
- ❏ Never say 'never' in politics – never claim that you would never work with another party.
- ❏ Give space to coalition or cooperative partners to differ on specific issues – the whole coalition does not have to agree on all matters all the time.
- ❏ If you are a smaller partner, do not specifically demand a speakership or mayoralty, even if you hold the balance of power. Be aware of your position in the pecking order.
- ❏ It is not necessary to air all issues about which there may be disagreement in public. Not every issue about which there is

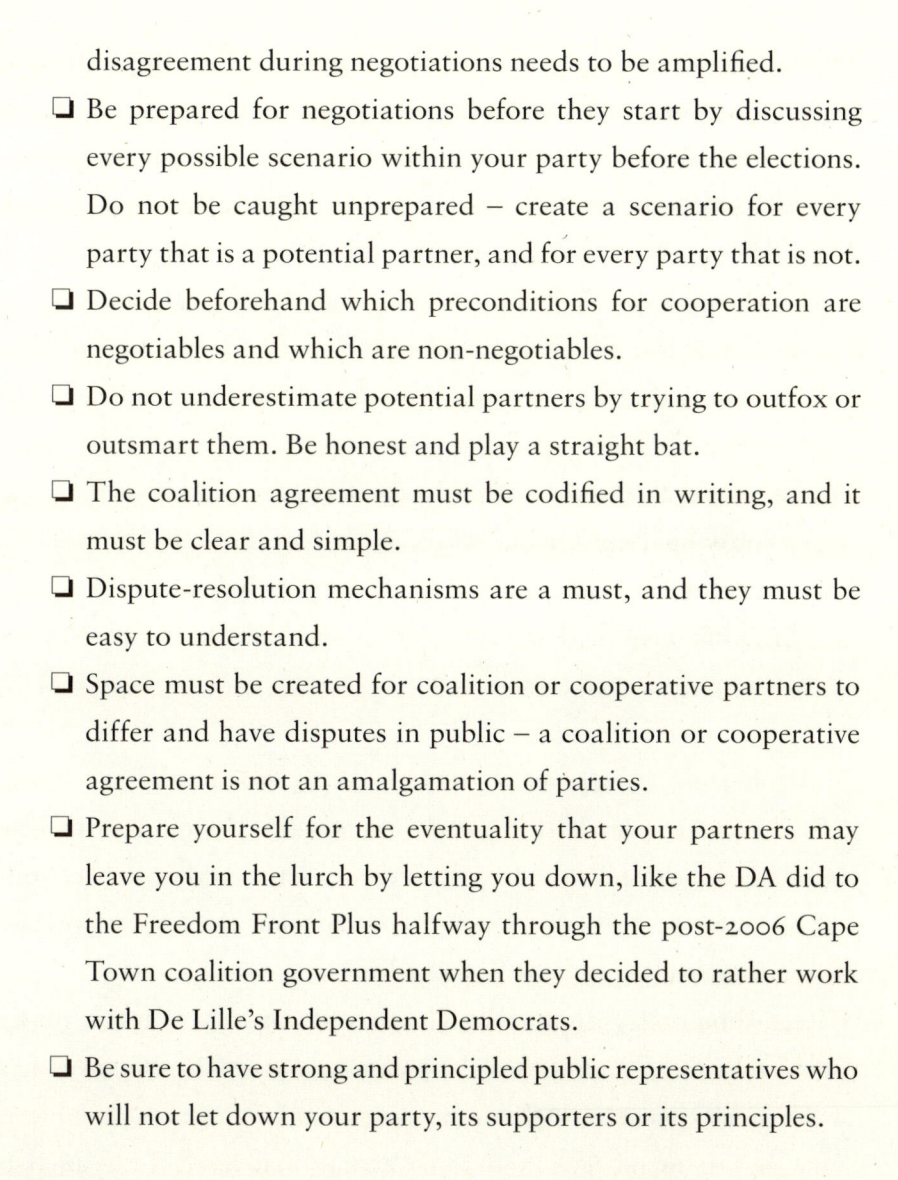

disagreement during negotiations needs to be amplified.
- Be prepared for negotiations before they start by discussing every possible scenario within your party before the elections. Do not be caught unprepared – create a scenario for every party that is a potential partner, and for every party that is not.
- Decide beforehand which preconditions for cooperation are negotiables and which are non-negotiables.
- Do not underestimate potential partners by trying to outfox or outsmart them. Be honest and play a straight bat.
- The coalition agreement must be codified in writing, and it must be clear and simple.
- Dispute-resolution mechanisms are a must, and they must be easy to understand.
- Space must be created for coalition or cooperative partners to differ and have disputes in public – a coalition or cooperative agreement is not an amalgamation of parties.
- Prepare yourself for the eventuality that your partners may leave you in the lurch by letting you down, like the DA did to the Freedom Front Plus halfway through the post-2006 Cape Town coalition government when they decided to rather work with De Lille's Independent Democrats.
- Be sure to have strong and principled public representatives who will not let down your party, its supporters or its principles.

Groenewald said that a fine balance had to be struck between the interests and the trust of the voters who support your party. 'You should never sell your voters down the river or betray their trust. At the same time, any political party must strike a balance between core matters of principle on the one hand, and adaptability on the other. The most important thing is to never betray your voter.'

He offered several tips for coalition negotiations to be successful:

- ❏ Communicate individually and in confidence – not through the media because communicating with a potential partner through the media breeds distrust and misunderstanding.
- ❏ Ignore the social-media noise.
- ❏ Ensure that all mandates are acquired internally through existing and agreed-upon channels.
- ❏ Reach agreement with all potential partners about the issues on which agreement exists, as well as those about which no agreement exists, like the land issue, for instance.
- ❏ Don't believe that negotiations will remain secret. Nothing remains a secret in politics.

So which negotiating partner should make the first move?

'It depends on leadership,' said Groenewald. 'I would never wait, lest someone is faster than me. Keep the initiative and do not let yourself be ambushed. Finally, always be aware that the largest potential partner may well not be the best one.'

Regarding policy differences, Groenewald insisted that it is important to take into account the sphere of governance where management of the specific issue resides. 'Some issues can be tackled at local level, some at provincial level and some at national level. Take an issue like land, for instance. This cannot really be addressed at local level because it is a national concern. You have to come as close as you can to realising your own party's policy mandate and preference,' he said.

The Freedom Front Plus feels strongly about several policy issues, especially constitutional safeguards of language, and cultural and property rights, as enshrined in Sections 185, 235 and 25 of the Constitution, Groenewald said.

He added that the party would be prepared to enter into cooperative agreements with the EFF, but would prefer not to put the EFF in a position where it could implement its policy preferences by going into coalition with it. The Freedom Front Plus is willing to work with all other opposition parties within reason, Groenewald said.

He maintained that the Freedom Front Plus would not work with the ANC to hand it a majority where the ANC failed to achieve 50% of the vote.

African Christian Democratic Party

The ACDP contested its first election in 1994, appealing to the fundamentalist Christian vote. It has known only one party leader – Reverend Kenneth Meshoe.

In 1994, the ACDP won two seats in Parliament, rising to the party's high point of seven MPs in 1999 before declining to settle on its current cohort of three MPs. Currently the party struggles to reach 1% of the national vote.

Strategically, the ACDP's greatest problem is that its support is so scattered across the country that it has no real geographical base. It picks up a handful of votes here and a few there, but never enough for a voting bloc. That means it is perpetually stuck in the role of junior coalition partner to the larger parties. The ACDP has never sided with the ANC in government, and has remained a staunch ally of national opposition parties in local governments across the country.

The party's policy line is very socially conservative: it opposes abortion and gay marriage, and supports the death penalty and the right of parents to spank their children. It did not support the vote to pass the Constitution into law in 1996. Its policies on issues like finance and governance are generally conservative and capitalist, although it acknowledges the role of the state in inclusive upliftment in a society as unequal as South Africa's.

The party's public representatives tend to be diligent and skilful. The ACDP's negotiator for coalitions is Jo-Ann Downs, who is a veteran in these matters and widely regarded by other parties as tough but fair. The Durban-based politician is unfailingly polite, consistent and well informed – a dream interviewee for any political journalist.

She admitted to me that the ACDP has burnt its fingers many times before but has emerged older and wiser as a result: 'Our first experience of coalitions was in Cape Town in 2006, when we were the biggest partner to the DA in ousting the ANC. In fact the ACDP took the lead to bring all the opposition parties together to build a coalition because none of the other opposition parties trusted the DA as a negotiating partner, which makes what happened in the end just all the more ridiculous.

'In the coalition agreement we negotiated, the ACDP's Reverend Andrew Arnolds held the position of deputy mayor. All went well until the DA decided to start wooing Patricia de Lille and the Independent Democrats in order to rather go into coalition with them.

'We learnt a lot from that experience – mostly to be more pragmatic and to put South Africa first, not our own preferences. We must keep an open mind and not let the past dictate what we do. We did learn,

THE SMALLER OPPOSITION PARTIES AND THEIR OPTIONS

though, and we ensured, when we negotiated the 2016 coalition agreement, that it differed from previous agreements, in that it gave us more power to hold the DA to account.

'I have no doubt that the 2016 agreement is much better than before, mostly because it makes the DA more dependent on the will of the smaller partners. Initially, the DA wanted to limit the public role of the smaller parties to hold high-profile positions and differ from the majority partner in public, but we opposed it successfully.

'Following the 2016 local-government elections, we are now in three governing coalitions – Johannesburg, Tshwane and Nelson Mandela Bay. Thus far, this time, the DA has stuck to its word.'

Given the ACDP's negative history with the DA, specifically in Cape Town, would they consider rather working with the ANC?

'As the ACDP, we voted for an ANC candidate once – when Zweli Mkhize became premier of KwaZulu-Natal after the 2004 general election. But that was a decision endorsed by the whole provincial legislature – all parties voted for him in light of the election results of that year.

'In essence, we have never worked with the ANC in coalition and we are not considering working with them. They have enjoyed such a huge majority and yet they have governed so poorly. There is no indication that they would govern better than they have been doing.'

My next question to Downs, namely when negotiations for a coalition should start, provided an interesting insight into the changing nature of relationships between opposition parties in the run-up to the 2019 elections: 'Normally, I would say negotiations should start only after the election results have been announced. But, currently, all the opposition parties in coalition and cooperation agreements are looking at 2019 – and we are all singing from the same hymn book. The inclination is to get the ANC out,' said Downs.

Asked who should make the first move to negotiate if an election result brings the possibility of coalition government, she said the biggest potential coalition partner – which, given the ACDP's reluctance to work with the ANC, is normally the DA – has to move first.

'The next step is to get all potential coalition partners to sit around the table and air issues. After the 2016 local elections, for instance, we as the ACDP wanted to get a major issue out of the way, namely the DA tactic in every election of telling the voters that voting for a smaller party is a wasted vote. Only after the DA agreed to change their ways did we get down to the nitty-gritty of coalition negotiations,' Downs pointed out.

So, how much detail about coalition negotiations should be shared with the public, and at what point? 'After every issue has been discussed and agreed upon by the prospective coalition partners, as the ACDP we take that issue to our federal council of provinces to ratify, after which we are happy to share that issue with the public. That is how everybody stays in the loop,' she said.

As for policy obstacles in the way of a possible opposition coalition in 2019, Downs said she did not expect any major stumbling blocks. 'The issues that we as the ACDP differ most strongly about from other parties are moral issues, like abortion and gay marriage, which are constitutional issues requiring a two-thirds majority to change. If an opposition coalition comes to power, it will have a small majority, so we have to be pragmatic and realistic. In practice, it will be impossible for us to implement those policy preferences.'

Downs was forthright about where the ACDP stands on other, broader policy issues, which may derail opposition coalition negotiations.

'On the vexed issue of land, we essentially make two points. First, we are absolutely in favour of restoration of rights which had been taken away. Second, we believe that the right to own property must be protected. No one can just be chucked off the property. We believe there should be a separate and independent evaluation court for such matters – not one in which the government has any role. Furthermore, we would prefer land restitution to focus on residential rather than farm land, which should address many of the current problems in this regard.

'Regarding labour, we believe the current labour regime is very negative in terms of the country's competitiveness. We also believe in fair wages and we are in favour of a national minimum wage.'

Downs emphasised that the ACDP is firmly opposed to nationalisation: 'Nationalisation does not work. It has not worked anywhere. The exceptions are the utilities, specifically water and electricity, because of the enormous levels of poverty in our country. However, these utilities can be run properly only if we have a capable state with a professional and well-functioning civil service. Without that precondition, nationalisation of even the most basic utilities would leave them in the parlous state we are currently witnessing.'

CHAPTER 7

Burning issues I: It's the economy, stupid!

When Arkansas governor Bill Clinton's presidential campaign was struggling to make an impact and the re-election of his opponent, President George HW Bush, looked likely, Clinton's campaign strategist, James Carville, came up with one of the greatest electoral catchphrases ever. He formulated three key issue-driven phrases at Clinton's campaign headquarters in Little Rock for his campaign workers, saying these were the main issues they had to focus on if they wanted to win the election.

'The economy, stupid' became the most legendary of these phrases, which soon morphed into 'it's the economy, stupid!' The phrase illustrates both the importance of the economy for the fortunes of politicians and, more pertinently, the importance of focusing on policies about the burning issues of the day to ensure a successful election campaign.

Zooming in on the issues of the day that voters care about most is a key factor when it comes to attracting votes. In South Africa the burning electoral issues in 2019 will be the shape and health of the economy, the land issue, nationalisation, labour battles (which are linked to the

BURNING ISSUES I: IT'S THE ECONOMY, STUPID!

unemployment crisis), black economic empowerment and tackling corruption.

The shape and health of the economy concerns all of us because the economy affects everyone's everyday lives. The luxury of a dogmatic choice between ideologies is no longer an option given the global interconnectedness of the modern world, weary as it is of the lessons learnt from the failed economic systems of the past. Nevertheless, in terms of pragmatic approaches to solving economic challenges, a stark choice presents itself insofar as the philosophical starting point of the future shape of the economy is concerned. That starting point concerns the role of the state in the economy.

Leading up to 2019, parties like the ANC, EFF and UDM are placing much emphasis on how the state should be at the fore in the development of the economy. Known as the developmental state, this model is based on economic success stories like Malaysia and Singapore. These parties' main argument, to varying degrees, is that the pro-market policies pursued by democratically elected South African governments since 1994 have not yielded the results hoped for in terms of reducing poverty, inequality and unemployment, and providing fair access for the black majority to the means of production from which they were, to a greater or lesser degree, excluded from 1652 to 1994. In fact, all measurements point to the fact that inequality has worsened since 1994. Therefore, a new approach is needed, the argument goes.

Supporters of such state-driven economic views point to capital flight and the brain drain (specifically of white professionals) to prove the selfishness they believe is inherent in the capitalist system has not served the poor well anywhere, and certainly not in South Africa. According to this school of thought, it follows that the state must take the lead in development.

Central to this view, and especially well articulated by EFF commander-in-chief Julius Malema, is that the levels of inequality in South Africa represent a time bomb with an ever shortening fuse that needs to be stopped in the medium-term national interest. The thinking is that the state, were it to be a capable state – which, with its dysfunctional civil service, at this stage it most definitely is not – is the only vehicle to address the wholesale poverty, unemployment and inequality that continue to characterise South African society.

Examples of projects where the state has done spectacularly well to provide access to basic services for those long denied them are housing provision, the mass roll-out of electricity and sanitation after 1994, the broadly successful introduction of the world's largest antiretroviral scheme to combat HIV/AIDS, the land-restitution programme and the introduction of social (welfare) grants for the poorest of the poor.

Anyone who argues against the relative success of these state-driven plans is politically callous or does not realise where the tyre hits the tar in the South African political discourse. The continued popularity of the ANC – despite its many faults, mistakes and corrupt practices – is not due to the fact that the South African voting population is stupid or even masochist. It is because the majority of the voting population believe that no political party will serve their interests better than the ANC.

These are South Africans who no longer live in shacks because they have the roof of an RDP house – for which they often paid a nominal fee or even nothing – over their head. This did not happen before the ANC made it state-led policy. These are people who no longer see their children having to study by candlelight or face the danger of that candle falling over and setting all their meagre possessions alight, because they now have access to the electricity grid. These are people who no longer have to bear the indignity and danger of having to use an outside, pit or bucket toilet or no longer need to collect water because they now have sanitation facilities and running water in their homes. Again, this was not possible before the ANC made them state-led policy.

These are the people who no longer necessarily see HIV as a death sentence leading to the social scourge of child-headed households, because they now have access to the biggest state-coordinated antiretroviral roll-out in the world. This was not possible before the ANC – admittedly belatedly and only after the party had removed AIDS denialist Thabo Mbeki from presidential office – made it state-led policy.

These are also the people for whom social grants keep the wolf from the door, even as economists and many of those fortunate enough to pay income tax grumble that the social-welfare net is unsustainable. If that grant is what stands between you and hunger, you will not vote for those who you believe might abolish or diminish the system. And these are the people who either regained the land their forebears had lost after 1913 because of the policies of segregation and apartheid, or have seen other communities regain such land and live in the hope that one day they, too, will be able to own the land they regard as their home and their birthright. This was not true before the ANC made it state-led policy.

The examples given above are very deliberate and aimed at the all too many South Africans, especially in the middle and upper classes who glibly, and often privately, underestimate the intelligence of ANC voters and misinterpret the reasons for their continued loyalty to the party. I have given but a few examples to show why the choice of voting for the

ANC is not an unthought-out or ignorant reflex reaction for many voters. Many South Africans continue to vote ANC not because they are blind to the faults of the ruling party, but to give them credit for what has been achieved despite those faults, and perhaps also in the hope that, if they have not yet benefited from the system created by the ANC, they might still be able to do so in the future.

At the same time, however, the developmental-state model has also failed in many regards, as critics, including opposition parties, will quickly point out. Sticking to the examples pointed out above, shoddy workmanship and lack of quality control has been way too common in the state-led housing programme. Furthermore, especially in areas where the state has kept ownership of housing projects, upkeep has been poor and social ills have continued to persist. This is because free enterprise is throttled by a state-driven economy, opponents would argue.

Electricity roll-out has also been hampered by an inability or unwillingness, often of those newly connected to the grid, to pay for the new service they have received from the state. This so-called culture of non-payment has had a crippling effect on municipalities and on the national power utility, Eskom. In addition, an undisclosed but huge number of South Africans have connected themselves to the power grid illegally, at great physical danger to them and their children. The extent of this problem is clearly visible in areas where the poor live. Those who take power from the grid illegally and those who refuse to pay their electricity bills are stealing from those who pay, and place massive pressure on Eskom and municipalities.

It is also true that the ANC government has lacked the political will to seriously clamp down on those who steal electricity. Is this maybe out of sympathy? Unfortunately, being in government sometimes means

BURNING ISSUES I: IT'S THE ECONOMY, STUPID!

one must take the tough decision to enforce unpopular policies. This is something that the ANC in government has not always excelled at.

Social grants have been criticised mainly on two grounds. First, according to the Institute of Race Relations, by 2016 there were 15 545 000 people with jobs in South Africa while 17 094 331 were receiving social grants, and the number of South African income-tax payers was put at around 5 million. Therefore, many economists doubt the sustainability of social grants. However, this is a false and lazy argument, as the tax paid by the average taxpayer easily outstrips the meagre amounts (adjusted upwards every six months) paid out to grant recipients.

Land policy has been implemented so disgracefully that it is a massive blight on the name of the ANC government, with maladministration, corruption and poor follow-up so rampant that it has turned many of these newly resettled areas into precisely the types of bantustan/homeland hell holes they were supposed to replace and provide salvation from.

Despite setbacks, large parts of the ANC have persisted with statist, redistributive policy preferences and for the past few years have said that so-called radical economic transformation is needed. This term, which has never been clearly defined, is generally used as the converse of the concept of white monopoly capital.

Only an idiot would take issue with the argument that the South African economy must be transformed to give black people a meaningful stake in it. Two questions arise, however. First, exactly how should this be done, bearing in mind that the economy has to keep growing at the same time. And, secondly, what is the biggest factor holding back black economic growth? Is it white monopoly capital – or is it perhaps the role of the state? Much empirical research will hopefully be done so that the standard of debate can at least improve.

President Cyril Ramaphosa has added another term to the wealth of options for South Africa's future economic trajectory, this time borrowing a phrase, if not the substance, from Franklin D Roosevelt – the 'new deal'. Ramaphosa unveiled his idea during a campaign speech in Soweto in November 2017. His new deal will focus on clean and effective governance, economic growth, improving business confidence, fixing the criminal-justice system, turning around the quality of education and investing in infrastructure. It is a grand plan indeed, but we'll have to see whether it will be implemented in practice – there's many a slip 'twixt the cup and the lip. The Soweto speech laid the foundation for Ramaphosa's state of the nation address and I believe he will return to it in due course.

Given the criticisms levelled at state-led economic interventions, it is not surprising that parties like the DA, IFP, ACDP, Freedom Front Plus and COPE are in favour of a different economic model. All these parties favour a greater role for the individual rather than the state, and greater freedom for the individual above statist prescriptions.

This does not mean that these parties foresee no role for the state but they believe the state's role should be limited to providing an environment for private enterprise to thrive in. Much as the realities of historical South African inequality have forced the market-oriented parties to temper their expectations, they would still no doubt find it hard to deny their Thatcherite policy preference for as small a role for the state as possible and for privatisation above nationalisation.

These reality checks have put the brakes on especially the free-market cowboys who tend to support the DA in the absence of any other party

BURNING ISSUES I: IT'S THE ECONOMY, STUPID!

to support. The economic shape of smaller and medium-sized DA-run municipalities has not been much different from that of those run by the ANC, for various reasons, including the lack of a tax base that would enable them to implement an alternative financing model.

The obvious exception has been Cape Town, under DA control since 2006 and a powerhouse of DA support. There the party took 66.1% of the vote in the 2016 local-government elections. Although Cape Town mirrors many of the inequalities bedevilling other South African metros and municipalities, it has nevertheless taken many steps to invite foreign and local investment, cut red tape, fight crime and clean up inner-city grime. Cape Town has managed clean audits and has taken important steps, such as opening up its tender bid processes to public scrutiny. Although Cape Town certainly isn't heaven and has its fair share of scandals and pathetic palace revolutions involving politicians with oversized egos, and the city has struggled to deliver basic services to some communities, these challenges are still addressed much better than they are in other metros. Cape Town has also outperformed other metros in its levels of foreign direct investment.

The question other political parties need to ask themselves is whether there are not lessons to be learnt from Cape Town's successes with the free market. It is a fact that unemployment and poverty levels are lower in Cape Town than in the other metros, despite Johannesburg, for instance, having more money. Critics of Cape Town claim that the apartheid government always favoured the city and that it is not truly African. With every passing year, these arguments sound more and more like sour grapes, especially because the Western Cape – the only province the DA governs – has also, according to every objective measurement, outperformed the other eight provinces, all of which happen to be run by the ANC. Would it not serve the ANC well to stop being so bitter about the Western Cape and instead see whether some of its solutions could be implemented in other municipalities and provinces – and even on a national level?

That said, the DA does face serious perception challenges in the run-up to the 2019 general elections. The perception is that it runs its municipalities and its province so strictly and with such an iron fist that it does not care about the poor, the vulnerable or the destitute. And, as is often the case, this perception contains a kernel of truth.

All political parties are made up of a group of individuals who joined them for their own reasons – be it for policy, principle, self-interest, the will to serve, the desire to be a leader, etc. In South Africa, because of the country's past of systemic racial discrimination, race and economic class still overlap to a large degree. It is true that among its number the DA has racial bigots who show their bigotry every so often.

Although the party has taken action unfailingly against such people and requires its members to sign a pledge against racism, it should perhaps ask itself why those people feel so at home within its structures in the first place. It should also ask itself whether the fact that these individuals seem at home in the party might send a message to potential supporters who, for that reason, just cannot bring themselves to vote for the DA.

The EFF believes in a state-driven economy aimed at equality. It believes that the public service should be strengthened to enable the sustainable transformation of the economy. The ethos of such a state should be developmental and very strong, with an emphasis on combating corruption. This is emphasised because the task of fundamental economic transformation requires a strong state with the ability to develop a clear, strategic vision, and the ability to implement and monitor the progress being made.

For this to happen, the EFF believes the state should build internal capacity to construct and maintain infrastructure, such as roads, railways and dams, and basic services, such as schools, houses, hospitals and recreational facilities. Its policy documents argue that the state's dependence on tenders limits the country's capacity to industrialise efficiently.

It believes the fight against corruption should not be a side show, but a fundamental component of the state apparatus that is used to increase public confidence in the state, which should be under the control of the working class.

As mentioned, the EFF favours a strong developmental state with such centralised power that it can decide the mandate of expanded SOEs in housing and road construction, cement manufacturing, food production, pharmaceuticals and mining. It also wants the state to direct much of the mandate of private corporations.

Furthermore, the EFF proposes that state companies must be buttressed by state ownership of critical parts of the value chains in which these companies operate, for example, petrochemicals (Sasol) and steel (Arcelor-Mittal), so that they produce essential inputs into the economy on a non-profit-maximisation basis.

The days of sovereign economies are largely over. For this reason, it is important for South Africans to take note of foreign perceptions of the country's future economic trajectory and the shape of its economy, so that everyone can have a better idea of whether we will be able to gain the direct foreign investment boost we need to thrive.

WHO WILL RULE IN 2019?

For this book, I had the opportunity of interviewing two leading London-based economic analysts who take a specific interest in South Africa. They spoke to me on condition of anonymity. Both of them felt the consensus among international investors with a South African interest is that after the 2016 elections, it seemed obvious that the ANC might lose the 2019 elections given its declining support, growing anger as the extent of state capture became apparent and lack of policy coherence in the Zuma government.

However, they also took the difference between national and local elections into account – 2016 was a local election and 2019 is a national and provincial election, and usually the ANC fares better in national elections, which means the ANC might still win in 2019. They are aware that it was essentially a stay-away vote that cost the ANC in 2016. The belief among international investors is that even though ANC supporters may be unhappy with their party, many are not ready to support any other party – at least not yet.

Turning to projections for 2019, investors generally cap EFF support at between 12% and 13%, believing the party has only niche appeal. There is a feeling that while the DA could attain more than 30% of the vote in 2019, it has a tendency to shoot itself in the foot and stymie its own growth potential. One example is Zille's comments about the relative benefits of colonialism, which she made in early 2017 and persisted with before a very public climb-down several damaging weeks later. The comments undermined her own standing, but, more importantly, they undermined the standing of her successor, Maimane, and the levels of black support that the DA has been at pains to build up.

By the end of 2017, support levels for the DA among black South Africans had still not recovered from the fiasco, which is to be expected given the levels of support Zille's comments had received from white DA voters. Clearly, many black voters wondered whether, despite the changes in the complexion of its leadership at a national, provincial and local level, the reins of power and the hearts of many of the DA's supporters had really moved on from the kind of party that Zille represented to the more social-democratic DA that Maimane represents.

From discussions with diplomats, international investors and analysts interviewed for this book, it was clear that there are still concerns about the battle for the soul of the DA – despite the levels of black representation now seen in the party's ranks.

Among foreign investors, there is a belief that given the ANC's pull with certain smaller parties, to whom it can make certain small policy concessions (like the African Independent Congress, who really only want the Eastern Cape Matatiele district to be reincorporated into KwaZulu-Natal), the ruling party needs only about 48% support to guarantee a victory for itself. It will get over the 50% hurdle with a little help from its smaller friends.

Whereas many international investors believe that there is an insufficient level of fear among the ANC of falling below 50% (which could help the opposition), others believe that as long as the DA remains under 30%, the ANC will win under any leader.

The feeling in London seems to be that the expected global economic upturn moving into 2019 should benefit the ANC. International analysts expect a fall in South African real household income and a populist ANC campaign in 2019. If the fall in household income is absorbed and contained, it may not have such a big effect, but if it happens against a backdrop of a slow global economy, it would be to the detriment of the ANC. There is also a belief that much as the ANC has been hurt by

South Africa's downgrade to junk status, it may well be that voters will feel that everything bad that could have happened has happened, which means the only way is up.

As for the DA, international analysts believe that by 2019 the party's dogged campaign against state capture may have a positive effect among supporters and push up core DA voter turnout, but it may simply leave others in the contested voter pool feeling cold. Picking up on a very real concern confirmed by much research, independent analysts believe that a phenomenon that the DA could benefit from is the marked xenophobic tendencies among many black South African voters, especially against immigrants from elsewhere on the African continent. It would require the DA to take a definite stand against illegal immigration. This tendency has also been picked up by DA pollsters and has been discussed within its parliamentary caucus as a possible vote-getter. However, many others in the DA believe such a xenophobic electoral tactic would not only be uncouth, irresponsible and illiberal, but also backward and immoral. We will have to wait and see who wins this specific fight within the DA.

What investors want above all is certainty. Before the ANC elective conference in Johannesburg in 2017, analysts and investors hoped for a Ramaphosa win because he represented a more market-friendly, non-racial, non-corrupt option than the Dlamini-Zuma slate did. Their joy at his victory proved to be short-lived, though. It lasted as long as it took for Mabuza to be elected as his deputy and Magashule as secretary general. Mabuza and Magashule are not highly regarded in responsible investor circles.

In short, then, the choice South Africans will exercise in 2019 will be for a greater or a lesser role played by the state in the economy. This choice will be watched very carefully in South Africa, but also from abroad, because the future shape of the economy will guide not only domestic, but also foreign levels of direct investment in South Africa.

The NDP may also play a role as we approach the 2019 elections. The NDP was drawn up by a group of distinguished South Africans under the leadership of Trevor Manuel, then Minister in the Presidency, and was finalised in 2012.

It is a detailed blueprint for how the country can eliminate poverty and reduce inequality by 2030, including how to attain economic growth of 5.4% a year and create 11 million new jobs over a 20-year period.

Principally, it focuses on practical steps to increase job creation, stimulate economic growth, improve education – specifically for black children – maintain and improve infrastructure, combat spatial divides, make the South African economy less resource-intensive, create a better-quality public-health system, improve public services, fight corruption and unite South African society.

Although the NDP was drawn up during the Zuma presidency, it has not been followed and has become something of a melancholic, bad joke in political circles. An ANC under Ramaphosa, however, is expected to focus strongly on its implementation. That would bring the party very close to the DA, whose policies are compatible with those contained in the NDP. However, implementing the NDP will cause tensions between the ANC on the one side and the EFF and Cosatu on the other, because both the EFF and Cosatu oppose the NDP.

CHAPTER 8

Burning issues II: Land and the power of perception

Since the beginning of time, the world over, the changing ownership and control of land and territory have been among the human race's greatest contestations and the chief causes of war. In South Africa, the land question is an especially emotive issue because it has its roots in – and has become synonymous with – the racially based patterns of dispossession stratifying and defining South African society.

For anyone wanting to tackle the land issue, it is incredibly important to understand how the role of history and context interlink with present realities and future solutions. Generally, many white South Africans become irritated or embarrassed when the historical context of the land issue is raised in relation to the present situation and future solutions. They tend to disregard the weight of history, believing that as a society we should move on and focus solely on how the issue can be tackled in the context of present and future concerns.

Anyone who follows the national discourse playing out on the streets, on talk radio, in the readers' letters that newspapers publish and on websites will not fail to miss that, by and large, black South Africans tend to express the same kinds of sentiments when it comes to the land issue. They feel the past is too often forgotten, and that present and future solutions tend to brush aside the historical context of the land issue.

In acknowledgement of these sentiments, I feel it is important to provide here a brief historical overview of land and race to explain how we got to the situation we are in today.

Although wars of conquest and dispossession of land occurred among the groups living in southern Africa before European colonisation, the arrival of Dutch settlers led by Jan van Riebeeck at the Cape in 1652 changed these patterns in three ways: the colonisers added race as a distinguishing factor, they made the battle for possession a one-sided affair and they created a chronicle of dispossession – a written record of wrong.

The element of race was introduced by the fact that the conquerors were white and the conquered black. This was the start of a harsh and persisting societal trait where race and class overlapped.

Of all racially defined issues, the land issue has proved the most divisive and explosive, because in South Africa land signifies self-reliance as well as the ideal of a rural idyll (even if it's unrealistic given South Africa's climate). For many in the black community, rural life represents an idyll lost alongside the loss of power in bloody colonial conquests. Now that power has been regained, the argument goes, it is time to regain the idyll. This view carries much emotional appeal for many black South Africans.

White colonisation turned dispossession into a one-sided affair, because of the technological gap between coloniser and colonised. European firepower, and the interrelated concepts of guns, gospel and gold (or guns, germs and steel, as Jared Diamond would have it) used to colonise Africans, meant that wars of land dispossession could have only one winner. African land, minds and wealth were captured in a series of violent frontier wars that wrested ever more land from whomever first occupied it. Few people would be able to argue with the emotional truth of Malema's point that no one ever asked permission or provided fair and just compensation when black South Africans lost their land – so why should this apply when that trend is reversed?

For many in the white community, land on the one hand represents a link to an agrarian and frontier past when their position of power mostly went unchallenged. On the other hand, present-day attacks on white farmers feed into a myth of white victimhood that is associated with the loss of political power to a government dedicated specifically to the interests of 'blacks in general, and Africans in particular' (to quote from ANC policy). The unstated flip side could (perhaps disingenuously) be read as that the government does not specifically prioritise the needs of white people in general, or white, coloured and Indian South Africans in particular. Hence the symbolism and emotion that have come to define the land issue.

The final way in which colonisation changed contestation for land in South Africa was that it kept detailed records of its conquests. In contrast to the Mfecane, the Difaqane or any other intra-black period of conquest, violent European conquests of land were proudly and triumphantly recorded for posterity – only to come back to haunt their white kith and kin many years later.

The recording of wrong was not the only way in which written records changed the history of conquest and dispossession. In fact, the biggest contribution of writing was codification – turning segregation and discrimination into law – written law enforced by the power of the

BURNING ISSUES II: LAND AND THE POWER OF PERCEPTION

sword wielded by the state. This became especially true after 1948 when the National Party was elected into government and implemented its policy of racially based and unequal separation, which became known as apartheid.

Through the Population Registration Act, written law defined every South African according to race. The Prohibition of Mixed Marriages Act stipulated that people could marry only within their own racial group. The Immorality Act declared sex outside the strictly defined racial groupings immoral and unlawful, and the Group Areas Act proscribed people of different racial definitions (as defined by the Population Registration Act) from living in the same area.

The Group Areas Act and the homeland system – which allowed permanent residency for black people only in racially and tribally defined pieces of rural land – in effect provided the codified and most recent causes for the emotionally charged mess in which the land issue finds itself in South Africa today.

Whereas the Group Areas Act removed many black (i.e. African, coloured and Indian) South Africans from relatively well-to-do areas and dumped them – without fair compensation – in dormitory townships as reservoirs of cheap labour and purchasing power for their white masters, the homeland system went one step further and robbed them of their South African citizenship, granting them instead the bogus citizenship of ethnically defined homelands whose 'independence' was a ruse recognised nowhere but in the minds of the apartheid apparatchiks.

In colonial conquest, segregation, the apartheid Population Registration Act, Immorality Act, Prohibition of Mixed Marriages Act, Group Areas Act and homeland legislation (notably the Natives'

Land Act of 1913, the Natives' Trust and Land Act of 1936 and the various acts establishing and regulating the territories of the homelands) lie the germs of the contested South African land issue.

This situation was exacerbated over many generations by the creation of a skewed labour system that created a class of masters – mostly white – and a class of serfs, which included almost all black people. These labour-exploitation practices started during the wars of conquest when the defeated would become labourers in the service of the victors, and they became institutionalised after the discovery of South Africa's mineral wealth led to the migrant labour system, which placed black men in single-sex hostels far from home, breaking up family units. But they bore their full fruit under the homeland system when men had to leave the homelands to which their families were repressively confined by law to find an income in the mines or towns, and they needed passes to stay in confined areas as 'temporary sojourners' (to use apartheid prime minister Hendrik Verwoerd's words) without property or civilian rights.

One cannot ignore that this toxic mix from history constitutes the current South African land and property issue.

Since 1996, land and property rights have been regulated by Section 25 of the Constitution, which guarantees the existing right to property currently held. That means that any South African can now hold title and ownership to land anywhere in South Africa, but critics of the current constitutional order point out that the skewed ownership systems of the past are largely unchanged.

This is one of the many legacies of apartheid and, for this reason, many previously disadvantaged South Africans feel the state should take measures to correct the imbalances of the past in terms of land ownership.

Section 25 of the Constitution allows for the expropriation of land, but only for certain very limited and specific reasons. Chief among these are expropriation for a public purpose (such as the building of a road or a dam, or the laying of a power cable, for instance) or expropriation in the public interest (such as land restitution). In all acts of expropriation, the current owner is guaranteed the right to fair and just compensation. If the state and the owner, after a period of negotiation, cannot agree on what such fair and just compensation should be, the court is the final arbiter. Section 25 states that property

> may be expropriated only in terms of law of general application for a public purpose or in the public interest; and subject to compensation, the amount of which and the time and manner of payment of which have either been agreed to by those affected or decided or approved by a court, adding that the amount of the compensation and the time and manner of payment must be just and equitable, reflecting an equitable balance between the public interest and the interests of those affected, having regard to all relevant circumstances, including the current use of the property, the history of the acquisition and use of the property, the market value of the property, the extent of direct state investment and subsidy in the acquisition and beneficial capital improvement of the property, and the purpose of the expropriation.[1]

Furthermore, Section 25 states that 'the public interest includes the nation's commitment to land reform, and to reforms to bring about equitable access to all South Africa's natural resources, and that property is not limited to land'.

It goes on to say that 'the state must take reasonable legislative and other measures, within its available resources, to foster conditions which enable citizens to gain access to land on an equitable basis', and that 'a person or community whose tenure of land is legally insecure as a result of past racially discriminatory laws or practices is entitled, to the extent provided by an act of parliament, either to tenure which is legally secure or to comparable redress'.

Referring to the date the Natives' Land Act of 1913 was adopted, Section 25 says that 'any person or community dispossessed of property after 19 June 1913 as a result of past racially discriminatory laws or practices is entitled, to the extent provided by an act of parliament, either to restitution of that property or to equitable redress'.

The section also states that 'no provision of this section may impede the state from taking legislative and other measures to achieve land, water and related reform, in order to redress the results of past racial discrimination, provided that any departure from the provisions of this section is in accordance with the provisions of section 36(1)' of the Constitution, which is the section limiting all rights to what is justifiable in an open and democratic society.

While on the issue of land, let's get one bogeyman out of the way: there is no such thing as a willing buyer, willing seller principle in South African expropriation law – and there never has been. The concept of willing buyer, willing seller – that land would be bought or expropriated by the state only if the current owner were ready, willing and able to sell it, rather than the state unilaterally expropriating it – has never existed.

BURNING ISSUES II: LAND AND THE POWER OF PERCEPTION

It is a ruse used to explain away the incompetence of the state in not implementing expropriation and land-reform policies – as mandated by Section 25 of the Constitution. It is nothing other than an attempt to pass the buck to another for lacking the political will and competence to implement existing policy. Basically, 'willing buyer, willing seller' is an invalid excuse offered by the government to explain away the mess of incompetence and failure that land reform and land restitution have become on its watch.

Before the ANC's 2017 elective conference, the policy as mandated by the 1996 Constitution was broadly supported by all mainstream political parties except the EFF, although there is broad consensus that it has not worked well at all. There was an attempt to remedy the situation when Parliament passed a new Expropriation Bill in 2016. Steered through the parliamentary committee process by Deputy Minister of Public Works Jeremy Cronin (a dyed-in-the-wool, dinkum communist), the bill tried to clarify the expropriation process within the ambit of Section 25 by defining terms more precisely and putting a timeline to events.

Clearly, these steps were not satisfactory to the ANC rank and file, because at its 2017 conference, by far the most controversial resolution passed by the ANC dealt with the land issue. In fact, it almost caused fist fights between ANC members. The resolution was taken to allow for the expropriation of land without compensation – but subject to a feasibility study to ensure that food security and the health of the economy would not be threatened. How any thorough feasibility study will be able to find that expropriation without compensation will not endanger food security and harm the economy is, quite frankly, beyond me. Maybe the ANC conference resolution is a sheep in wolves' clothing and not as potentially harmful as one may have thought?

For many, it is concerning for the ANC under Ramaphosa to opt for expropriation without compensation. The ANC resolution has been slated as irresponsible by economists, investors and organised commercial agriculture lobbyists, but it has let the genie out of the bottle and opened the door to cooperation between the ANC and the EFF on this matter. The ANC conference resolution was indeed a jump to the left, bringing the party closer to the EFF's land policy. Only as recently as February 2017, the ANC caucus had voted against an EFF motion proposing expropriation without compensation after a parliamentary debate. Not that it was uncontested territory in the ANC – almost exactly a month later, in March 2017, Zuma called for expropriation without compensation during a speech to the National House of Traditional Leaders.

The EFF has always been in favour of wholesale change and the replacement of the current system with a radical and potentially disastrous policy of expropriation without compensation. Quite why and how this policy will work has never been adequately explained by the EFF. The example of Zimbabwe, where land expropriation helped to turn Zimbabwe from a regional breadbasket into an agricultural basket case, has been wholly ignored.

Where the EFF has a point, of course, is in claiming that the current system of expropriation and land reform has failed. Their basic argument is that, where something has failed, it is madness to keep doing the same thing and expect a different result (as Albert Einstein famously said). Therefore, so the EFF alternative argument goes, it may be worth going down the state-led, radical route. (One is left to wonder why they don't apply the same logic about not repeating the same mistake as Zimbabwe and draw some conclusions from the failed Zimbabwean example.)

BURNING ISSUES II: LAND AND THE POWER OF PERCEPTION

Before we get into the reasons why the EFF argument is reckless and does not hold water, let's first look at why the current expropriation and land-reform system has failed.

Currently, government policy aims to restore land to owners who had lost their land since the passing of the 1913 Natives' Land Act, and tries to restore the African landowning agrarian class, which was systemically destroyed by colonialism, segregation and apartheid. It is a noble aim, which has, sadly, been very poorly executed. Billions of rands later, figures from the government's Department of Rural Development and Land Reform indicate that only a negligible percentage of land has been redistributed to black farmers and farming communities. The reasons why this policy has been such an abject failure are fourfold: poor implementation, corruption, focus on communal rather than individual commercial farming and poor follow-up support.

It is a widely accepted fact that the post-1994 South African government has been better at formulating than implementing policy at almost every policy level, and not just land reform. Reclaiming land lost since 1913 has proven to be a bureaucratic nightmare, all too often characterised by civil servants who are out of their depth at dealing with the complexities and competing contestations of land reform. Much money is at stake and, especially at the start, the necessary checks and balances were simply not in place. Corruption was therefore rife. The situation has improved but much harm was done and several senior officials were forced to resign.

At least some progress has been made with redress. The current system allows any community or individual who lost land due to the apartheid system since the passing of the 1913 Natives' Land Act to claim restitution either through the return of the land or by means of a cash payment.

In the event, although much has rightfully been made of the heartbreak of losing land, around 90% of claimants prefer a cash payout to settling on the land again, which somewhat gives the lie to the school of thought glorifying the rural idyll of land above everything or, in the words of the erstwhile PAC slogan, 'The land first, the rest shall follow'.

This leads to an important point that cuts to the heart of the matter: is the whole issue of land really, deep down, a matter of money, of base redress – an opportunity cost? Is the matter of land redistribution merely a proxy for the absolutely necessary process of wealth and opportunity redistribution, given how wealth and opportunity were stolen from the majority of the population in the periods of colonial conquest, segregation and apartheid? And, if so, is land, and the focus on land, truly the right way to go, given that, as I have argued above and as the preference for monetary compensation seems to show, land dispossession really is a symbol for wider dispossession?

Put simply, do most people really wish to be compensated in land at all, or do they just want something instead of nothing, a chance, a way out of the hell of systemic deprivation? Is land truly the solution? Far be it from me, or any other individual, to settle this with a definitive answer, but questioning perception cannot be a bad thing ...

In terms of the realities of land-reform measures, the focus on communal rather than individual commercial farming has not yielded the results hoped for. While this is hardly surprising, the preference for communal farming is understandable given that the governing ANC and the EFF view themselves as forces of the political Left and thus inclined to socialism. Nowhere in the world has communal farming equalled the yields achieved by commercial enterprises. If the ANC continues to favour communal farming in a country that has a rapidly urbanising environment and rapid population growth, the impact on food production and food security will be as disastrous for South Africa as it was in neighbouring Zimbabwe.

Regarding follow-up support, government policy is to lend these newly settled African farmers a hand by providing know-how, seed, tractors and the like. Unfortunately, the policy has been an abysmal failure, with more than 90% of land-reform projects (the resettlement of forcibly removed communities or the support of new black farmers) going under for many reasons, some of which cut very close to the bone, possibly revealing some uncomfortable truths.

One of these is that commercial farming in South Africa is a precarious business, with a larger number of South African commercial farmers than the EFF may want to acknowledge already deeply indebted to the government-controlled Land Bank and the commercial banks. Figures listed by Omri van Zyl, executive director of AgriSA (the largest organisation representing South African commercial agriculture), claim that by 2016, the total value of South African commercial agriculture, if measured in terms of land, implements and animals, was about R430 billion, and that farmers borrow about R153 billion annually from the banks with their property as security.

A second uncomfortable truth is that commercial farming in South Africa is not just a matter of fencing an area, putting seed in the ground or animals in the fields and then harvesting the crop or slaughtering part of the herd. Much of the land yield is poor, and much of the climate is unstable, with periodic drought and flash flooding. It is a risky business requiring fortitude, much low-return investment and even more skill – skills that were denied generations of black people through systemic segregationist and apartheid deprivation. For the unfairest of reasons, history has left many South Africans with a skills backlog that will probably take a generation or two to erase.

Another nail in the coffin of the ANC government's land policy is its fixation on size and foreign ownership. The ANC is forever discussing the possibility of capping land ownership, especially for foreigners. There seems to be very little comprehension that a one-size-fits-all land cap makes no sense in a country as climatically divergent as South Africa. Table grape and wine farming in the Western Cape may not require much land for them to be profitable, but sheep farming in the arid Northern Cape requires incomparable land size and economies of scale for profits to materialise. This fact also makes a mockery of the whole government focus to have 30% of agricultural land transferred into black possession (initially by 2014, but since postponed). If it were just a matter of transferring 30% of land, all the government needed to do was transfer the Northern Cape and *voilà*! Except of course that everyone looks at you funny when you make this suggestion.

So much for 30%, then.

Speaking of figures, one of the most contentious issues regarding the land debate is who owns what. At long last, the Department of Rural Development and Land Reform published the government audit of land ownership in January 2018. Unfortunately it was too hopelessly inconcise to be of any use. It found that in 67% of instances the race of the land owner could not be ascertained. Where the department did decide the race of the landowner, it often used the surname of the owner to guess at the race, which surely is pathetically flawed. It found that black individuals owned 1.2% of rural and 7% of urban land and that whites owned 23.6% of rural and 11.4% of urban land.

BURNING ISSUES II: LAND AND THE POWER OF PERCEPTION

AgriSA had claimed for many years that the government was understating the level of black land ownership by not taking into consideration the land bought by black South Africans on the open market, and by not measuring black land ownership empirically. All the information was available, said AgriSA, if someone just had the will to collect and calculate it. So, in 2017 AgriSA and agricultural weekly *Landbouweekblad* pooled resources and did the research. Their findings were that black South Africans now own 26% of the land in South Africa. This of course means that white people, who make up 9% of the population, still own the vast majority of the land. This figure may well be skewed, but much less so than those still using the apartheid figure of 13% black land ownership have been claiming.

We can take home two lessons and one important caveat from the AgriSA land audit. The first lesson is that it is always better to use facts rather than emotion as the basis for an argument. The second is that the market has a role to play. Neither the state-led development model nor the completely free-market approach can alone solve the land-ownership problem – both interventions are needed. The caveat is that although the market has contributed to addressing the racial imbalance, it still only benefits white and black elites. The poor and dispossessed do not benefit from it as much as they should. A purely free-market approach does not speak to the point argued above, namely that the land issue is but a proxy for the inequality issue.

Which brings us to the last of the major weaknesses among the current government's land bugbears, namely the hang-up about foreigners owning land in South Africa. It seems like some sort of xenophobic paranoia dressed up as patriotism – which is the last refuge of a scoundrel, as Samuel Johnson quite correctly called it.

Heaven knows why we don't want foreigners to invest directly in our country – be it in industry, mining or, indeed, land! It has a knock-on effect. Just look at what foreign interest at the high end of the market has done to benefit the Cape Town housing market across the board.

In the run-up to 2019, it is clear that land ownership will be one of the most difficult topics for potential coalition and cooperative partners to agree on. So, where do the different parties stand on the issue of land reform and is there any way that they can meet each other halfway on this contentious issue?

The 2017 ANC elective conference agreed that land reform had to be fast-tracked. Two options were on the table. The moderate option was to fast-track land reform by pursuing it more aggressively by implementing redistribution through just and equitable compensation of current owners more aggressively, as defined in Section 25 of the Constitution. The second option was to move towards the populist left, and into EFF policy territory (albeit a less refined and considered version than the one the EFF offers) and embrace expropriation without compensation.

The latter option won, with no indication of how it would be implemented, and subject to the feasibility study, which should take a while.

Now, we have learnt over the years that the fact that an ANC conference takes a policy decision does not automatically mean that it will be implemented. But if it were to implement expropriation without compensation it would be very destructive to the economy – for two main reasons. First, it would make all land and property worthless, nullifying the investments made therein by all South Africans hoping to use land or

BURNING ISSUES II: LAND AND THE POWER OF PERCEPTION

property as security against the ravages of life – including those Africans whose treasured first home will now be under threat.

And, secondly, if you're going to make investment in land worthless, why stop at land? In principle, if land is made worthless by the stroke of a bureaucratic pen against the express guarantees of the Constitution as the highest law in the land, what investment is safe? And if all investment, all value, all worth, is unsafe, why should anyone invest or indeed reside here?

A final point on ANC land policy is its evolving relationship with traditional leaders and communal land ownership. Although traditional leaders played a huge role in the founding of the ANC in 1912, over the years it came to the realisation that in practice he who pays the piper tends to call the tune and that traditional leaders, therefore, tend to support whichever government is in power. Under apartheid, traditional leaders were paid by the apartheid government, and by and large did that government's bidding. Back then, the ANC believed traditional leaders were counter-revolutionary and branded them as such. However, since 1994, the ANC has realised that traditional leaders and their supporters have become some of its strongest and most reliable reservoirs of support, especially outside the IFP's northern KwaZulu-Natal heartland. The ANC, in turn, has become much more supportive of traditional leaders and communal land ownership.

Moving on from the ANC's policy proposals to those of the DA, first let's get one point out of the way, which will resurface with unfortunate repetitive tedium throughout any policy discussion. The DA's policies aren't always all that clear.

On land, the DA acknowledges that the systemic wrongs of the past must be addressed through a more equitable system of land ownership. The party is clear that this should be done in terms of Section 25 of the Constitution, which means through just and equitable compensation, as decided by a court if all other efforts at reaching consensus fail.

Interestingly, the DA also places much emphasis on providing title deeds to individuals living in communal areas under traditional leadership. Although this may represent a laudable step forward for the rights of some of South Africa's most vulnerable and impoverished people (especially women still labouring under the repressive, undemocratic, hereditary and often sexist, absolutist system, which is so at odds with democracy, dependent as it is on accidents of birth rather than gifts of ability for access to power), it is highly unlikely to become the policy of any coalition that includes the DA's presumed coalition partner, the IFP. In fact, it is hard to imagine anything that would represent greater anathema to everything the IFP stands for and its regime of traditional leadership and communal ownership.

Furthermore, the DA makes the valid point that much could have been achieved if the options detailed in Section 25 had been implemented with greater gusto and political will, and with less corruption.

At the same time, as with many other issues, it often seems as if the DA is somewhat deaf to the emotional depths from which so many of the landless poor hunger for the land denied them for so long. Much as the DA's proposal to give title deeds to individuals in communal areas, while simultaneously respecting the property rights of food-producing commercial farmers, seems better thought through than many others, it risks underestimating the zeitgeist.

To be an attractive voting option and coalition partner come 2019, the

BURNING ISSUES II: LAND AND THE POWER OF PERCEPTION

DA would have to factor in the emotional appeal to the majority of voters of changing the status quo on land policy. At the same time, it does not want to alienate the large numbers in its core constituency for whom safeguarding property rights is a paramount concern. It has some very tough choices to make. But such is politics.

The EFF has the most detailed and radical land policy of all the mainstream parties. In short, it wants the Constitution to be changed, so that the state takes ownership of all land, much in the same way that it has taken ownership of the country's mineral wealth. South Africans who wish to farm would have to apply to the state to do so, and would have to declare what they intend to farm. If the state agrees, the prospective farmer can put his or her idea into action. After a certain period of time, the state will assess whether the farmer has made a success of the endeavour. If so, the farmer can continue; if not, the farmer must abandon the project.

The EFF concedes that such a policy presupposes a competent state, which, given South African reality, is one hell of an assumption to make.

The EFF also envisages a system whereby prospective farmers will be supported with know-how, seed, livestock and equipment. How this would work in practice and how it would be paid for remain unclear. Although EFF leaders have often said that despite its often racially motivated anti-white rhetoric, it will not take away all white land ownership, quite why the current white commercial farming class should see a future for itself in such diminished circumstances is a good question. The question the EFF would at some stage have to ask itself very carefully is whether South Africa can afford to alienate and practically chase away its commercial farming class, white as it may be, or whether the country needs all hands on deck to address its many challenges.

The IFP view on the land issue is seemingly somewhat contradictory. On the one hand, the IFP fully supports private land ownership and rejects expropriation without compensation. On the other, it is totally rooted in the system of traditional leadership and communal ownership. The IFP way would be to create space for the two systems to co-exist, thereby largely maintaining the status quo, although the size of the land allocated to each system may change.

Of the smaller parties, the UDM is in favour of a more state-led developmental approach but has called for a land convention, so that all views can be heard before a final decision is taken. The ACDP and Freedom Front Plus favour a more market-driven system. All of these parties acknowledge that inequalities and the wrongs of the past must be addressed, but they are not quite in agreement how this should be done.

In the 2019 election, land will be one of the great debating points for any grouping that will end up in government. It is a potentially explosive issue, with firm fault lines and much emotional baggage. On the one hand, there is the group consisting of the EFF, the UDM, a part of the ANC and some minuscule leftist groupings, like the PAC and Azapo, who favour a constitutional change to simplify expropriation without compensation in an effort to accelerate redress. This could include fast-tracking expropriation, maybe even without compensation. This carries the danger of huge foreign and local disinvestment, and the collapse of the economy under the weight of populist policy decisions.

BURNING ISSUES II: LAND AND THE POWER OF PERCEPTION

On the other hand, there is a grouping represented by the DA, IFP, Freedom Front Plus, ACDP and many hidden commercial interests, who favour a more market-driven approach. This option carries the danger that it may alienate the huge South African economic underclass from peaceful and constitutional ways of solving problems, fomenting the violent change many have always expected in South Africa and which the country has thankfully been spared thus far.

Surely the two extremes would have to find a middle way, whereby the toxicity can be taken out of the land issue. A first step would be for the state to get its basics right and do an independent land ownership audit. That it has not done so is almost unthinkably reckless. Furthermore, those entrusted with governance in 2019 would do well to know exactly which policies can realistically be put into practice. If the current commercial farming class is not prepared to contribute to creating equality and assisting redress, it will lose everything. If populist leftists continue to preach simplified revolutionary slogans, they, in turn, will find there is nothing much to take over.

Because of its emotional nature and the enormous impact that could be made by new policy decisions on land, the land issue will be one of the toughest nuts to crack for any government post-2019. Realistically, the needs of those on both sides of the divide – those with land hunger and the commercial food-production sector – must be taken into consideration. Focusing on either at the cost of the other will be disastrous. And yet, treading the middle ground, as the Constitution attempted to do with its Section 25, has not satisfied many South Africans.

The land issue, and how political parties propose to address it, may well be pivotal to the 2019 election outcome, and to how political parties are perceived in their heart of hearts by voters. Such emotional appeal is important and beguiling to political parties, especially during times of contestation, which is precisely why it must be treated circumspectly.

Potential political partners would do well to try to smooth out as many of the practicalities as possible even before the voters cast their ballots. It is going to be tough. An overemphasis on the idealism of ideological purity will benefit no one in the long run. This is South Africa, not utopia. A very South African compromise will have to be found, in the national interest and for the common good.

CHAPTER 9

Burning issues III: Labour and black economic empowerment

The debate on future South African labour policy may be less heated and emotionally charged than the debate on land, but it is much more important because it affects more people. At issue is the problem of unemployment and how to address it.

As with all major South African political challenges, its roots can be found in the country's racially divided past. Labour relations were a central discriminatory tenet in the wars of colonial conquest and the systems of segregation and apartheid that followed.

Slavery was not abolished in South Africa – then a British colony – until 1834. So opposed were the Boers to this step by their British colonial masters that it became a major contributing cause to the Great Trek, when thousands of Dutch *trekboers* left the confines of the then Cape Colony to start their own Boer republics of the Orange Free State and the South African Republic. One of the mainstays of the legal systems in both Boer republics was the principle of no equality in church or state, which meant there was no equality between racial groups and these laws kept black (i.e. African, coloured and later Indian) South Africans permanently subservient to whites in all aspects of life.

The discovery of South Africa's mineral wealth in the late 19th century (especially diamonds in 1867 and then the Witwatersrand goldfields around 1886) increased the need for cheap unskilled labour, which, in the racially stratified realities of colonialist South Africa, meant black labour. Competition for such labour was fierce, both from white commercial farmers and mining companies. Local black men were not keen to work on the farms or in the mines, so a system was created to indirectly force them to become a pool of cheap labour.

This was done in two ways. First, the state started demanding taxes from rural African subsistence farmers. To pay these taxes, they had to find a source of income. The main way to do so was to sell their labour cheaply in a situation where there were no modern labour rights, either on the farms or in the mines.

If these taxes, in the form a hut tax, a dog tax or whatever, were not paid, violent reprisals were meted out, as evidenced by the murder of the Zulu chief Bambatha between Greytown and Nkandla in 1906. Bambatha was beheaded by Colonel Duncan McKenzie's colonialist men for not paying a hut tax, and his severed head was paraded around Pietermaritzburg. On another occasion, in 1922 General Jan Smuts sent the fledgling South African Air Force to bomb the Bondelswarts in the then South West Africa (now Namibia) for not paying their dog tax.

The second way of forcing Africans into labour happened somewhat more indirectly and over time. As the black population grew, the side effects caused by dumping people in homelands without extending their size – overpopulation, overgrazing and lack of commercial opportunity – turned the homelands into economic wastelands. In order to earn an income, men were compelled to leave the homelands to work on farms or in mines. This was a system of indirect but very effective labour coercion by design.

Black South Africans were given the right to unionise after the government-appointed Wiehahn Commission recommended it in 1979, partly to let some steam out of the political pressure cooker as the country entered what proved to be the last decade of white minority rule. In 1985 the biggest trade unions amalgamated into Cosatu, which became a staunch ally of the liberation movement, specifically the ANC.

Through Cosatu's links to the liberation movement, workers' rights became firmly associated with general political and economic liberation in South Africa. Labour rights became ever more consolidated in the years after 1994, as Cosatu wielded much power behind the scenes in the ANC government. It is said that if the ANC provided the heart of the ruling Tripartite Alliance after 1994 and the SACP provided its brain, Cosatu provided the brawn.

Since 1994 the formalisation of labour legislation and labour positions in South Africa has continued apace. The new labour legislation has made it easier for workers to strike and harder for bosses to fire workers, and has enshrined benefits such as sick leave, maternity leave, pensions and equal work for equal pay (racially and in gender terms). Legislation also protects workers against exploitation by employers, and when one considers the grim examples of worker abuse still periodically occurring in South Africa even today, the situation could well have been untenable without this protection in law.

All of which is excellent news if you have a job, but less so when you are unemployed, as more than a quarter of the potential South African labour force is at any given time. The reason why the South African labour regime is so harsh on the unemployed is that all this formalisation of employment with job security, benefits and a lesser likelihood of being fired means that employers are less likely to hire people in the first place. Also, it is hard on start-up businesses and their entrepreneurial founders, who often cannot afford the expense and associated risk of appointing staff with benefits before the business has even proven its viability.

What the current labour regime has achieved, even if many South Africans do not realise it at present, is that it has created different realities for the employed and the unemployed. At some point that cannot be foreseen with certainty, the penny will drop that it has also set up the working class who are employed and the unemployed in competition with one another. This is an issue any post-2019 government would have to tackle with some alacrity, but the prognosis for finding general agreement over the kind of ideological pragmatism needed to solve it is not good.

Under the Zuma government and the tenure of his labour minister, Mildred Oliphant, the labour policy terrain was one of reactive management, big promises, political paralysis, periodic crises and job losses.

On labour, the ANC policy is to maximise workers' rights and fight unemployment by increasing what Zuma called 'decent jobs'. This means jobs with benefits such as a pension, medical cover, unemployment insurance and maximum job security – permanent rather than temporary jobs. Although the ANC is also committed to fighting unemployment as one of its five apex priorities, this policy resulted in fewer jobs being created – no surprise considering that such benefits make employing someone more expensive, as they incur a greater unit cost per employee for the employer.

LABOUR AND BLACK ECONOMIC EMPOWERMENT

The reactive nature of labour governance was on show for all to see during the labour unrest in the Cape winelands in late 2013. It was left largely to the churches and the minister of agriculture, Joemat-Pettersson, to contain a violent situation. Oliphant was missing in action.

The biggest tangible promise by the ANC on the labour policy front is to ban labour brokers. It is a promise that has not been kept, which is probably a good thing given how many South Africans depend on temporary jobs to get by.

According to its 2013 policy document on labour, the DA has a five-point plan for job creation:

- ❏ To invest in integrated energy, transport and information and communication technologies infrastructure for job creation.
- ❏ To give more people the education and skills they need to get a job.
- ❏ To radically reform the labour regime to support job creation.
- ❏ To provide direct incentives for job creation.
- ❏ To create a nation of entrepreneurs by making it easier for South Africans to start and grow their own small businesses.

The DA's labour policy seems somewhat vague, an unhappy mix that is neither fish nor fowl. The party has stated in its policy papers that the most fundamental challenge facing South Africa today is that too few people are employed. It believes that high barriers to entry in the labour market exclude millions of South Africans from accessing employment opportunities.

These barriers relate to two things, the DA says – South Africa's inflexible labour regime and the failure of the education system to equip South African job seekers with marketable skills.

The DA therefore believes that labour policy must balance the protection of workers' rights with the need to build greater flexibility into South Africa's labour market to make it easier for businesses and other organisations to create jobs. If this balance is not achieved, labour policy is protecting the employed at the expense of the unemployed.

The DA admits that labour policy on its own will not be sufficient to create the number of jobs South Africa needs to establish a truly inclusive economy. It argues that, in addition, appropriate labour regulation must be accompanied by an economic policy that stimulates growth, an education and skills-development system that empowers job seekers to participate in the labour market in a changing global economic landscape and social policies that facilitate access to job opportunities.

The DA has said that, if elected to government in 2019, it will strive to create circumstances that allow every citizen to have the skills that are needed to be employable and to be able to participate in the economy.

This it wants to do by democratising labour negotiations, challenging the dominance of large unions and ensuring that the labour regime serves not only the representatives of workers, but the workers themselves. It says it wants to make it easier to hire employees by making key changes to the Labour Relations Act, by strengthening recognition of temporary work (by supporting a regulatory system for such work that does not stifle its job-creation potential) and by 'easing the burden of labour regulations that are inhibiting job creation in the small business sector'.

In short, with certain checks and balances, and allowing for vagueness in its labour policies, the DA, more than any other major South African political party, believes that an emphasis on regulation may stifle the job market. It wants to free up the job market to a greater extent in the belief that thereby more jobs would be created.

Ideologically, the EFF is poles apart from its cooperative partners the DA and IFP on labour matters, while the ANC is divided, as ever, but generally leans to the left – towards the EFF. Among the smaller parties, the UDM also leans to the left on labour policy, and the ACDP and Freedom Front Plus to the right.

For its part, the EFF makes six points about job creation:

❏ Within the context of a state-led industrial policy, the state should protect infant industries, particularly in areas where the country does not enjoy competitive advantages. The industrialisation South Africa should adopt ought to be both export-led and import-substituting industrialisation. Internal capacity must be built, in collaboration with established industrial and manufacturing corporations, in order to locally manufacture the goods and services we currently import from other economies. This will lead to industrial and manufacturing investments by corporations that manufacture the goods and services South Africa currently imports, further building internal skills capacity to expand on these areas.

❏ In all other industries, the state should introduce minimum wages, which would improve the living conditions of the people.

❏ South Africa's inequalities are, among other things, a result of the wage gap between top managers and ordinary workers. This, therefore, means that levels of underemployment are at a crisis level because an absolute majority of workers are not adequately remunerated.

❏ By fighting for increases in minimum wages, the EFF will organise and play a leading role in the struggles of workers in

various sectors, with the minimum demands of adequate minimum wages, and better working conditions.
- ❏ The EFF will call for legislation on incomes policy, including regulation of the pay of chief executive officers, directors, chief financial officers and managers in all sectors of the economy. Laws should be passed that executive pay should be a certain proportion of the wages of the lowest-paid workers in respective firms.
- ❏ The EFF is especially bothered about the recruitment and promotion of Africans in the workplace, and the opportunities for workers to move up the career ladder through opening up access to tertiary institutions so that workers with experience can benefit, as must be reflected in employment equity reports.

Political parties on the left have mooted a cap on the pay of top executives. This is perfectly understandable given the difference of income between the best and most poorly paid staff in many organisations, but it can never be sustainable to limit income without limiting the enterprise, upon which all workers depend. If you are going to limit income, it might be best to limit it to a sliding scale dependent on profit – for everyone.

The issue of labour brokers also remains vexed. The ANC and the EFF remain utterly opposed to the practice of labour broking because they believe labour brokers exploit desperate job seekers by offering them temporary job opportunities without benefits and with no job security.

Given South Africa's past and present realities in terms of labour relations, it would be foolhardy and callous not to protect workers against exploitation by ruthless employers. But to ban labour broking altogether seems like a simplistic answer to a complex situation. Surely it is impractical to argue that in a developing country like ours all jobs have to be permanent and come with fringe benefits. The consequence will be that fewer people will be employed, leading to even greater numbers without jobs and leaving many of the most vulnerable South Africans completely up the creek. No one wants that. So, given that some jobs will always be casual jobs, what is the point of banning labour brokers? Who would those in desperate need of casual jobs (i.e. casual workers) turn to in the absence of labour brokers?

Taken to its logical conclusion and admittedly being hyperbolic, it sometimes seems those so implacably opposed to labour brokers do not realise that economics is always a balancing act hemmed in by the confines of practical reality. Surely, the answer must be stern regulation rather than a ban, and a better effort from the Department of Labour to police and enforce such regulations.

An important labour question that any post-2019 South African government will have to address is how to balance the rights of the workers with those of the unemployed. Although the ANC and EFF have rightly complained about jobless growth, they have also taken up strong positions against a two-tier labour system, which would allow certain categories of jobs and certain categories of employers some respite from the stringency of the current formalised labour regime.

Continuing with the current slapdash approach is not an option. Any country with South Africa's levels of inequality, as reflected in its high Gini coefficient, has a revolutionary potential that must be taken very, very seriously. The EFF recognises this fact through its periodic and well-founded warnings that the country is sitting on a ticking time bomb of inequality. Whether its solution will avert what it intends to avoid remains to be seen – it certainly is no given!

Among both the left-leaning and right-leaning political parties, one sees a certain inability to adapt their ideological views to contestation and the need for compromise. It is the only way to explain the nonsensical insistence on banning rather than strictly regulating labour brokers. In this regard, the UDM's Holomisa may have provided the direction needed with his proposal for an economic version of Codesa – based on the very successful, in fact globally iconic, Convention for a Democratic South Africa, whereby seemingly irreconcilable views were accommodated to varying but surprisingly full degree in deciding upon South Africa's interim constitution, which lay the foundation for the eventual Constitution of 1996.

Black economic empowerment

Black economic empowerment has been a mainstay of ANC economic policy since the Mbeki presidency. Its basic logic rests on the assumption that because the disempowerment of black South Africans was effected systemically by the state, the empowerment of black South Africans – the righting of the wrong, if you will – must, in turn, be effected systemically by the state.

Quite how to do this has proved a huge challenge. In practice, it has boiled down to the requirement that 26% of ownership in companies that want to have dealings with the state must be in the hands of black people. In such a way, the ANC government hoped to resurrect the black entrepreneurial class who – with notable exceptions, like Herman Mashaba (who became mayor of Johannesburg in 2016 on a DA ticket) and Richard Maponya – were crushed to near extinction by the jackboot of the apartheid state.

And so began the era of empowerment deals and its ugly stepsister, fronting. The initial policy of black economic empowerment increased inequality and failed to uplift the poor for a number of reasons. First and most importantly, it was not structured as a mass empowerment tool. It was basically a way for the white business elite to empower (actually to enrich) a chosen few among the black elite.

Money is where money goes. Established (overwhelmingly white) business therefore did not as a rule enter into these empowerment deals for altruistic reasons. They did so because they were compelled to do so if they wanted their thriving business deals with governing authorities to continue. Empowerment scorecards were introduced – a box-ticking exercise to show just how far the ownership of a company had been transformed, which meant to what degree it had become owned by so-called 'designated groups', which meant black people, women, people with disabilities, in fact just about anybody except the able-bodied white men who had always been in control of business.

Because business moguls took part in empowerment deals out of necessity rather than virtue, it follows that the same black people were 'empowered' again and again. This was because most successful white business moguls did not want to change the way they made their money to any greater extent than the law and regulations now compelled them to do. By and large, they did not, primarily, embark on empowerment deals because they wanted to transform themselves or society. They embarked on these deals because it empowered them – the moguls – to continue making money.

Therefore, these deals were done either with black people (so-called empowerment entrepreneurs) who had proven through their participation in previous empowerment deals and their subsequent conduct that they understood business (meaning they would stick to established convention in the company and not rock the boat too much) or with black people who took no interest in running the company. The latter conduct became known as fronting, and sometimes bordered on the ridiculous. Tales of business owners listing their gardeners as empowerment partners abounded, although some of them may fall within the realm of urban legend.

There were two other main reasons why the initial model of black economic empowerment failed. The first was that although these new black-empowerment partners were often granted shares in companies on a preferential basis, they were generally not just given their shares for free. They still had to find money to pay for these shares and, given the extent of these massive empowerment deals, this amounted to large sums of money. Many empowerment entrepreneurs therefore became heavily indebted, reasoning that the dividends paid to them as shareholders would cover and exceed their debt repayments. Of course, success in business is not guaranteed, so many of these empowerment partners/entrepreneurs fell to the wayside.

Another reason why the initial model of black economic empowerment was unsuccessful was that there was no requirement, or even implication, that the black empowerment partner or equity partner needed to land that key state contract, or add any value to the deal, for that matter, except their blackness. All too often, therefore, these black-empowerment entrepreneurs or black-owned equity partner firms became a burden, adding very little except 'connectivity' – to use fraudster Schabir Shaik's term. Some unscrupulous black entrepreneurs quite openly traded on exactly this connectivity as their main, and sometimes only, asset if lucrative state tenders were to be won.

LABOUR AND BLACK ECONOMIC EMPOWERMENT

It led to abuse that became so widespread that a new term – 'tenderpreneurs' – was coined to refer to people who used their race and/or ANC connectivity to win state tenders that they were not capable of carrying out, ending, often, in unfinished or unsafe work. Such actions, in turn, fed into a prejudice in certain bigoted circles that connectivity was all that black business had to offer – an obvious untruth that many competent black-owned businesses had to work very hard to overcome.

So, over time, and to an accelerated degree in the latter years of the Zuma presidency, it was broadly realised that the model of black economic empowerment had to be changed from elite empowerment to what became officially known as broad-based black economic empowerment (BBBEE). This policy has, however, not really been implemented with any gusto or political will. If we turn to possibilities for 2019, this has created a gap for the opposition to exploit, because the main opposition parties have an alternative view of black economic empowerment, which overlaps to a surprising extent, and they will probably have much more political will than the ANC to implement it, given that it was largely ANC supporters and donors, rather than the opposition parties' supporters, who benefited most from empowerment and BBBEE deals.

The DA has had a very uncomfortable relationship with black economic empowerment because it professes fundamentally to believe in non-racialism. It took the rise of black leaders such as Lindiwe Mazibuko, the erstwhile DA parliamentary leader, to start addressing the issue that a non-racial solution to a racial problem – the structural disempowerment of black people through colonialism, segregation and apartheid – may not be adequate. It has also been one of the hallmarks of Maimane's leadership that he has tackled this issue head-on and has attempted to craft a coherent and decisive DA policy favouring black economic empowerment and affirmative action.

Under Maimane, the DA has come out for empowerment of the many, not the few, and has declared itself to be in favour of the empowerment of the poor. This is deft footwork, because, as we have seen, for the precise reason of colonial and apartheid systemic planning, the poor in South Africa are overwhelmingly, if not quite exclusively, black. The fact that race and class overlap to such a degree in South Africa means that a largely non-racial solution may well present itself, counter-intuitively. Under Maimane, the DA is now unstintingly in favour of black economic empowerment, but it believes it should be implemented in a fundamentally different way from how the ANC has chosen to do it.

The DA's specific policies on this issue, however, have not been finally formulated and are therefore as much a mystery as many of its other policies. But it is fair to say that their utterances on this matter have been in favour of mass empowerment. This brings the party very close indeed to the EFF's much clearer policy on the empowerment of workers by giving them shares in the organisation in which they work. Such a model would link productivity to income, although it would also open the worker to the risk of loss should the business not perform or should some unforeseen calamity overtake it.

A focus on the empowerment of workers, as opposed to black entrepreneurs, presents four challenges of its own. First, if, say, 26% of a corporation is broken up into little parts and divided among each worker, it is probable or at least possible that it would leave them with such a small share each that it won't uplift them in any meaningful way. Secondly, if individual workers own such a small part in the company, would they have any real power or say if their views collided with those of management?

A third and related issue is whether management would have enough leeway to make unpopular decisions, or decisions that cater to the medium to long term rather than short-term interests of all concerned should the workers disagree? In this case, a practical example from land reform on citrus farms could serve as an illustration.

In citrus farming, parts of the orchard must be uprooted every so often and replenished with new, young trees because every tree has a limited lifespan. So, if the whole orchard ages at the same rate the day will eventually arrive when the orchard is too old to bear fruit in a financially sustainable way. At the same time, it is very costly to replace citrus trees and many a farmer leaves it too late, ending up having to sell the farm. The same problem occurred with depressing reality at citrus farms that were handed over to beneficiaries of land reform. For understandable reasons, workers would all too often vote to invest money in, say, education bursaries for their children rather than buying young trees. In time, such decisions led to crop failures because unpopular but imperative investment decisions could not be implemented. It is easy to see how such a situation could repeat itself if workers were to be given a meaningful input into strategic corporate decisions.

Finally, a system would have to be created to address the issue of what would happen to shares if a worker leaves the company. So, all in all, it is not merely a matter of handing workers shares and everything will be fine and dandy, as the EFF policy envisages.

In the run-up to 2019, prospective political partners would do well to iron out at least some of their differences on black economic empowerment. Otherwise the election pressure cooker could cause their negotiations or even their cooperative and coalition agreements to become unstuck on this important and complicated issue. In contrast with issues like land, nationalisation and the structure of the economy, this is an issue on which opposition parties can find much common ground.

Partly linked to black economic empowerment is affirmative action, a policy intervention that is used, with varying success, all over the world to the benefit of vulnerable and economically excluded demographically defined groups. The aim is to put members of such groups in positions of preferential employment. In South Africa, the intended beneficiaries of affirmative action are members of the black *majority*. This is very different from other countries, where affirmative action is normally aimed at righting the wrongs done to *minorities* who were historically discriminated against.

It follows that affirmative action, when implemented after South Africa's democracy in 1994, had a much greater effect on South African society than on most other societies around the world where it has been implemented, because the extent and reach were so much greater.

South Africans tend to accept affirmative action as a fact of life, and as, over time, the worst racial imbalances of the past were corrected and staff components started to better reflect South Africa's racial mix, affirmative action became viewed increasingly less as a form of reverse discrimination (against capable white people) that its opponents claimed it to be. The emergence of ever more suitably qualified black South African professionals as the systemic discrimination against black people lessened also improved affirmative action's sometimes tawdry image. Indeed, affirmative action is no longer the contested issue it used to be in South Africa – even though political parties on the extreme right, of which the Freedom Front Plus is the largest, still oppose it.

CHAPTER 10

Burning issues IV: Nationalisation and tackling corruption

On the issue of nationalisation, the country's two most unlikely cooperative partners, the DA and the EFF, are, yet again, completely at odds while the ANC seems to be divided on it.

The ANC believes, as mentioned, in the developmental state, which places the state at the centre of development. To understand why the ANC holds this view, you need only attend an ANC conference of your choice. The party's conferences always contain several discussions on how the ANC is 'in government but not in power' – meaning that it gained a political majority but that true power resides elsewhere – in what it calls the 'commanding heights of the economy'. Therefore, it is understandable that the ANC would argue that development must be steered from where it can be controlled – by the state.

In 2012, at its Mangaung elective conference, the ANC was careful to steer clear of explicitly supporting nationalisation. The ANC favours a less stringent, more social-democratic policy, preferring to support a developmental state. There is, therefore, clear blue water between its policies and those of the EFF, which is in favour of nationalisation.

Of course, a record exists of exactly how the South African state fares when it involves itself in managing key strategic parts of the economy. Sadly, it has been implemented very, very poorly. In fact it has been an unmitigated disaster. Very few SOEs have not been the very definition of mismanagement.

Whereas power utility Eskom, the South African Broadcasting Corporation (SABC) and SAA have become synonymous with corporate failure in the public mind, the worst results have been chalked up by PetroSA, which recorded a whopping R15 billion loss in a single year. In December 2015, the Strategic Fuel Fund, which, like PetroSA, answers to the Energy Portfolio Committee in Parliament, managed to sell off the country's strategic oil reserve at basement bargain prices, quite illegally.

What these state-owned companies have in common is incredibly incompetent managers, a disregard for how taxpayers' money is spent and the ability to duck and dive when things go wrong rather than be held to account.

At the heart of the incompetent management at state-owned companies is the ANC's policy of cadre deployment, which was formulated at its national elective conference in Mahikeng in 1997. This means that the ANC has pushed its own members into positions of influence, notably positions filled by presidential or parliamentary decision, whether they are best qualified for the job or not.

The aim was to achieve greater power and control, but the results were as predictable as they were disastrous to the country. It follows like night on day that if you are put in a position because of your ability to serve a political party rather than the public, you will always put the interests of that party and its power brokers above the interest of the public, because that is where your power derives from – it is how you got your job, after all – finish *en klaar*.

It really is that simple: for South Africa to have a functional civil service and therefore a capable state, cadre deployment must be relegated to where it belongs – the dustbin of history. Unless the best person is appointed to every job, the ideal of having a capable state is not worth the paper it is written on. Mediocrity breeds mediocrity.

One extreme example among many will suffice – the tenure of Dudu Myeni at the helm of SAA. If you put a primary-school teacher in charge of an airline, she is most likely to be as unsuccessful as a pilot who is put in charge of a grade-one class. Neither will succeed, and both will cause immense damage – each in his or her own way.

Myeni – cheekily referred to in Parliament by the EFF as Mrs Dudu Myeni-Zuma – wreaked havoc at the airline. It lost billions. She alienated pilots and made the wrong financial decisions, and hogged the headlines for all the wrong reasons. But she refused to go. Called to account by opposition MPs, notably the DA's David Maynier and Alf Lees, at sittings of the Parliamentary Portfolio Committee on Finance, she dodged responsibility, blamed others, made populist statements and claimed a racial agenda to unseat her. Her arrogance was something to behold, matched only by her vacuousness. To their eternal disgrace, all too many ANC MPs played along, keeping her in position until she was finally removed in October 2017.

How did Myeni land the job in the first place? She was very, very close to Zuma – she even headed his charity education foundation (which, incidentally, also belly-upped under her guidance leaving financially struggling students high and dry after it failed to meet its bursary obligations). Her tenure as head of the uMhlathuze Water Board, serving Richards Bay, Empangeni and surrounds, did not inspire confidence either. But she was close to the president, so she was kept in her positions

NATIONALISATION AND TACKLING CORRUPTION

until Zuma's star waned. Power is where power goes, evidently.

Closeness to the president, incidentally, was also key to the appointment of Ellen Tshabalala for a disastrous stint as head of the SABC board, not to mention Busisiwe Mkhwebane (nominated by the Presidency) as Public Protector, and that after the bar had been set so high by her predecessor, Thuli Madonsela. Two very controversial and damaging appointments by Zuma need to be added to this list of shame: Tom Moyane as the head of the South African Revenue Service and Shaun Abrahams as the head of the National Prosecuting Authority (NPA).

With most of these positions, ANC Members of Parliament were absolutely complicit and even more to blame than Zuma, or whoever pulled the strings within the Presidency. They were very happy to turn Parliament into a rubber stamp. Ever since the days of the post-World War II Nuremberg tribunals, the principle in this regard is clear: one does not merely take instruction; one chooses to take instruction.

This said, and the blame game over, one has to hope for improvement, which can happen in one, two or all of three ways: ANC MPs can be held accountable for their actions (hugely unlikely); they can mend their ways and actually appoint civil servants who are competent and prepared to put the public before politics (but can a leopard change its spots?); or they can be replaced by another government – but that would assume politicians from other parties would fare better, which, were I a betting guy, would not be a bet I'd be willing to make.

Turning to 2019, then, what are the views of parties potentially in government, firstly on nationalisation and, secondly, on its ugly twin sister, cadre deployment?

The ANC, still styling itself as a force of the Left, has certainly not let the facts stand in the way of the good story it believes it has to tell. Its 54th conference in Johannesburg in December 2017 gave a nod to the pro-nationalisation Left with its resolution that a state bank should be formed, but without going all the way and asking for the nationalisation of commercial banks. With this, it has remained true to its vision of the developmental state where a state bank serves those who fall outside the ambit of the commercial banking sector. Let's just hope such a state bank performs better than just about every other state institution.

The party also held on tight to its vision of a state mining company, which, it can only be hoped, will fare somewhat better than the one it already has, Alexkor.

What the ANC did do at its Johannesburg conference was to decide that deployed cadres had to have the requisite skills before they are deployed. That sounds fine, but actually this has always been a requirement in many government jobs, honoured mainly in the breach. It is hard to believe that the conference resolution will, all of a sudden, lead to excellence being valued above party interest and ensuring jobs for fellow cadres.

In fact, the ANC resolution misses the point on two scores. First, as long as people are appointed because they are party deployees, they will always be party servants first, before they are public servants. Secondly, there is no way the job will be done as well as it could have been had the best-qualified people been appointed. Logical, not so?

Two of the most controversial resolutions of the Johannesburg ANC conference also boil down to a form of nationalisation – the decisions on land and higher education. On land, should the constitutional amendment actually be made to legalise expropriation without compensation, then the government will effectively be in a position to nationalise land in South Africa. Only time will tell how an ANC led by Cyril Ramaphosa will action this decision.

The adoption of a policy of fee-free tertiary education carries with it the potential of massive future government interference in higher education, as if the interference permitted by the Higher Education Amendment Act of 2017 is not already draconian enough. At the national conference, the ANC endorsed the reckless announcement by Zuma of fee-free higher education for all families earning less than R350 000 a year. If the state in time starts to regard taxpayers' money as 'its' money – as states the world over tend to – it is more likely that a time will come when the state will argue that, as 'it' pays for students' tuition, lodging, books and food, 'it' should have a say in what is taught at university. Zuma's announcement has placed the ANC straight on the road to nationalising higher education, unless cooler heads prevail.

The EFF strongly favours nationalisation, believing it needs to be given a chance given the failure of market forces to uplift the poor and combat inequality in South Africa since democratisation in 1994.

Most controversially, the EFF favours the nationalisation of mines. It does so very loudly – which is very reassuring for those who agree with it but scares the living daylights out of those who disagree. The EFF sees the nationalisation of mines as a basic prerequisite for the economic transformation that, it believes, did not happen after the dawn of South African democracy in 1994.

Those in favour of nationalisation argue that only 5% of mining interests are owned by black South Africans. Shivambu has argued that the current system expects prospective black investors to borrow money to attain shares, either from the companies they are buying shares in or from the banks, which leaves them powerless.

One of Shivambu's major political hobby horses since he joined Parliament in 2014 has been illegal asset and financial transfers from South Africa to foreign destinations by big companies – notably in the mining sector. This gives such companies the option of declaring very low profits locally, leading to very low return on investment for these black capitalists.

As a solution, the EFF believes that a not-for-profit state mining company could save the flagging mining industry – once the dynamo driving South Africa's industrialising economy but currently very much a sunset industry in South Africa.

Such a company, the EFF proposes, should have the interests of South African society at heart, rather than be driven by a narrow profit motive. Importantly and, to my mind, positively, the EFF favours giving mineworkers a stake in the mines where they work, thereby linking their productivity to the income they can derive as shareholders. This could be a major step towards shifting black economic empowerment away from being a policy that benefits a few among the black elite to one that benefits the masses.

In terms of possible coalitions, this position could provide a starting point for discussions between the EFF and the DA, who may surprise each other, and themselves, by finding some common ground on this matter, since the DA view of broad-based black economic empowerment is based on a model of giving a stake in the economy to the masses rather than the select few. That is not wholly incompatible with the EFF preference for mass worker empowerment, although much negotiation on any potential policy overlap would still have to be done.

In another important EFF mining policy proposal, the party suggests that a separate framework for small-scale mining should be introduced. This policy has not been explained in detail, but seems to be a move away from dogmatic nationalisation and towards entrepreneurship in the small-scale mining industry. This brings me to why I have always admired the EFF's thinking on economic matters, as exemplified by Shivambu. Much as it is rooted in the ideology of the Left, it is not blindly dogmatic. It will take from the market economy whatever good it can find there. It is as if the EFF finds itself in less of an ideological cul-de-sac than some of the other opposition parties. If this kind of open-mindedness can persist, the EFF can make a very valuable input – maybe the most valuable of all political parties – to the discourse on the future of mining in the build-up to 2019.

As we have seen, the EFF also favours nationalisation of farmland, which would then be farmed according to plans the state has agreed to; the land would be taken away from farmers who did not make a success of it.

The EFF has pointed out that South African history is replete with examples of state-led industrial growth, such as Iscor, which was once the foundation and champion of the country's steel industry, and Armscor, the driving force behind the South African weapons industry. It has argued that Afrikaner upliftment by the National Party and its predecessors after the Union of South Africa in 1910 would not have happened without large state-sponsored projects involving the railways or irrigation works. While it has a point, there is a counter-argument: would this National Party policy have proven to be sustainable in the end?

The EFF's state-centred view is strongly challenged by many of its opponents, who claim that state-focused growth is discredited and has been abandoned globally. To this, the EFF argues that it has simply not been properly implemented globally. The party also points out that the poor do not benefit from the selfishness that is inherent in the capitalist system, which has worsened global inequality, and has had to be bailed out and hemmed in by states worldwide, even the US.

As mentioned, the EFF includes the caveat that the state has to be a capable state with the best people working for it. Given the current underperformance of the civil service, it is hard to understand how the EFF would achieve this ideal.

The EFF has committed itself and its members to the selfless vision of the 'upright man', an ideal that Thomas Sankara embraced during his tenure as president of the West African nation of Burkina Faso from 1983 to 1987. Sankara, known as the African Che Guevara, emphasised pride in one's roots, acting rather than procrastinating, living within one's means, perseverance, care for the environment (especially by planting trees), feminism, leadership through service, opposition to leadership personality cults, emphasis on personal style and the importance of physical fitness.

It has to be said that the EFF has walked the talk in terms of living out this philosophy and putting the public good before personal gain. It instructed its municipal councillors to be cooperative partners rather than coalition partners with other opposition parties in municipal councils where no party holds an overall majority. This means those councillors forfeit the money they would have received if they had taken up the executive positions they would have been offered had there been a coalition agreement.

Nevertheless, it would be a surprising and amazing feat if the EFF were to succeed in keeping this ideology of disciplined selflessness intact as the party grows. Sadly, all too many people prefer to place more emphasis on improving their own material well-being before that of society at large.

My own experience with politicians tends to suggest that they always believe their leadership qualities are underestimated and that – with very few exceptions (among whom I count the SACP's Jeremy Cronin as a truly selfless servant of the public) – they believe they deserve to reap material rewards, which they come to view as their due.

But, heck, maybe the EFF vision will survive. It would be wonderful if it could.

At the other end of the nationalisation spectrum stands the DA, which certainly does not favour nationalisation. In fact, it is probably fair to say nationalisation is anathema to the DA. On state-owned entities, DA policy goes as follows:

- ❏ SOEs must sell off existing ageing or underutilised assets and then reinvest the proceeds in new infrastructure projects.
- ❏ Various large infrastructure projects should be listed, so as to raise equity capital from the financial markets.
- ❏ SOEs should also be listed, whereby a majority of shares could be retained by the state but capital could be raised on the sale of the remainder on global markets.
- ❏ Private-sector players should be allowed to build and manage infrastructure assets. This could include allowing more independent power producers in the energy sector or permitting mining houses to build their own rail connections to the ports.

The DA favours selling off non-performing state-run enterprises, such as SAA, which it considers a black hole into which good money follows bad. The DA favours putting the money to what it considers better use, that is, investing in education and training, and strengthening the social-security net by increasing the welfare grants upon which so many of South Africa's poorest citizens depend. The DA also favours cutting back on – rather than expanding – the civil service.

It believes the economy will grow faster if there is more private investment from local and overseas investors. It proposes achieving this by freeing up more sectors in the South African economy to be market-driven – the polar opposite of nationalisation. It often points to the billions of rands that local businesses prefer to keep as liquid assets rather than reinvest the cash in what it – and more than a few leading figures in business – claims to be an investor-unfriendly South Africa.

The DA argues that very few economies that have nationalised on a large scale have proven to be successful. It claims the world is littered with examples of the economic havoc nationalisation has caused, for instance in the erstwhile Soviet Union and its socialist satellites, Venezuela, China (before its liberalisation), Cuba – the list goes on.

This stance has left the DA vulnerable to attacks by its opponents to the effect that it is in the pocket of big business and does not care about (or certainly does not care for!) the interests of the poor. In South Africa, given the historical overlap between class and race, only half a step is required for the argument to move on to the accusation that the DA favours big monopoly capital (in South African parlance, this is often equated to 'white' monopoly capital). The temptation to overlay the economic argument with the racial one has proven just too juicy to resist for many a DA opponent.

NATIONALISATION AND TACKLING CORRUPTION

The IFP is also not in favour of nationalisation. It has always aligned itself with the market-oriented powers globally and is unlikely to change tack now – the IFP has, after all, never really been known for its fondness for change. It has also always prided itself on the philosophy of self-help rather than state handouts to ameliorate poverty.

The same goes for the ACDP, which is on record as saying that only the utilities should be nationalised, and the party is not shy to list local and international failures of nationalisation policies when pushed on the subject. The Freedom Front Plus finds itself in the same ideological corner as the IFP and the ACDP, with the UDM the odd one out among the smaller opposition parties on this matter. The UDM is in favour of greater state intervention in the economy, believing in the ideal of a developmental state. It has stopped short, however, of endorsing nationalisation, rather sticking to its call for an economic 'Codesa' to deal with these matters.

Nationalisation is one of the matters that could strongly divide potential partners if talks about forming a post-2019 government were to start in earnest. The EFF and the UDM are ideologically much closer to the ANC on this matter than they are to the DA, IFP, ACDP and Freedom Front Plus. Very small parties, such as the PAC and Azapo, would also find themselves close to the positions of the ANC, EFF and UDM.

Nationalisation is a vexed issue, one that the ANC could use to divide the opposition and gain certain allies. It is an issue with which opposition parties would do well to engage and reach certainty – even consensus – before 2019 if they wish to keep the ANC out of government.

Tackling corruption

In order to be corrupt, you must have the power to act corruptly. Corruption and maladministration seem to have become an intrinsic part of South African daily life. Under the trusteeship of Zuma, the term 'state capture' was added to our lexicon, and corruption became synonymous with ANC governance.

Although no political movement in the world supports it in its policies, no political movement is free from corruption. The measure of any political movement is therefore how it deals with corruption when it surfaces. In this regard, the ANC's performance has been woeful. The callousness with which it has been tolerated was probably best illustrated by Bathabile Dlamini, who, when certain members of the ANC threatened to blow the whistle on corruption in 2016, did not choose to deny it but warned that 'we all have smallanyana skeletons'.

Some of these skeletons are, unfortunately, not so small, and it is very important to realise that they manifest in all spheres of government – local, provincial and national. The malfeasance is probably most prevalent at local level, where many municipalities are so poorly governed that the Auditor-General gave a form of a disclaimer when he said that their affairs are so chaotic that they cannot really be audited to any meaningful extent.

In 2017, in the whole of North West province, not a single municipality received an unqualified audit. Each of these municipalities is run by the ANC. By contrast, in the Western Cape, where the DA is in government in 28 out of 30 municipalities, almost all municipalities received unqualified audits in 2017. This does not necessarily mean that the ANC is a bunch of crooks, or that the DA are angels. (Anyone who followed the nasty fallout in the halls of power within the DA-controlled city of Cape Town in the final months of 2017 would know that this is not the case.) What it does highlight, though, is that the ANC needs to muster the political will to be as strict on the spending by the municipalities it controls as the DA is on theirs. This may seem like an easy decision but, on the other hand, poor compliance is a very hard habit to change. It means adhering to the Public Finance Management Act as if it were the Bible and the day of reckoning were imminent. It means being that person no one wants to be socially – like the schoolma'am or teacher's pet who sticks to every rule – no jobs for pals and nothing for personal gain.

The extent of corruption and maladministration over many years in South Africa is well documented by the Office of the Auditor-General. In 2016, the incumbent, Kimi Makwetu, said that the provinces with the highest proportion of municipalities with clean audit outcomes in 2014/15 were the Western Cape (73%), Gauteng (33%) and KwaZulu-Natal (30%). Striking a hopeful note, he said that audit outcomes of municipalities in the Eastern Cape, Free State and Mpumalanga were starting to emerge from many years of negative audit outcomes, but that the audit outcomes of municipalities in Limpopo, North West and the Northern Cape were 'disappointing at best'.[1]

Regarding the audits of national departments in 2017, Makwetu said there had been a slight improvement in outcomes, with the number of clean audits increasing to 30% of the total population under review. At the provincial level, the Western Cape and Gauteng continued to produce the best results. It is also clear that these results are being sustained from year to year – the result of leadership emphasising a culture of accountability.

Makwetu also acknowledged improvements in the audit outcomes in both the Eastern Cape and Limpopo, attributing these positive trends to the leadership roles of the provincial treasury and the premier, respectively. In contrast, outcomes in Mpumalanga, the Northern Cape and KwaZulu-Natal were erratic over the past four years, caused by a lack of urgency among leaders in responding to the root causes of the audit outcomes in these provinces.

In North West and the Free State, Makwetu singled out 'lack of accountability and commitment towards clean administration' as factors that influenced the poor showing of these provinces.

But the worst example of corruption was not to be found in the reports of the Auditor-General. It was recorded in news reports (for instance about the #GuptaLeaks emails) and Madonsela's 'State of Capture' report, which reveal how the state was captured by the influential Gupta family. This family, who moved from India to South Africa in 1993, gained South African citizenship through the express and highly questionable interference of the then Minister of Home Affairs (later Minister of Finance) Malusi Gigaba.

Over time, as expounded by Pieter-Louis Myburgh in his excellent book *The Republic of Gupta*,[2] the Guptas became very influential and very wealthy, mostly through their friendship with and favours for the extended Zuma family, other well-placed people in the state and those in charge of SOEs. They certainly did not think small and they lived large, in a heavily guarded compound in the posh Johannesburg suburb of Saxonwold.

The family scored billions in government tenders, many of which became legendary for their brazenness and extent in strategic sectors ranging from uranium to coal contracts and many commercial endeavours. Gradually, ordinary South Africans became aware of the influence

NATIONALISATION AND TACKLING CORRUPTION

the Gupta family had in the highest citadels of power – and they did not like it one bit.

The day the Guptas overplayed their hand can probably be pinpointed to 30 April 2013, when a plane carrying wedding guests from India to a Gupta family wedding held at Sun City was allowed to land illegally at Waterkloof Air Force Base in Pretoria – a national key point. The guests were escorted to the wedding venue without having to go through customs at OR Tambo International Airport, like the rest of us unconnected mortals. The government official forced to take the fall for this situation, Bruce Koloane, insisted the orders came from Number One (a code name for Zuma). Shortly after the saga, Koloane was appointed by the president as South African ambassador to the prized posting of the Netherlands. It was all just so brazen.

Volumes have been written on the Gupta family and the stories need not be repeated here. However, two aspects should be aired in the run-up to the 2019 general elections. The first is the persistent allegations that, during the Zuma presidency, the Guptas influenced cabinet appointments, which are supposed to be an exclusive presidential prerogative exercised after consultation with the ANC leadership. A senior ANC MP, Vytjie Mentor, has gone public with the way in which she claims the Guptas offered to organise her the position of Minister of Public Enterprises if she guaranteed a lucrative flight route to India to one of their airlines. She refused. Mentor never did become a minister in a Zuma (Zupta?) cabinet.

The second aspect is the closeness of the Guptas to Zuma. Among all the pictures and visits to the Saxonwold compound that South Africans have become all too familiar with, one shocking example stands out. On 17 October 2015, I had been watching South Africa beat Wales in the

Rugby World Cup at the home of two friends. We were channel-hopping when we spotted Zuma on the Gupta-owned television channel ANN7. The garish spectacle that followed is difficult to do justice to in words.

The show was called the *ANN7 South African of the Year Awards* and if you ever wanted to see state capture in motion, this was it. It was basically the kind of razzmatazz award function with dancers, presenters and little award trophies that are a dime a dozen these days, but this one was particularly awful. Many of the presumably Gupta-sponsored awards were presented by cabinet ministers known to be especially close to both Zuma and the Guptas. This was political toadyism the likes of which I had never seen before, and never witnessed since.

And there, lording over the event, seated on a couch, was the president himself, looking as captivated as captured. Then the apparent highlight (ethically, the low point) of the night came – the announcement of the winner of the South African of the Year award, jointly presented by Zuma and one of the Gupta bothers. It went to Nkosazana Dlamini-Zuma, who actually went on stage to receive a cheque from her former husband and a Gupta. I kid you not ...

It showed exactly what the score was on live television – a Gupta brother and the president physically handing over money to the woman who, in December 2017 at Nasrec, would come within a whisker of beating Ramaphosa and capturing the ANC presidency.

I choose to mention the examples of the Waterkloof scandal, Vytje Mentor's allegations and these TV awards because they have implications for the upcoming general elections. Ramaphosa was elected president on the ticket that he would rid the ANC of the corruption and state capture gnawing at its core. These three examples illustrate how tough his task will be, because they show the apparent complicity

NATIONALISATION AND TACKLING CORRUPTION

in state capture by ministers who are still senior members of the ANC's NEC, by the former ANC leader, Zuma, and by the person Ramaphosa pipped to the post in the race for the ANC presidency, Dlamini-Zuma. And these are just a few of the people who will have to be investigated if the extent of state capture is to be ascertained.

On a provincial level, two of Ramaphosa's colleagues in the top six were premiers in provinces that will also have to be probed. The Free State under Magashule was the place that sanctioned and subsidised a Gupta-owned dairy farm in the Vrede district of the province, when Gupta favourite Mosebenzi Zwane was Magashule's MEC of agriculture. That probe started in January 2018, within a few weeks of Ramaphosa's election as ANC president.

In early February 2018 a number of state officials and Gupta associates were arrested and charged on 12 counts, including theft, fraud and conspiracy to commit theft and fraud, in connection with the investigation into the dairy farm project.

Mpumalanga, which was under the premiership of Mabuza, may prove as interesting if a thorough probe is conducted – the province is just far enough from the bright spotlight of pesky journalists to warrant some looking into. Speaking of the ANC top six, Deputy Secretary General Jessie Duarte's son-in-law has also been alleged to have Gupta links, the extent of which a somewhat more energetic NPA post-Shaun Abrahams may find interesting to investigate.

So, the test for Ramaphosa leading up to 2019 is a basic and very tough one – just how far is he prepared to go in cleaning the proverbial Augean stables of the ANC? Will he be willing to have the lid lifted on the actions of the former ANC president, those of his main opponent for the ANC crown and three of his five colleagues within the ANC's top six?

Given that Ramaphosa, after he was elected, has called for unity in the ANC – and the whole theme of the conference was unity in the ANC – will he not be failing that call if he probes wrongdoing in the ANC too deeply? What will his decision be if he had to choose between unity and cleaning up the ANC, especially if those two priorities are at odds, even mutually exclusive? And if he chose unity by offering an escape mechanism for prominent ANC members possibly guilty of misconduct, what does that do to his brand of clean governance and his promises to clear out corruption? South Africans might wonder what the point was of his taking over the ANC if he just provides more of the same.

On the other hand, if he does allow a thorough probe, it could be debilitating for the ANC. As we have seen, ANC support in the 2016 local-government elections came to only about 53% and has dipped since then in by-elections. Even allowing for a large 2016 stay-away vote and resultant turnout differential in favour of opposition parties, and for the non-representative nature of by-elections, these are trends that should leave any thinking ANC supporter (and no one would seriously class Ramaphosa as unthinking) at least somewhat worried. To unleash a civil war inside the ANC by acting harshly on signs of wrongdoing could jeopardise the unity a party needs to perform well in an election, and could cause ANC support to fall below 50% for the first time.

Then again, if Ramaphosa doesn't act, he gives credence to Maimane's charge that his election as ANC leader means very little – that it is a case of a different driver for the same bus with the same passengers travelling towards the same destination. A lackadaisical approach to allegations of corruption could also scupper efforts at cooperating with the EFF given its commitment to its seventh policy pillar – which opposes corruption and favours clean governance. The third option is to replace

NATIONALISATION AND TACKLING CORRUPTION

the rotten eggs and promote people in the mould of the squeaky-clean Naledi Pandor to positions of real power (as happened in February).

There is a final way open to Ramaphosa's ANC, namely to throw the Gupta family completely under the bus, and possibly a few other shady high-profile characters with little or diminishing political clout, while keeping and protecting certain ANC members with future political clout. The success of such a strategy would depend on the extent to which South African voters will be prepared to accept the Guptas as the true villains in the story, and that powerful ANC figures of the present and recent past were mere fellow travellers led up the wrong path.

After sensing the prevailing wind of power shifting to Ramaphosa, Bathabile Dlamini lost no time to ask forgiveness for state capture – and to demand that such forgiveness be granted in the same way that perpetrators of apartheid had been granted forgiveness. If such an amnesty (surely only after full disclosure) were to be an option, it would be interesting to see how many South Africans would buy into it at election time – especially if the idea is that those who own up to state capture are either given some kind of indemnity from prosecution or even continue in their current positions. If the voters buy into it, it could improve the ANC's electoral fortunes. If not, it could all backfire badly.

Ramaphosa faces an even tougher choice – as morally simple as it is strategically complicated – regarding possible steps against potentially corrupt ANC councillors. Given the horrendous audit record of many ANC municipalities, this could be a gargantuan task. If it had to be done as strictly as it should be, the ANC could be incapacitated at the local-government level. If, however, it is not done, voters may wonder whether Ramaphosa is much of an improvement on Zuma.

The DA has built its reputation as an alternative government mostly on its record of clean governance and for taking strict action against corruption. Its firm stance against party members who are found to be guilty of maladministration, corruption or conflict of interest has differentiated it from the ANC, as has its near obsession with, and success in obtaining, unqualified audits from the Auditor-General in the areas where it governs.

An unqualified audit, it is important to note, does not mean the Office of the Auditor-General necessarily agrees with exactly how public money is spent. It means the Auditor-General knows where the money went, and that it was used for the intention it was budgeted for. Actually, it is not the highest of bars. That DA local governments attain unqualified audits speaks more to the incredible weakness of many ANC governments than to the strength of DA governments. I am reminded of Bill Clinton, who liked to say that the central question in elective politics is always 'compared to what?' Compared to ANC local governments, DA governments do indeed excel at obtaining clean audits, which, as a rule of thumb, means less wasteful and fruitless expenditure, and more money spent on providing municipal services.

Ensuring relatively clean government has taken up much time and effort from the DA, leaving less time and energy for other matters. DA members have told me what a mission it is to clean up the governance mess left by their ANC predecessors – to the extent that they do not always have the time to focus on new policy interventions. Their efforts are crowded out by the first activity. Also – and this is important in the run-up to the 2019 elections – many in the EFF believe the DA does not have much real policy outside of clean governance. As many an EFF member has told me, clean governance or being opposed to corruption is a principle, not a policy – it cannot be a substitute for the DA's lack of policy coherence on issues such as labour or land.

The DA knows that the good name it has for clean governance and opposition to corruption at the provincial and local levels is its strongest weapon to win voter support in the build-up to 2019. It will, no doubt, play that hand for all it is worth, and it would be correct to do so. It would also do well, though, to realise that this will not be enough to ensure partnerships with other parties, and that it needs to finalise policy issues. Once again, it will be wiser to discuss these policies informally with prospective partners before the pressures of the election season are upon them.

The EFF has taken a very strong stance on corruption and has been steadfast in holding the ANC to account on this score. Still, it has not quite built up the credibility the DA has on the issue, mainly because of the rather chequered past some of its leaders have regarding their own conduct. Its problem, not unrecognised by many of its leading lights, is that for all its criticism it has not shown that it can govern in a non-corrupt way. That is the major weakness of its policy of cooperation rather than coalition – no one knows what the EFF would be like as a government or as part of a government.

Laudable as it is that EFF members do not take up executive positions for financial gain, it also means the party has not taken responsibility for governance matters where it was in a position to do so. By not taking up this responsibility, it has played into the hands of those among its opponents who paint it as something of a political juvenile delinquent – entertaining and bright, but not willing to apply itself when it matters. I believe this to be an unfounded argument, but the EFF would do well to take up the responsibilities of leadership in the municipalities where it holds the balance of power.

The problem the EFF faces is that it has to live down the reputation of its leaders, and especially its commander-in-chief. When he was leader of the ANC Youth League, Malema did not pay his taxes as he had to, ending up in court and having property sequestrated. At the time, he also held much sway in his home province of Limpopo and became a lucrative tenderpreneur whose company On-Point's shoddy dealings and poor workmanship was exposed for all to see in Madonsela's report 'On the Point of Tenders'. Tenders awarded to On-Point Engineers by the Limpopo transport department were unlawful, and Malema benefited improperly from the deals, Madonsela found.

In *The President's Keepers*, Jacques Pauw aired an issue long in the public domain – the allegation that alleged illicit tobacco kingpin Adriano Mazzotti paid R200 000 to the EFF for their registration fees to participate in the 2014 elections. Mazzotti himself has made the claim. Mazzotti has made many claims, some more believable than others, but the EFF has never denied this one.

Which all begs the question often put by those South Africans who remain sceptical of Malema and the EFF: much as the EFF opposes corruption, would they walk the talk when Malema has the power in his hands? Put differently, can a leopard change its spots?

I had the opportunity to ask Malema this question some years ago. His answer was: 'We are not proud of some of the things we have done in our past, and we have learnt from it.'

A good answer, I thought, which many will believe – and many won't. All the more reason for the EFF to realise that they should put their money where their mouth is – they should consider showing South Africans that they can govern cleanly in the places where they have the opportunity to do so.

NATIONALISATION AND TACKLING CORRUPTION

The issue of corruption, and prosecuting the corrupt, has been a major policy stumbling block hindering possible cooperation between the EFF and the ANC since 2014. It started with the parliamentary hullabaloo about the Public Protector's report on the improvements to Zuma's homestead at Nkandla, 'Secure in Comfort'. The EFF was the most outspoken party when it came to pointing out that Parliament's whole exercise in 'reviewing' Madonsela's findings rather than implementing them was an illegal ruse. The EFF was the first party to refuse to take part in the pathetic charade and was the first to take the matter to the Constitutional Court, where Parliament was given a severe and well-deserved dressing down by Chief Justice Mogoeng Mogoeng. Prosecution of the corrupt was also one of the issues on which cooperation talks between the EFF and the ANC stalled after the 2016 local elections.

So, on the issue of combating corruption the EFF has found itself more on the side of the DA, the IFP and other opposition parties than on the ANC's side. It has proven to be the dividing line between the ANC and the ruling coalitions — held in place by the EFF through cooperative agreements — in various municipalities, including the metros of Johannesburg, Tshwane and Nelson Mandela Bay. In the run-up to 2019, it is a point on which the opposition is in agreement, across ideological divides.

Another opposition party that has taken a very strong and successful stance against corruption is the IFP, which grew the number of rural KwaZulu-Natal municipalities it governs from two to 14 with its simple slogan, 'Trust us'. The party claims that its record in governance, including its time at the helm of the erstwhile KwaZulu government, is much better than that of the ANC, and that it was never guilty of the same venality which, it claims, typifies ANC rule.

A tough stance on corruption can be reasonably expected to provide a rallying point to opposition parties in the 2019 general election, and it will be a very tough argument indeed for the ANC to counter in any meaningful way, given its record.

CHAPTER 11

Coalitions – lessons learnt from the past and the present

Coalitions are no one's idea of a happy political marriage. They are at best dysfunctional marriages of convenience or necessity, brought about when voters do not give a clear governing mandate to those politicians who believe that their views and principles mean they should be the only governing party. It is often a loveless marriage.

Still, coalitions are a reality of political life. In light of the great likelihood that the 2019 national election could bring about a coalition, what can be learnt from past efforts, especially from the Government of National Unity of 1994 to 1999, and more recent cooperative agreements? Is it possible to identify the factors that would make such political marriages succeed or fail?

So, firstly, what does history tell us about South African politics and coalitions? Paradoxically, while coalitions have not really been a way of life in South African politics, its national, provincial and major local governments (i.e. metros) have never seen a change of government control without a coalition – neither in the pre-democratic nor democratic phase. The one exception is the DA's win in the Western Cape provincial elections of 2009.

In 1910 the government was initially made up of a loose coalition between the Afrikanerbond (Cape), Orangia Unie (Free State), Volksbeweging (Natal) and Het Volk (Transvaal), which won the October 1910 election under the banner of the Governing Party, and which later became united as the South African Party in 1911. The South African Party ruled until 1924, when it was unseated by an unlikely alliance between the National Party and the Labour Party, which stayed in power until 1933, only to be replaced by a coalition between the South African Party and the National Party, which merged into the United Party and governed until 1948.

The United Party lost the 1948 election to a coalition between the Reunited National Party (it was 'reunited' from 1939 by the United Party's decision to become involved in World War II) and the Afrikaner Party, which merged in 1951 under the name of the National Party and which governed the country until the start of democracy in 1994.

The first democratic elections of 1994 were decided in terms of the interim constitution, which guaranteed a forced coalition – called the Government of National Unity (and provincial unity, on a provincial level) – until 1999 on a proportional level for any party that achieved more than 10% of the vote and wanted to serve in such a government. The National Party served in the Government of National Unity until 1996. The reasons why it walked out offer helpful tips on potential pitfalls to avoid in a coalition, discussed later in this chapter.

The IFP continued to exercise its rights to remain in the Government of National Unity until its expiry in 1999, after which it continued to serve in national government at the pleasure of President Mbeki. This was not out of some generosity of spirit on Mbeki's part, but as a result of horse-trading: The ANC made the IFP part of the national government in exchange for a share of provincial power in KwaZulu-Natal, where the IFP needed a coalition partner to govern.

That KwaZulu-Natal government was a very unhappy political marriage. In fact, so unhappy and filled with intrigue that it led to an interregnum where the DA joined the rocky KwaZulu-Natal alliance in 2004 under the banner of the Coalition for Change – dubbed the Collision for Change because it failed so spectacularly.

These failures in coalition can be weighed up against successful coalitions in the Western Cape. First was the successful cooperation between the National Party and the Democratic Party to shut the ANC out of provincial government between 1999 and 2001, leading to the formation of the DA in 2000 and, later, the seven-party coalition that shut the ANC out of the government of the City of Cape Town in 2006.

South Africa's first Government of National Unity was mandated by the country's interim democratic Constitution. It stipulated that there would be a Government of National Unity from 1994 to 1999, proportionally made up of all parties willing to serve in it, provided they received more than 10% of the vote in the national ballot. In the event, three parties qualified constitutionally for cabinet positions in the subsequent Mandela government – the ANC with 62.7%, the National Party (20.4%) and the IFP (10.5%).

The ANC and the IFP stayed the course in the Government of National Unity from 1994 to 1999, but the National Party left it in 1996, shortly after the final Constitution was adopted. It was a controversial decision.

Interestingly, in due course, Mandela also offered a cabinet position to the Democratic Party, headed at the time by Tony Leon. He surprised many by declining Mandela's offer in the interest of building a strong opposition, which he and his party believed was something the fledgling South African democracy needed dearly. Many were surprised and many more were delighted – it was a key moment in Leon's achievement of building the Democratic Party from the nowhere mark of 1.7% support nationally to 9.5%, attaining the coveted spot as national official opposition in the 1999 general election.

It also laid the foundation for the Democratic Party component to become the main contributor and the strongest power within the DA when it was founded in 2000 – and to remain so as it grew to its strength of 22%, which it polled in the 2014 general election. It also laid the foundation for the current DA view on governments of national unity in the case of an ANC majority, as put forward by Maimane and Selfe in their interviews for this book, namely that the DA would decline the offer in view of the need for a strong opposition in South Africa.

In retrospect it is fair to say that the Government of National Unity worked better from an ANC perspective than from a National Party perspective. In my research for this book, I returned to an interview I did in 2002 with the late Professor Jakes Gerwel, who served as cabinet secretary to the Government of National Unity from 1994 to 1999. In that interview, he shared valuable insights into the strengths and weaknesses of the Government of National Unity, which Ramaphosa might do well to take into consideration should he maintain his initial preference for such a coalition.

Gerwel, whom I was blessed to know very well in his later life, used his position as vice chancellor of the University of the Western Cape before 1994 to formulate strong views and take strong action against the apartheid regime and its ideology. He ensured that the university became a home of the Left during his tenure. In his later life, he became a very successful businessman and throughout he remained a committed ANC stalwart.

He was one of the most intellectual, knowledgeable, honest, well-mannered and humorous people you could ever meet. When he was chairman of the Naspers board of directors and I was political editor of several of its publications (successively, not at once), we would meet every few weeks – and in times of rapid political development, every few days.

In that 2002 interview, he told me that the role of the cabinet secretary to the Government of National Unity was quite challenging at times. 'A new party [the ANC] was in charge, a new Government of National Unity had to find its feet and there was great interest from everywhere and everyone about what the Government of National Unity would look like and how, and whether, it would function.

'In 1994, three parties made up the Government of National Unity. … They were not only opposed ideologically. Their supporters were fighting, violently.

'The party leaders of the National Party, FW de Klerk, and the IFP, Mangosuthu Buthelezi, chose their parties' cabinet members after consultation with Madiba. I was surprised to find very little political ganging up against each other in cabinet.

'If you did not know any better, you could believe the ministers were from a single party, not from three different ones. Kader Asmal [ANC Minister of Water Affairs and Forestry] and Dawie de Villiers [the National Party's tourism minister] would often take up a policy position against Pik Botha [the National Party's Minister of Minerals and

Energy] and Mac Maharaj [the ANC's transport minister]. One knew there would be differences between the political parties on issues such as abortion and the death penalty, but generally everybody was committed to consensus,' said Gerwel.

'Madiba never chaired cabinet – well, almost never. The deputy president, Thabo Mbeki, was in the chair and maintained order. Madiba's hearing was poor, it was not his style to be a formal chairperson and he was focused on moral rather than technical issues.

'So, in cabinet Mbeki did the technical work and Madiba took the moral lead in keeping the peace and uniting the people. It was a matter of give and take. All three parties had to be prepared to sacrifice and cooperate. I found it inspirational to see the ANC, the National Party and the IFP cooperate after all those years of division in South Africa.

'Nevertheless, it was a period of massive tension between political parties, especially in KwaZulu-Natal, where open conflict between the ANC and IFP was the order of the day. Surprisingly, Buthelezi was not a problematic member of cabinet. He was a friendly and cooperative colleague. In fact, we used to refer amongst ourselves to the Wednesday Buthelezi and the Saturday Buthelezi as if they were two different people because on Wednesday in cabinet meetings he was so affable whereas on Saturdays in public meetings he was so aggressive,' Gerwel recalled.

'That said, there were many obstacles in cabinet. Apartheid was not overcome by military conquest. It was a gradual and partial transfer of power.

'Madiba believed very firmly in informing opposition leaders on issues of national importance. He really went out of his way to do so, and it did much to establish and build trust between political parties.

COALITIONS — LESSONS LEARNT FROM THE PAST AND THE PRESENT

'Within cabinet, the consultative tradition of the ANC played a huge part in allowing discussions to flow. The ANC has always been a broad church and in cabinet there were a thousand views on every issue. Nobody ever complained that a discussion was too broad.

'Cabinet was also notable for the excellent manners characterising inputs, specifically the politeness shown by De Klerk and Buthelezi. As cabinet secretary, it was easy for me to maintain very good relations with both leaders. De Klerk was especially easy to discuss matters with,' said Gerwel.

'I will always remember Madiba's amazing memory. He recalled the details of meetings with people from all walks of life effortlessly. This made for great relations with the media, and with people in general, because it was second nature to him to engage and listen to people.

'Working as Madiba's cabinet secretary required me to change my ways. Great people have the ability to think simply and get straight to the heart of the matter. Madiba was very direct and to the point, whereas I had spent almost all of my professional life at universities. Theorising comes naturally to me. I distrust simple or simplified answers, but Madiba told me time and again, "Jakes, it must be simpler than that."

'Madiba simplified everything, even when reading nuances. In meetings, he would not speak much – he would listen. Often, his way would remind me of the way of a traditional leader. He would listen, decode and decide. Madiba could cut to the core, simplify and come to a conclusion. He could take a definite decision on a matter – within five minutes, if required,' said Gerwel.

However, Gerwel's views differ greatly from those of Dr Kraai van Niekerk, who served in the National Party contingent of the Government of National Unity as minister of agriculture. Van Niekerk, who holds a doctorate in agricultural science, became a National Party MP in 1981. He served on the parliamentary committees that scrapped the apartheid Immorality Act and Prohibition of Mixed Marriages Act.

In 1989, Van Niekerk became minister of agriculture in the FW de Klerk cabinet and held the position until 1996, the last two years as part of the cabinet of the Mandela Government of National Unity. After serving in the Northern Cape provincial legislature for a couple of years as the National Party's provincial leader, he became an MP for the Federal Alliance, which became part of the DA in 2000. Van Niekerk served in Parliament until 2009, the last few years as chairman of the DA parliamentary caucus.

Van Niekerk is a deeply intelligent and diligent person – a disposition so often lacking in politicians – and he can laugh at himself. During his time in the National Party, he was known as an independent thinker who did not allow himself to be put into a box or confined to an internal political camp. This attribute, together with the ability to observe closely and intelligently, and then pithily formulate those observations, are some of the reasons why he was such a wonderful source for this book. But, most importantly, he served in the Government of National Unity and was part of the National Party's decision to leave it, although he disagreed with the manner and timing.

Interviewed for this book, Van Niekerk's view differs from Gerwel's observation that the Government of National Unity cabinet was largely united: 'Oh no, most certainly there were divisions and groups in cabinet – and more interestingly, groups within groups!

COALITIONS — LESSONS LEARNT FROM THE PAST AND THE PRESENT

'One of the most interesting things I picked up on from the corner of my eye was the non-verbal communication between ANC members in cabinet, and especially SACP cabinet members. Tito Mboweni [minister of labour in the Mandela cabinet and later a respected governor of the South African Reserve Bank] was specifically interesting to watch.

'I came to realise that ANC and SACP members often arrived at cabinet with their respective or joint strategies for that meeting, which would not always be apparent at first. But then, when the discussion became intense, I'd focus on ANC and SACP colleagues, observing a nudge here, a wink there or a small hand signal and so forth. I came to realise that, more often than not, these colleagues arrived with a subtle but carefully prepared plan, in which each had an assigned role to move the discussion to the conclusion they desired.

'Very often, it was Buthelezi, who had years of governance experience in the KwaZulu cabinet, who kept everything together. This did not mean that he was co-opted or overly charmed by Mandela or the ANC at all. Already at the second meeting of the Government of National Unity cabinet in 1994, Buthelezi arrived with a memorandum tackling the issue of the 400 IFP leaders murdered in the KwaZulu-Natal civil war between Inkatha and the ANC. He wanted to know what Mandela was going to do to bring the perpetrators to book.

'Mandela never gave him an answer, but Buthelezi never gave up. He kept raising the point. It made me realise that the IFP was unlikely to merge with the ANC, and also that Buthelezi was a straight dealer – he meant what he said and he said what he meant.'

Van Niekerk said the most important consideration for a smaller party in a coalition or a Government of National Unity is to know its rights and the guarantees it has to disagree with and advocate against policy decisions it doesn't support. That is rule one – that is what one refers back to when in doubt.

'One must have some sort of guarantee – constitutional or by virtue of holding the balance of power, which could sink the Government of National Unity or coalition. If you don't have that power, you are at the mercy of the larger party – in the cut-throat world of politics, you are at their beck and call.'

Van Niekerk told me of the following showdown he witnessed between Mandela and De Klerk in a cabinet meeting of the Government of National Unity. This is not widely known, though it was described in Inus Aucamp and Louis van der Watt's book *Die einde van 'n groot party*, which deals with the demise of the once powerful National Party.

According to Van Niekerk, at times cabinet members of the National Party often differed strongly with members of the ANC, leading to uncomfortable stand-offs. The relationship between Mandela and De Klerk could at times be particularly strained. 'I recall a specific cabinet meeting where we discussed the future shape of the economy, and differed about it fundamentally. FW then exercised his right to publicly state the National Party's view – which was at odds with the ANC view and thus at odds with the majority view in cabinet.

'Mandela was furious and called a special cabinet meeting. In a break with convention, he chaired the meeting, not Mbeki. Mandela was purple with rage. Three times he told De Klerk to leave the cabinet. Mandela was, as we say in Afrikaans, *de moer in* – beside himself with anger. He lectured De Klerk on the concept of joint responsibility for cabinet and on accepting the majority decision. In the end, he shouted: "I don't want you in my cabinet!"

'De Klerk took his briefcase and got up to leave the room. After he had taken a few steps, he turned on his heels and faced Mandela. De Klerk then told him: "Mr President, I am not here because you put me here. I am here because it is my right to be here, guaranteed by the [interim] Constitution and by the votes my party received from the voters of South Africa. It is the voters who put me here, not you. It is not up to you to decide when I should leave cabinet. I do not serve at your pleasure." And he stayed,' Van Niekerk said.

'This is also why we in the National Party decided to leave the Mandela Government of National Unity cabinet once the final Constitution was adopted. It did not include the Government of National Unity guarantee. That provision had lapsed, which meant we served at the pleasure and mercy of the president.

'The issue we differed about within the National Party was the timing. Many of us felt we should wait for a serious policy difference to arrive, stand our ground against the ANC and walk out or be kicked out, so that we could keep the initiative. But FW had had enough. He took the decision on behalf of the party, as was his right as leader,' said Van Niekerk.

The National Party officially left the Government of National Unity on 30 June 1996. It cited three main reasons for doing so: the exclusion of joint decision-making from the final Constitution; the National Party's lack of influence on government policy; and the fact that the National Party had adopted a new role as a fully fledged opposition party.

Ever the diligent academic, in his preparation for our interview Van Niekerk drew up a list of 12 points that he believes will make or break a Government of National Unity, whether after 1994 or after the 2019 election:

❏ It is imperative to realise whether a party is in government by legal right (such as the constitutional provisions up to 1996, or if it holds the balance of power) or by invitation. The former guarantees a position of strength in relation to the governing party, the latter guarantees a position of weakness.

❑ Smaller parties must ensure that there is a written consensus on how and on which issues they are allowed to differ publicly from cabinet decisions.

❑ Smaller parties must realise that the true battle of ideas take place in cabinet committees. By the time cabinet committee decisions reach cabinet sittings, it is very hard to change them, especially if your party did not take part in the committee discussions. It is therefore important for smaller parties in a Government of National Unity to keep abreast of the exact happenings in cabinet committees, which, because of the large number of committee meetings and the small number of opposition cabinet members, they cannot always attend.

❑ Long, hard and thorough preparation is needed before every cabinet meeting, especially when legislation is discussed. Every word must be studied and the fine print must be understood, so that you are not caught napping by your political opponents.

❑ Be aware that your political opponents in cabinet may slip in new ideas, wording or strategies at any time. Be very vigilant to safeguard the interests of the voters whose mandate you carry.

❑ Be very aware of the internal camps, and the camps within those camps, dividing your cabinet colleagues from other political parties. Be aware of any sign of division, but also any sign of unexpected alliances on any specific issue. In the case of the ANC in the Mandela Government of National Unity, it served Van Niekerk well to observe, note and act on the way the democrats, the socialists and the communists in the ANC worked against or with each other on different issues.

❑ It is imperative for any political party newly joining a coalition or Government of National Unity cabinet to study exactly how the cabinet system, and especially the cabinet committee system, works. If you do not master the system, you can be hoodwinked. How are decisions taken? How are differences accommodated? Who are the key players? What are the scenarios? How is power obtained? How is influence assured? For the leadership of smaller cabinet parties, it is important to be vigilant about how their members conduct themselves in cabinet committees. Because of their relative seclusion, long work hours and often more informal nature, these committees are where members of the larger coalition or cabinet partner parties will try to lobby the ministers from the smaller partner parties to their cause, or even entice them to join the larger party. 'The ANC tried it with me,' said Van Niekerk, 'but they learnt soon enough that I will never be an ANC supporter.'

❑ It is important to be aware of the internal rules, regulations and decision processes of other parties with whom you find yourself in coalition or in cabinet. You need to know your opponent. You need to know when a view they give you is also a mandate or an internal decision. 'We learnt this the hard way regarding the ANC. We would reach a specific decision or formulation in a cabinet committee or even in cabinet, and then the ANC would add the proviso that their NEC had to pass it first. The next thing you know, the NEC has selectively changed crucial parts of the decision or legislation, effectively allowing the ANC a second bite at the cherry. Be aware and be vigilant, always,' he said.

❏ Where it seems that two parties in cabinet are very close to agreement on an issue, it is particularly important to look at the formulation of the final decision or policy. Colleagues from different parties will often try to change the whole gist and meaning of a decision with seemingly innocuous word choice changes. An excellent example during the negotiations for the 1996 Constitution was the wording of the property clause in Section 25, where the Democratic Party's Tony Leon did excellent work.

❏ Be especially vigilant regarding the interests of the country and the voters you represent when your cabinet colleagues from other political parties seem more friendly, laid back, jolly or accommodating than usual. This could be exactly the moment when they try to hoodwink you, and then the pawpaw could hit the fan big time.

❏ Be very careful when the wording of the cabinet statement or any press statement is being finalised, because it shapes the public's perception of the decision and, in politics, unfortunately, perception is almost as important as truth. 'In the Mandela Government of National Unity cabinet, it sometimes took us an hour to reach a decision and three hours to formulate it.'

❏ As a final rule of thumb, when you decide that you agree with a proposal by a member of another political party, think again and then consider it carefully for a third time before you put your name to it.

Moving from the past to the present – while South Africa does not have a Government of National Unity at the moment, since 2016 it has had more coalition governments than ever before. Of the three metros with coalition governments, the consensus seems to be that the one in Tshwane, which serves Pretoria and surrounds, is functioning best. That would be no surprise to anyone who knows its mayor, Solly Msimanga.

Msimanga, who served as the DA's Gauteng chairman before, is one of the most likeable, down-to-earth, informed and hard-working politicians in the country. He is also the only one of the three metro mayors presiding over coalition governments (the other two being Herman Mashaba of Johannesburg and Athol Trollip of Nelson Mandela Bay) who has not had a motion of no confidence proposed against him. Msimanga has been lauded by politicians from other parties for the consultative nature of his rule.

He therefore seemed a natural choice to ask about what it takes to make a coalition government work in South Africa. According to Msimanga, one of the most important aspects is to maintain an 'open-door policy for all parties, including the EFF, with whom we are not in coalition but whose cooperation and support we need in order to govern.

'It is important that when politicians interact, we realise that it is fine to differ and to argue but, in the end, the lives of the people in the communities we serve need to be improved. I think that even some ANC politicians have come to understand that – ANC councillors in Tshwane, but perhaps more especially ANC leaders on a provincial level.

'I always invite everyone to all meetings, including the metro's portfolio committees, such as the crucial finance committee. Multi-party inputs are crucial – that is how we grow. It is imperative to always be honest and forthright about what is doable and what is not. In this way, politicians who are interested in finding solutions rather than creating problems will find each other.

'I think that in Tshwane, we found each other.'

Msimanga said the cooperation process with the EFF was helped by the fact that he had met and worked with some EFF councillors before his election, and knew how capable and committed they were.

'It assisted all of us in being frank and establishing a cordial and personal relationship. Cordiality, in fact, is key. I can pick up the phone and call any coalition or EFF councillor, and they can do the same with me. This has developed into a situation where the EFF raises the issues they have with me personally, and we solve it together. The same goes for all parties – COPE, the ACDP, Azapo, everyone. They'll call on all sorts of issues, whenever they felt it was necessary. It remains important to keep communicating with as many councillors as possible, as often as possible.'

Msimanga said that, as a mayor, it was important for him to remember and inculcate in others that solving Tshwane's challenges required not just a political effort. Only a community effort with all hands on deck would do.

'Once you are in power you absolutely have to develop a true understanding of what is expected and required of government. When in government, you must look at all possibilities where problems exist and in which problems may develop. Then you must tackle them honestly and cordially. It is no use throwing your hands in the air.

'What has also worked very well thus far is the creation of a safety net of non-political professionals to help tackle Tshwane's many challenges. Professionals from institutions like the University of Pretoria, the University of South Africa and civil society. It really has been quite inspiring,' said Msimanga.

So, what can we learn from these bits of history? Surely that a Government of National Unity or a coalition functions much like any relationship, or marriage: it must be based on trust, honesty, openness and wanting to make it work, and the willingness to give is paramount. Gerwel's main points were that in the Mandela cabinet, everyone wanted to put the country first, put partisanship aside and that Mandela was quite willing to be the bigger person in the interests of providing moral leadership rather than scoring political points.

In his rather more critical assessment, Van Niekerk raised some very important points of his own regarding the position of smaller coalition or cooperative partners. He emphasised that trust in politics is finite and rather limited – even more so between political opponents. His inputs and warnings in the run-up to 2019 are all specifically relevant and astute, and chief among them is that one needs a formal guarantee (either articulated in the Constitution or through the balance of power) against being bullied or used by the bigger partner, and that vigilance is the price of liberty.

But, in the end, the will to make the arrangement work is a paramount concern, and Msimanga has shown in Tshwane that nothing beats goodwill and the willingness to bring all well-meaning people on board.

CHAPTER 12

Who will rule in 2019?

Making projections and predictions about election results in a country where the news cycle is as fast and fluid, and the political issues as wild and divergent as they are in South Africa is a risky and precarious business.

In the end, the ball is in the hands of the more than 26 million voters, in all their diversity, who will decide on the morning of election day whether they will vote at one of the 22 612 voting stations nationwide and, if so, who they will vote for. The way they vote will embody their deepest hopes and fears, which are often buried so deep that the voter remains unaware of them. Each voter will make his or her own decision, in secret.

Although making projections and predictions about the 2019 national election may seem foolhardy, it needn't be if we draw up a provisional checklist noting some of the information contained in this book, a few personal insights and access to the back rooms of South African politics.

I will be able to make more exact predictions only after the 2019 registration figures are in, and once they have been calibrated and I have imposed them on previous results and population trends, and after I have taken the probabilities of differential turnout into account, as explained in Chapter 1. But, until then, let's consider the information we have, and work out trends and probabilities on that.

Our first question should be whether the 2019 election will be free and fair. Since 1994 the IEC has managed, without fail and against massive odds, to ensure free-and-fair national and provincial elections. There is much reason to have full confidence in the IEC's chief electoral officer, Sy Mamabolo, and his team – they have proven themselves over the years, despite persistent allegations that the ANC has been trying to capture the IEC.

However, while this is a spectacular record, the IEC will be under threat as never before if the 2019 election results prove to be a close race.

The electoral system has also shown itself to be strong but the IEC faces the daunting challenge of fully updating the voters' roll with their addresses, as instructed by the Constitutional Court. There are other worrying factors. In the 2016 local-government election, an abnormally high number of applications to cast early special votes (special voting is mainly meant for legitimate absentee ballots, voting by the aged and infirm, and voting by essential services, like the police, who must work on election day) were recorded in Mpumalanga. That is one of the few ways to potentially commit voting fraud in South Africa. In 2019 the fate of our democratic process will again be in the IEC's hands, and they may have to be even more vigilant than ever.

The ugly issue of election violence returned to haunt us during the 2016 local elections after being in welcome hibernation for several election cycles. When election violence occurs, voter turnout is lower.

WHO WILL RULE IN 2019?

The political parties perceived to cause election violence tend to lose support in South Africa. In 2016 the perpetration of serious election-related violence – and even killings – was almost exclusively limited to the ANC. Let us all hope it does not recur in 2019.

The most important party-political aspect that will influence voter behaviour and election results in 2019 will be whether the ANC can self-correct under Ramaphosa. There can be no doubt that his election as ANC leader had everything to do with the belief that he stands a better chance than his opponent, Dlamini-Zuma, of maximising the ANC's vote in 2019.

Having attained only 53% of the national vote in the 2016 local elections and having lost a median of seven percentage points in support in by-elections between then and Ramaphosa's election as ANC leader, the ANC knows it is staring down the barrel of electoral defeat in 2019. The key question is, can Ramaphosa turn the tide?

The information provided for this book by and on behalf of Ramaphosa's supporters in the ANC, as well as the information contained in his 'new deal' speech delivered in Soweto in November 2017 gave a greater understanding of what his goals, and therefore his wish list, were when he was elected party leader. This information can be used as a checklist to measure his success at attaining his goals. In the upcoming months, it should help us to measure how strong his control of the ANC is, and whether he has the ability to turn words into actions – i.e. policy into practice.

A crude and simplified Ramaphosa wish list could look as follows. Mark it off at your leisure. You'll see that much of it has already been achieved. Also keep in mind that some preferences, priorities and possibilities have changed since his election as ANC leader in December 2017:

- ❏ Get rid of Zuma as president.
- ❏ Appoint a preferred candidate as caretaker president, with the initial choice being Baleka Mbete. (This did not pan out as planned.)
- ❏ Appoint Pravin Gordhan as Minister of Public Enterprises in place of Lynne Brown.
- ❏ Stop the trillion-rand Russian nuclear deal.
- ❏ Offer a Government of National Unity in the run-up to the 2019 election, especially if ANC support dips below 50%.
- ❏ Replace Zuma acolytes as chairpersons of cabinet committees, thereby breaking their hold over cabinet, and bring in respected politicians from the Ramaphosa camp.
- ❏ Ensure that committees in the NEC are headed up by capable members, such as Gordhan and Tito Mboweni.
- ❏ Keep ANC internal kingmaker extraordinaire David Mabuza on side and in check.
- ❏ Minimise ANC infighting.
- ❏ Shift the national discourse back to reconciliation rather than polarisation.
- ❏ Take a tough line against corruption.
- ❏ Take tough action on corruption.
- ❏ Isolate corrupt high-profile ANC leaders.
- ❏ Institute a programme by which ANC branches can act against local corruption.
- ❏ Institute a public inquiry into corruption in provincial governments.

❏ Allay fears about expropriation without compensation by delaying its possible implementation.
❏ Take effective steps to accelerate economic growth.
❏ Start the process to reverse the sovereign downgrade to junk status.
❏ Oversee a strengthening rand.
❏ Propose a drastically smaller national cabinet, especially after 2019.

A further indication of the shape of South African politics after 2019 will be the reaction of large opposition parties to any ANC proposal of a post-2019 Government of National Unity. From my interviews with the DA and the EFF, it seems as though the initial chances of the two largest opposition parties agreeing to such a proposal must be regarded as very slim indeed.

This impression was strengthened by Maimane and Malema's reactions to events at the 2017 ANC elective conference. Maimane said only the driver had changed, the bus remained the same and South Africans had to build a post-ANC future.

Malema said that nothing had really changed – the core of what he called the corrupt premier league (i.e. Mahumapelo of North West, Mabuza of Mpumalanga and Magashule of the Free State) were now the centre of the ANC top six.

Malema warned South Africans not to become too excited, although he welcomed the humiliation of the Zupta faction.

Despite the negative response of the two largest opposition parties, I believe the planned proposal of a Government of National Unity by the ANC would be a master stroke by Ramaphosa and a game changer for reasons already covered in this book.

To my mind, that is precisely why Maimane and Malema's initial reactions were so strongly negative – they realise that, if many of the other aspects covered in this final chapter fall into place for Ramaphosa and the party regains the moral high ground, the DA and the EFF may well be the big losers. Also, many officials in the DA, and many in the EFF, would be tempted by the offer, and the bite at the power cherry that it implies. So, if the offer materialises of a Government of National Unity, expect the ANC to do much better in the 2019 election than it would have otherwise.

And if Ramaphosa maintains or regains the marvellous momentum and hope of his first few days as the country's president, expect a huge ANC win in 2019.

To project the 2019 election result, it would also be important to know how the ANC's stance on the country's big policy issues will play out. The ruling party's 2017 conference did not make many policy pronouncements. But, it is fair to assume that should the ANC move more to the left, it would eat into the EFF's policy space and gain more votes from those who might have considered supporting the EFF. In such a case, the EFF's support would decline. If, on the other hand, the ANC moves to the right, the DA would lose potential supporters.

For instance, if the ANC moves more firmly in favour of expropriation without compensation, it would take away votes from the EFF. If the ANC moves more firmly in favour of property rights, the EFF would gain votes and the DA would lose votes.

From a strategic point of view, the ANC needs to decide where more votes are to be had, although of course it also has to consider the impact of its policy actions on the economy and the population.

In practical politics, it is also always the prerogative of the larger party to appropriate some of the better and more popular ideas of its smaller opponents and use them in its own policies. This is known as stealing the opponent's clothes, and it could benefit the ruling party at election time.

If the ANC remains as lackadaisical as it has been on fighting corruption, both the DA and the EFF will gain votes in 2019. If the ANC can change the perception that it is soft on, or even synonymous with, corruption it will gain votes in 2019 and all opposition parties will lose out. In this regard, it will be interesting to see how successfully those who stand accused of complicity in corrupt practices – specifically the Gupta family and Zuma – are dealt with.

Will they be treated as the cause of state capture, or merely as its beneficiaries and manifestations? A populist and easy but ineffective way for the ANC to be seen to be dealing with corruption would be to hound the Guptas out of the country or into prison. That will be popular, but South Africans would have to ask themselves whether this action will suffice. Merely blaming the Guptas would be a red herring – officials and politicians lower down the corruption food chain should also be targeted.

If so, what will the effect be on the image, membership and support levels of the ANC? In 2019, the ANC will benefit if it is seen to act against corrupt individuals, but such actions could boomerang if it exposes the rot within the ANC to be worse than the voter had anticipated. In such a case, the ANC would be weakened in 2019.

It will also be important who emerges in the mind of the voter as the true leader of the ANC, or, to phrase it differently, the leader of the true ANC. If the voter's image of the ANC is Ramaphosa, the ANC will benefit in 2019. If the opposition convinces the voter that Mabuza and Magashule represent the true power in the ANC, and Ramaphosa is just a smiling front man, the ANC will not do as well.

The ANC's fear of losing power in 2019 will be a contributing factor to the election result. If this fear galvanises it to campaign with greater gusto, it will gain in 2019. If it is lackadaisical or in denial about losing, it will experience greater loss of support. If it turns to violence, its results will plummet.

Internal dynamics in and between the DA and the EFF will also affect the 2019 election result. The EFF will, at some stage, have to deal with an internal rebellion of sorts. How it handles such a major difference of opinion, and whether it can maintain its unity, discipline and purpose will be a big test.

The four biggest tests for the DA will be whether it can deal with the many nasty differences of opinion in its own ranks better than it did with the fallout between De Lille and Alderman JP Smith in the Cape Town city council in 2017 and 2018, whether it can finalise coherent and exciting policies, whether it can maintain municipal coalitions and cooperative agreements and whether it can stop voter leakage, especially to an invigorated, Ramaphosa-led ANC government.

The DA's performance in 2019 will be influenced by its ability to manage internal schisms. Over the last few years, the party's image and brand have suffered as infighting increased. These internal battles, of which outrage over Zille's colonialism tweet and the De Lille Cape Town palace revolution have drawn the most attention, have certainly harmed the DA. If it does not find a way to handle such internal tiffs in a less vicious and malicious way, it will turn off current and potential voters and will underperform in 2019.

In Gauteng, its performance will be greatly influenced by how it governs the populous metros of Johannesburg and Tshwane. If mayors Herman Mashaba (Johannesburg) and Solly Msimanga (Tshwane) continue to impress, the ANC can be unseated in Gauteng. If the coalition and cooperative agreements between opposition parties in Johannesburg and Pretoria collapse, however, the ANC will score in 2019. The Ramaphosa factor can also help the ANC spectacularly in regaining lost ground in Gauteng.

An important contributor to the 2019 election results will be the relationship between the DA and the EFF. Their relationship on a municipal level has held up remarkably well against many an internal upheaval and ANC onslaught. If the DA and EFF continue to attack the ANC in the pincer movement that has worked so well for both opposition parties since 2014, the opposition vote could benefit and the ANC vote will suffer.

However, if the cooperative agreements between the DA and EFF were to collapse, it would of course benefit ANC support levels in 2019. At the same time, the DA and EFF would have to fiercely guard their respective independent natures. The ANC would also gain votes from both parties if it could convince the voter that a vote for the EFF is actually a vote for the DA, or a vote for the DA is actually a vote for the EFF. In that way, it would capitalise on the fact that there are many hard-core members of the DA who are opposed to working with the EFF and actually despise them so much that they don't want anything to do with the EFF. The same goes for the distaste many hard-core EFF members feel for the DA. This mutual disdain is something the ANC can capitalise on in 2019.

It would also be interesting to watch whether the EFF believes a bump in its support levels can be achieved by breaking off its cooperative agreements with the DA shortly before 2019. Such a step would be a huge gamble for the politicians in red, and would probably be triggered only if an ANC campaign to paint them as being in cahoots with the DA were started and was looking successful.

In this regard, the DA has missed many an opportunity to have the policy discussions with the EFF that the EFF craves. The DA may come to rue these missed opportunities.

The EFF will be walking a tightrope between revolutionary fervour and a more responsible approach in the build-up to 2019. It faces tough choices. On the one hand, its plucky and disruptive style and radical policies have ensured that it has a loyal following of core voters. On the other hand, its brashness constrains its growth in new voter markets. A good example is the way its stance on the admission of students to universities at the beginning of 2018 raised its profile but isolated it. The most radical disruptors face off continually with those in the EFF who want to be appreciated as a positive and constructive influence rather than the juvenile delinquent at the back of the class who may be entertaining but is also disrupting. How the EFF deals with this tension will influence its performance in 2019.

One view that is held of the EFF, which its opponents feed continually, and which will catch on increasingly before 2019, is the notion that it is actually an ANC project and that its members will return to the ANC in due course. Important sources, especially in the ANC, and specifically in the Gauteng and Eastern Cape ANC, keep feeding that narrative. In the more neo-conservative parts of the DA liberal wing, the EFF is typecast as a mere revenge project by Malema against his expulsion from the ANC, and that it is inevitable that the EFF will return to the ANC fold eventually.

This is an important matter, but it is hard to get to the bottom of it. The claims are hotly denied by EFF sources – to which the obvious retort is that naturally they would deny it. It boils down to who and what you believe. I believe that for some in the EFF it may be an ANC project, but for the majority it is not. Some may aim to use the EFF as a vehicle to take over the ANC but, for others, joining the ANC would be akin to 'worshipping alien gods', as the EFF's national spokesperson, Mbuyiseni Ndlozi, was once quoted as saying in the newspaper *Rapport*.

Much will depend on Malema's preference, as he is the leader and face of the EFF. Malema has always shown himself to be closer to the ANC than many other EFF members. Maybe the EFF did start off as an ANC project and then acquired a life and momentum of its own. Time will tell who was speaking the truth on this matter, but if the EFF continues as a separate entity, it will be hurt in 2019 if the claims of it being an ANC project stick.

The 2019 general election will be the first since democratisation that the ANC will fight without a single KwaZulu-Natal representative in its top six. After the 2017 elective conference, this caused immediate resentment in the province. If this resentment persists and damages ANC support levels among Zulu-speakers, the opposition, and especially the IFP, could benefit from it. If the IFP could couple this with maintaining its upward trajectory in by-elections since 2016, the 2019 elections could see the first improvement in IFP national and provincial electoral fortunes since 1994.

The UDM has proved a popular fall-back option for voters who regard the ANC as too corrupt, the DA as too white-oriented, the EFF as too hooligan, the IFP as too traditional, the ACDP as too fundamentalist and the Freedom Front Plus as too Afrikaner to vote for. Infighting and aggression by other political parties could benefit the UDM in 2019.

Local conditions will also play a role in 2019. Voters in relatively well-governed municipalities will be more likely to vote for whichever party runs their municipality well. Poorly governed municipalities, on the other hand, will mean lost votes to the parties that rule them so badly, especially among urbanised voters.

Local weather conditions on voting day could also be important, especially to parties like the IFP and the UDM, who get the lion's share of their votes in specific provinces. For instance, if it rains or it's bitterly cold in those parts of rural northern KwaZulu-Natal, where IFP support is concentrated, the lower turnout would mean a lower IFP vote. The same holds true for the UDM in the former Transkei. Bad weather affects turnout among poorer voters more than among wealthier voters. So, if the weather is poor, parties supported by wealthier voters tend to benefit.

The general mood in the country will be important. If the negative and generally depressed mood about the state of the country and the economy characterising the later years of the Zuma presidency persists, all opposition parties will benefit in 2019. However, if Ramaphosa, succeeds in turning the national mood around and voters believe the country is changing for the better, the ANC will definitely gain.

So, who will rule in 2019?

Always allowing for changes in the ever swirling world of South African politics, I believe that it won't be a single party who will govern after the 2019 national elections. To my mind, the best early bet is that a coalition will rule in 2019.

That would be a specifically safe and easy bet if the Ramaphosa grouping sticks to their great idea of offering a government of national unity. If the ANC scores between 47% and 50%, it should be able to cobble together a coalition of very small parties.

If the ANC scores below 50% and is prepared to give massive ground on important issues to either the left or the right, a coalition between the ANC and the EFF (if it concedes to the left) or between the ANC and the DA (if it concedes to the right) is unlikely but not impossible.

If the ANC dips below 47%, the most likely outcome is a post-ideological grand opposition coalition or cooperative agreement focused on service delivery and rooting out corruption, as we are already seeing in many metros and municipalities. Of course, the ANC could romp home if the initial Ramaphosa magic could be maintained or regained, and just decide to rule on its own.

In the end, it will be up to each and every South African voter to pitch up on election day and make his or her choice. As R Lee Sharpe wrote memorably in his poem 'Princes and Kings':

> Isn't it strange how princes and kings,
> and clowns that caper in sawdust rings,
> and common people, like you and me,
> are builders for eternity?
>
> Each is given a list of rules;
> a shapeless mass; a bag of tools.
> And each must fashion, ere life is flown,
> A stumbling block, or a stepping stone.

How to put a coalition together: A user's guide

Now, should you be one of the parties hoping for a win in 2019, what are the most important principles or tips to keep in mind if you want to put together a coalition?

When should you start negotiating coalitions? As we have seen from the inputs for this book by the chief coalition negotiators for the main opposition parties, the general convention is not to start negotiations before the results are known – or at least before they can be projected – so that potential partners know localised positions and relative strength. This may be the convention and the preference of the DA, IFP, UDM, Freedom Front Plus and ACDP, but it is clear that such a convention may well be challenged in 2019 by the preferences of South Africa's largest and third largest parties, the ANC and the EFF.

Early indications from the ANC were that Ramaphosa would prefer to run on a ticket of offering places in a post-2019 Government of National Unity, whether his party gains more than 50% of the votes or not, and that he would prefer to make it a rallying cry in the run-up to the election. That would mean that the ANC will put its cards on the table from very early on, thereby gaining both the moral upper ground and maximum turnout from its core voter base.

Sources in the EFF have given me every indication for a very long time that they want to discuss policy issues with fellow opposition parties long before the election season, but that they have no one to speak to because other South African political parties seem not to be as specific on policy issues as the EFF is.

The EFF's leaders have been highly frustrated for a long time by what they regard as a shallowness on the part of other political parties. Come 2019, other parties (especially the DA) may well come to rue their reluctance to address the EFF's need for early discussions as an opportunity lost to build both trust and policy certainty.

For those of us in the public who are on the outside looking in on the unfolding political drama, the place to watch carefully may well be the floor of the national election results centre in Pretoria from the night after the polls close. The next step would be to zoom in on the key players among each party, and to judge which journalists have, over time, built good contacts, so that one knows which pieces of information can be trusted and which are red herrings. But, most importantly, it will be a question of knowing what is going on behind the closed doors where the political future of the country will be discussed.

Who should make the first move in the coalition mating dance? The bigger parties should court the smaller kingmaker parties, and the smaller parties should signal their willingness.

How much should potential coalition partners be telling the public? As little as possible. Speaking too soon will limit room to manoeuvre and may very well paint a party into a corner, especially considering that power balances and possibilities may change as other parties shift allegiances, often quite independently, for their own reasons and without consultation. Anyway, the public is bound to know the score by the end of the 14-day period that South African electoral law allows for the formation of governments after the election results have been formally certified by the IEC.

How much should potential coalition partners be telling the media? During negotiations, both the interest of the public and the public interest (i.e. the importance of the matter) are at very high levels. Discussions and decisions are taken by a small group, often in relative seclusion, which also excludes politicians with a material interest in the outcomes. All of which means that a perfect storm for rumour mongering and self-serving lies can easily be created.

Information will flow, people will tweet, news stories will be published and the political events that the public are hungry to hear more about will be covered on the basis of whatever information is available. In the end, the media machine must be fed. Consequently, perceptions will develop and other parties – potential allies – will be guided by the available information.

At the same time, any political party going on record publicly too early in a fluid situation may find that it paints itself into a corner or has to repudiate itself before an uncomprehending public if the situation changes, triggering accusations of flip-flopping. If, on the other hand, no one puts their view across correctly at any given time, such a political party may find itself the victim of misinformation, or may be silenced out of the national discourse, missing out on opportunity.

So, if you are a politician, you would be advised to have a trusted media source (as in, trusted by yourself, the public and other influential politicians) to whom you can give information off the record on the understanding that the situation may change. In short, give information to selected journalists you trust to write the story correctly; give the information off the record, to be reported as possibility rather than fact because of the fluidity of the situation.

Who does the negotiating? It is important that a trusted person (or preferably a small group of two or three people) who can negotiate on behalf of a political party is identified before the election, and given a basic mandate, so that person or group can make initial contact with their counterparts in potential partner parties at the election results centre.

The party should have done basic scenario planning regarding potential partners and policy options before the election, subject to changes that may occur. Negotiators must have a mandate on which issues are negotiable and which are non-negotiable. There must be very specific safeguards – negotiators must report back and the results of negotiations agreed to formally by the party structures before they become binding.

As far as possible, politicians who stand to gain from the negotiations should not be part of the negotiations.

How important is a written agreement? It is important: everyone should know exactly what is agreed and how everything works. The agreement must be written in simple, clear language everyone can understand. It must be an attempt to deal with all foreseen eventualities. It must be made public so that voters can know what they are in for, and can judge for themselves who keeps to the agreement and who breaks it. Remember that a written political agreement is not legally binding – a coalition or a Government of National Unity can only ever be a marriage of convenience. Don't expect much love.

How should conflict be resolved? As in any relationship, conflict is to be expected in a deal forged between competing political parties. The test of a successful political agreement is not whether problems occur, but how they are handled.

Problem-resolution mechanisms should be an integral and crucial part of negotiations over a coalition or a Government of National Unity right from the start. They should be agreed to carefully and clearly, and be put in writing. It is important that problem resolution should not be restricted to only one sphere of governance. Disputes must be settled at as local a level as possible, but should that fail, it should be possible to escalate problems to a higher level to be settled by senior members of the parties involved. What must be avoided is a zero-sum game, where a whole political agreement or coalition crashes because a single problem cannot be solved by specific individuals.

What is the key building block of the relationship? Honesty, because it helps to build the trust on which the relationship depends. If one party tries to hoodwink anyone else in the negotiation process, it will come back to bite them. In the words of Freedom Front Plus leader Pieter Groenewald, 'Nothing in politics ever stays secret. And anyone who does back-room deals against their partners will reap what they sow. The DA still struggles to rebuild the trust it lost when it dropped its coalition partners in Cape Town to rather work with the Independent Democrats.'

How do you nurture the relationship? It is very important for parties in a partnership to have continuous contact when the going is good. This builds personal ties and trust for the times when the going is tough. Contact could also help minimise misunderstanding and festering resentment. I rather liked Holomisa's proposal of holding informal meetings between political partners, for instance at a Friday afternoon braai, where potential problems can be tackled in convivial circumstances rather than every issue becoming a strained, formal process.

When the going is tough, it is sometimes advisable not to have contact, but to give space for parties to cool off. In times of severe tension, a trusted go-between can be brought in to broker calm. Cool heads do not create a crisis over every disagreement. Be adult.

When does a coalition agreement end? Every partner is in the agreement out of their own free will and can withdraw from it at any point. In the world of political coalitions and governments of national unity, written agreements are not binding.

Notes

CHAPTER 2

1 William L Shirer, *The Rise and Fall of the Third Reich: A History of Nazi Germany*, Simon & Schuster, first published 1960.
2 JJ Joubert, Registration data give a read on August poll, *Sunday Times*, 15 May 2016, https://www.pressreader.com/south-africa/sunday-times/20160515/281633894459847.
3 Ibid.
4 Ibid.
5 Ibid.
6 JJ Joubert, ANC isolated as coalition race hots up, *Rand Daily Mail*, 7 July 2016, https://www.businesslive.co.za/rdm/politics/2016-07-06-anc-isolated-as-coalition-race-hots-up/.
7 Ibid.

CHAPTER 3

1 Not to be confused with differential turnout, the turnout differential is a measure of the differential turnout.
2 A minor political party, Icosa is the Independent Civic Organisation of South Africa.
3 This was a reference to the kanga (a traditional African garment) that Khwezi was wearing before she was allegedly raped.
4 These interviews were published in my article, Two negotiators, ten days, six meetings, four deals – Inside the talks that changed South Africa, *Rand Daily Mail*, 23 August 2016.

CHAPTER 4

1 Justice Malala, *We Have Now Begun Our Descent: How to Stop South Africa Losing its Way*, Johannesburg and Cape Town, Jonathan Ball, 2015.

CHAPTER 5

1 Tony Leon, *On the Contrary: Leading the Opposition in the New South Africa*, Johannesburg and Cape Town, Jonathan Ball, 2008.
2 PJ O'Rourke, *Holidays in Hell*, New York, Grove Press, 1988.

CHAPTER 8

1 Constitution of the Republic of South Africa, Section 25, Paragraphs 1 and 2, http://www.justice.gov.za/legislation/constitution/SAConstitution-web-eng.pdf.

CHAPTER 9

1 One of the Boers' most shameful chapters – vividly brought back to life in several recent publications by historian JC van der Walt – was their use of black child labour, mostly orphaned children they captured after vanquishing African tribes.
2 See the DA's labour policy document, www.da.org.za/why-the-da/policies/job-business/labour-policy.
3 See EFF, Industrial development for quality, www.effonline.org/on-industrial-development-for-jobs.

CHAPTER 10

1 Auditor-General South Africa, Auditor-General reports an overall, encouraging five-year improvement in local government audit results, 1 June 2016, www.agsa.co.za/Portals/0/MFMA%202014-15/section%201-9%20MFMA%202014-2015/FINAL%20MEDIA%20RELEASE%20(MFMA%202016)%20FN.pdf.
2 Pieter-Louis Myburgh, *The Republic of Gupta: A Story of State Capture*, Penguin Random House South Africa, 2017.

Index

Abrahams, Shaun 195, 209
African Christian Democratic Party (ACDP) 52, 84, 94, 98, 121, 131, 135–139, 172, 181, 203, 232, 245
African Independent Congress 151
African Muslim Party 84
African National Congress (ANC) 1–8, 10–13, 15, 17–18, 20–22, 24–26, 32–51, 53–62, 64–78, 82–84, 86–88, 91–92, 95, 97, 99, 109, 111–116, 118, 120–131, 135–138, 141–145, 147–148, 150–153, 161–162, 164, 166, 169, 172, 177–179, 181–184, 187–188, 192–193, 196–197, 203–205, 207–216, 218–219, 221–223, 225–230, 235–236, 238–247
African National Congress Women's League (ANCWL) 38, 64
African National Congress Youth League (ANCYL) 40, 57, 99, 214
Afrikanerbond 130, 218
Afrikaner Party 218
Afrikaner-Weerstandsbeweging 126
AgriSA 130, 165, 167
Alberts, Anton 26–27, 42
Alexkor 196
Al Jama-ah 39
ANN7 208
antiretroviral programme (HIV/AIDS) 59, 142–143

Arnolds, Andrew 136
Asmal, Kader 221
Aucamp, Inus 226
Azanian People's Organisation (Azapo) 123, 172, 203, 232

Bambatha & Bambatha Rebellion 176
Biko, Steve 36
Black Consciousness Movement 37, 58, 111
black economic empowerment 141, 175–191, 198
Bobani, Mongameli 93, 98, 121
Bondelswarts 176
Bongo, Bongani 67
Botha, Pik 221
Botman, Russel xii
Brown, Lynne 237
Buffalo City Metro 9
Burrows, Roger 116
Bush, George HW 140
Buthelezi, Mangosuthu 41, 111–114, 221–223, 225

Cape Town Metro 9, 12, 22, 31, 33, 40, 60, 83–84, 86, 95, 98, 122, 133, 136–137, 147, 205, 219, 241, 251
Carville, James 140
Chicago Tribune 16

Christian Democratic Union
    (Germany) 91, 117
Christian Social Union (Germany) 91,
    117
Clinton, Bill 140, 212
Coalition for Change 97–98, 116–117, 219
coalition politics 2–3, 5–6, 12–13, 18–21,
    24–26, 33–36, 39, 46–47, 49–52, 54–88,
    90–99, 109, 113–114, 116–119, 122–125,
    128, 130–139, 168, 170, 190, 198,
    200, 213, 215, 217–221, 223, 225–233,
    241–242, 246–252
Coetzee, Ryan 24
Congress of the People (COPE) 25, 39,
    42, 52, 60, 94, 99–100, 121, 124, 126,
    146, 232
Congress of South African Trade Unions
    (Cosatu) 4, 58, 153, 177
Conservative Party (South
    Africa) 126–129
Constitutional Court 47, 66, 215, 235
Convention for a Democratic South
    Africa (Codesa) 184, 203
corruption, prevalence of & policies
    against 3, 17–18, 40, 44, 49–50,
    59–60, 68–69, 73–75, 82, 89–92, 96, 98,
    105–106, 108, 120–122, 125, 141, 145,
    148–149, 153, 163, 170, 192–215, 237,
    240, 246
Cronin, Jeremy 161, 201

Defiance Campaign 57
De Klerk, FW xii, 58, 123, 221, 223–224,
    226–227
De Lille, Patricia 51–52, 83, 100, 133,
    136, 241
Democratic Alliance (DA) xi, 3, 10–12,
    17–19, 21, 26, 33–34, 36, 38–39,
    41–46, 49–54, 71, 80, 82–99, 109,
    113, 116–119, 121–122, 124–125, 128,
    130–133, 136–138, 146–153, 169–170,
    173, 179–181, 187–188, 192, 194, 198,
    201–205, 211–213, 215, 217, 219–220,
    224, 231, 238–243, 245–248, 251
Democratic Party 82–83, 90, 92, 219–220,
    230
De Villiers, Dawie 221
Diamond, Jared 155
Difaqane 156
Dlamini, Bathabile 38, 45, 67, 75, 204,
    211
Dlamini-Zuma, Nkosazana 61, 63–67,
    152, 208–209, 236
Dlodlo, Ayanda 46
Donson, Jeffrey 34, 95
Downs, Jo-Ann 136–139
Duarte, Jessie 37, 46, 61–62, 67, 209
Du Plessis, ID xvi–xvii

Economic Freedom Fighters (EFF) 3, 6,
    10–12, 14–16, 18–21, 25–27, 32–54,
    69–70, 71, 91, 94, 96–97, 99–110,
    113, 117, 121–122, 124, 131–132, 135,
    148–149, 153, 161–164, 168, 171–172,
    181–183, 188–189, 192, 194, 197–203,
    210, 212–215, 231–232, 238–248
education, free 47–48, 107, 124, 196–197
Einde van 'n groot party, Die 226
Ekurhuleni Metro 9, 40, 55, 93
Eskom 76, 103, 106, 144, 193
eThekwini Metro 9
Expropriation Bill 48, 161

Federal Alliance 82, 224
Freedom Front Plus 26–27, 39, 42, 52, 84,
    99, 123, 126, 128–135, 146, 172–173,
    181, 191, 203, 245, 247, 251

Gardee, Godrich 34–35, 38, 43, 54, 100
Gerwel, Jakes xii, 220, 222–224, 233
Gigaba, Malusi 67, 206
Gini coefficient 183
Godfather, The 93
Gordhan, Pravin 67, 68, 73–76, 237

INDEX

Government of National Unity 59, 70–73, 78, 87, 92, 97, 114–115, 123, 125, 217–221, 224–231, 233, 237–239, 247, 250–251
Graham, Philip xi
Great Trek 175
Groenewald, Pieter 84, 129–135, 251
Group Areas Act 157
Guevara, Che 200
Gupta family 19, 47–48, 60, 68, 206–209, 211, 238, 240
Gupta leaks 206

Het Volk 218
Higher Education Amendment Act 197
HIV/AIDS pandemic 59, 142
Hlophe, Hlengiwe 101
Holidays in Hell 85
Holomisa, Bantu 42, 60, 84, 98, 120, 122–126, 184, 251

Immorality Act 157, 224
Independent Civic Organisation of South Africa (Icosa) 34, 253
Independent Democratic Party 83–84, 100, 133, 136, 251
Independent Electoral Commission (IEC) 1, 22, 28, 30, 45, 235, 249
Inkatha Freedom Party (IFP) 11–12, 25, 36, 38, 41–42, 53, 59, 97–98, 111–119, 124, 169–170, 172, 203, 215, 218–219, 221–222, 225, 244–245
Independent Party 90
Industrial and Commercial Workers' Union 111
Institute of Race Relations 145
Integrated Development Plan (IDP) 51–52

Jansen, Jonathan xii
Jesus Christ 1, 13
Joemat-Pettersson, Tina 79, 130, 179

Johannesburg Metro 1, 9–10, 13, 21–22, 26, 40–43, 49–51, 54, 60, 84, 94, 125, 137, 147, 152, 184, 215, 231, 242

Kadalie, Clements 111
kaMagwaza-Msibi, Zanele 119
Kannaland municipality 34, 95–96
Kganyago, Ntopile 121, 123
Khama, Ian 99
Khoisan Revolution 39, 93
Khwezi 45
Koloane, Bruce 207
Kopane, Patricia 52
Kriegler, Johann 30
Kubayi, Mmamoloko 79
Kwankwa, Nqabayomzi 26
KwaZulu-Natal 4, 11–12, 20–21, 38, 42, 53, 56, 58–59, 85, 97–98, 111–116, 118–119, 121–123, 137, 151, 169, 205–206, 215, 219, 222, 225, 244–245

Labour Relations Act 180
Labour Party 218
Landbouweekblad 167
land issue (also see Expropriation Bill) 19, 90, 117, 134, 140, 142, 154–158, 161, 167, 172–173
Lees, Alf 194
Lekota, Mosiuoa 60, 100
Lembede, Anton 57
Lenin, Vladimir 34
Leon, Tony 37, 80, 82–83, 220, 230
Liberal Democratic Party (Britain) 92

Mabuyakhulu, Mike 116
Mabuza, David 61–67, 75, 152, 209, 237–238, 240
Madikizela-Mandela, Winnie 40
Madonsela, Thuli xii, 15, 195, 206, 214–215
Magashule, Ace 61–64, 67–68, 74–75, 87, 152, 209, 238, 241

Maharaj, Mac 222
Mahlobo, David 67, 80
Mahumapelo, Supra 87, 131, 238
Maimane, Mmusi 43, 51, 54, 86–90, 150–151, 187–188, 210, 220, 238, 241
Makhaye, Dumisani 116
Makhura, David 46
Makwetu, Kimi 205–206
Malala, Justice 59
Malema, Julius 6, 15, 19–20, 36, 40–41, 44, 46–47, 54, 60, 99–100, 124, 142, 156, 214, 238–239, 244
Mamabolo, Sy 235
Mandela, Nelson xii, 48, 57–59, 70, 77, 92, 120, 123, 219–226, 228, 230, 233
Mangaung elective conference (ANC) 40, 192
Mangaung Metro 9
Mantashe, Gwede 37–38, 46, 60–62, 67, 124, 131
Manuel, Trevor 153
Maponya, Richard 184
Marikana 36, 49
Marshall, George 76
Marshall Plan 76
Mashaba, Herman 51, 54, 184, 231, 242
Mashabela, Reneilwe 17–18
Mashatile, Paul 46, 61–62, 67
Mau Mau uprising 38
Maynier, David 194
Mazzotti, Adriano 214
Mbeki, Thabo xi, 59–60, 65, 121, 123, 143, 184, 218, 222, 226
Mbete, Baleka 15–16, 49, 66, 237
Mboweni, Tito 68, 225, 237
Mchunu, Senzo 63
McKenzie, Duncan 176
McKenzie, Gayton 55, 93
Menell, Clive 48
Mentor, Vytjie 207–208
Meshoe, Kenneth 135
Meyer, Roelf 120

Mfecane 156
Mineral and Petroleum Resources Development Act 101
Minority Front 113
Mkhabela, Mpumelelo 11
Mkhize, Zweli 46, 131, 137
Mkhwebane, Busisiwe 195
Mogoeng Mogoeng 215
Motlanthe, Kgalema xi, 60, 121
Moyane, Tom 195
Mpofu, Dali 101
Msimanga, Solly 231–233, 242
Mthembu, Jackson 60
Mthethwa, Nathi 49, 68
Mtshali, Lionel 116
Mulder, Corné 27
Mulder, Pieter 128–131
Muthambi, Faith 67
Myburgh, Pieter-Louis 206
Myeni, Dudu 194

National Democratic Movement 90
National Development Plan (NDP) 71–72, 153
National Executive Committee (NEC, ANC) 64–65, 68, 229, 237
nationalisation 19, 47–48, 52, 89, 103–105, 120, 126, 139, 140, 146, 190, 192, 195–197, 199, 201–203, 209
National Party (NP) xi, 59, 82, 120, 126, 157, 199, 218–222, 224, 226–227
National Prosecuting Authority (NPA) 109, 195
Natives' Land Act (1913) 157–158, 160, 163
Natives' Trust and Land Act (1936) 158
Ndlozi, Mbuyiseni 32–33, 46–51, 54, 101, 244
Neethling, Ryk xii
Nel, Andries 46
Nelson Mandela Bay Metro 1, 10, 13, 21–22, 25–26, 32–33, 40, 42–44, 60, 84, 93, 96–98, 121, 124–125, 137, 215, 231

INDEX

Nene, Nhlanhla 67
New National Party (NNP) xi, 82–83
Ngcobo, Wilson 116
Nkandla (constituency & scandal) 11, 15, 41, 68, 113, 176, 215
Nquthu 11–12, 113, 119
nuclear deal with Russia 47–48, 67, 78–80, 237

Oliphant, Mildred 178–179
Oliphant, Nathi 12
On-Point 214
On the Contrary 82
'On the Point of Tenders' Report 214
Orange Free State Republic 175
Orangia Unie 218
O'Rourke, PJ 85

Pan Africanist Congress (PAC) 57, 123, 172, 203
Pandor, Naledi 61, 211
Papo, Hope 46
Patriotic Alliance 39, 55, 93
Pauw, Jacques 80, 214
PetroSA 193
polls, political 4–5, 9, 152
Population Registration Act 157
President's Keepers, The 80, 214
'Princes and Kings' 246
Progressive Federal Party 90
Prohibition of Mixed Marriages Act 157, 224
Public Finance Management Act 125, 205
Public Protector xii, 15, 109, 195, 215

Rajbansi, Amichand 113
Radebe, Jeff 46, 67, 119
Ramaphosa, Cyril xii, 3, 49, 56, 61–81, 87–88, 92, 119, 125, 146, 152–153, 162, 197, 208–211, 220, 236–237, 239–242, 245–247
Rand Daily Mail 22, 27, 253

Rapport 244
Republic of Gupta, The 206
Reunited National Party 218
Rise and Fall of the Third Reich, The 16
Roosevelt, Franklin D 146
Rupert, Johann xii

Sankara, Thomas 200
'Second Coming, The' 8–9
Section 25 of the Constitution (see also land issue & Expropriation Bill) 48–49, 87, 135, 158–159, 161, 168, 170, 173, 230
Section 185 of the Constitution 135
Section 235 of the Constitution 135
'Secure in Comfort' report 15, 215
Selfe, James 19, 33, 38, 46, 51–55, 84, 86, 90–99, 117, 130, 220
Shabangu, Susan 49
Shaik, Schabir 59, 186
Sharpe, R Lee 246
Sharpeville massacre 57
Shirer, William L 16
Shivambu, Floyd 37, 52, 94, 100, 109, 197–199
Sigcau, Stella 120
Singh, Narend 25, 114–119
Sisulu, Lindiwe 61
Sisulu, Walter 57
Skwatsha, Mcebisi 95
Slabbert, Frederik van Zyl xii
'smallanyana skeletons' 38, 75, 204
Smith, JP 241
Smuts, Jan 176
Social Democratic Party (Germany) 91
'Soet is die Stryd' xvi
Solidarity Party 115
Solidarity trade union 130
South African Airways (SAA) 106, 193–194, 202
South African Broadcasting Corporation (SABC) 193, 195

South African Communist Party
   (SACP) 4, 177, 201
South African Democratic Teachers'
   Union 106
South African Native National
   Congress 57
South African Party 218
South African Republic (ZAR) 175
Soweto uprising 58
Spies, Willie 129
Standing Committee on Public Accounts
   (Scopa) 125
state capture xi, 2, 40, 44, 47–48, 60, 67,
   74, 108, 150, 152, 204, 206, 208–209,
   211, 240
state-owned enterprises (SOE) 68,
   106–107, 149, 193, 201, 206
Stem, Die 47, 52
Strategic Fuel Fund 193
Sunday Times 20
Swart, Steve 26

Tambo, Oliver 57
Tau, Parks 49
Transvaal Agricultural Union 130
Trollip, Athol 43, 109, 121, 231
Truly Alliance 39
Tshabalala, Ellen 195
Tshwane Metro 1, 9–10, 13, 32, 40–43,
   51–52, 60, 84, 94, 137, 215, 231–233, 242
tuberculosis 90
Tutu, Desmond xii

United Front 25, 124
United Democratic Front (UDF) 58, 112
United Democratic Movement
   (UDM) 11, 25–26, 39, 42, 60, 84, 93,
   96, 98, 100, 112–113, 120–126, 131,
   141, 172, 181, 184, 203, 244–245, 247
United Independent Front 84

United Party 218
Universal Party 84

Van der Watt, Louis 226
Van Niekerk, Kraai 72, 224–227, 229, 233
Van Onselen, Gareth 5
Van Rensburg, Cornelius 129
Van Riebeeck, Jan 48, 155
Van Rooyen, Des 67
Van Schalkwyk, Marthinus 83
Van Zyl, Omri 165
Vavi, Zwelinzima 1
Verwoerd, Hendrik 17, 158
Viljoen, Constand 126–128
Volksbeweging 218
volkstaat 126–128
Vrede dairy farm scandal 68, 209

Walters, Thomas 52
Washington Post xi
Waterkloof Air Force Base
   scandal 207–208
We Have Now Begun Our Descent 60
Western Cape 4, 12, 34, 42, 56, 59, 82–84,
   95, 131, 147–148, 166, 204–205, 217,
   219–220
Wiehahn Commission 177

Yeats, WB 8–9

Zille, Helen 80, 95, 150–151, 241
Zondi, Musa 97
Zuma, Jacob xi, 1, 11, 14–15, 17–19, 40,
   45, 47–49, 59–63, 65–68, 74–77, 79–80,
   108, 113, 121, 124, 128–130, 150,
   153, 162, 178, 187, 194–195, 197, 204,
   206–209, 211, 215, 237–238, 240, 245
Zupta (Zuma & Gupta relationship) 19,
   44, 207, 238
Zwane, Mosebenzi 67, 209